THE PEACE CORPS IN TANZANIA

The Peace Corps in Tanzania

A History

LAWRENCE E. Y. MBOGONI

The Kent State University Press *Kent, Ohio*

© 2025 by The Kent State University Press, Kent, Ohio 44242
All rights reserved
ISBN 978-1-60635-488-9
Published in the United States of America

No part of this book may be used or reproduced, in any manner whatsoever, without written permission from the Publisher, except in the case of short quotations in critical reviews or articles.

Cataloging information for this title is available at the Library of Congress.

29 28 27 26 25   5 4 3 2 1

Dedicated to

Thomas "Tom" Houlihan

and all the

Peace Corps volunteers

who have served in Tanzania

CONTENTS

Preface ix

Acknowledgments xi

Introduction 1

1 Tanganyika One (T-1): Engineers, Surveyors, and Geologists 10

2 Race and Peace Corps Recruitment and Training 34

3 Tanganyika Two (T-2): Volunteer Nurses 64

4 Tanganyika Five (T-5): Civil Engineers, 1964–1966 78

5 Tanzania Six (T-6): Volunteer Teachers, 1964–1969 84

6 Termination of the Peace Corps Program in Tanzania 96

7 Return of the Peace Corps Program to Tanzania 116

8 Peace Corps Volunteer Mishaps in Tanzania 129

9 Anecdotes of Peace Corps Volunteer Experiences 143

10 Peace Corps Volunteer Early Departures 155

11 Peace Corps Volunteers and the Reentry Problem 167

12 The Friends of Tanzania (FOT) Make a Difference 184

13 Peace Corps Volunteers Who Died While Serving in Tanzania 191

Conclusion 194

Notes 205

Index 220

PREFACE

The aftermath of World War II and the early years of the Cold War saw the United States and the Soviet Union engaged in a global struggle for influence. To counter the spread of communism, the United States sought nonmilitary approaches to win hearts and minds in the developing world. The establishment of the Peace Corps was one of these approaches. It was supposed to tap into American idealism and desire for global engagement that was prevalent in the early 1960s.

However, public enthusiasm about Peace Corps volunteers as America's goodwill ambassadors abroad was tempered with skepticism, especially because of the 1958 publication of *The Ugly American* by William Lederer and Eugene Burdick. The novel is set in the fictional country of Sarkhan, which closely resembles Southeast Asian countries like Vietnam. The main theme of the book is the portrayal of the failures of American diplomacy and development assistance in Sarkhan, resulting from cultural misunderstandings, ignorance, and arrogance.

The title *The Ugly American* refers to the character of Homer Atkins, an unassuming and pragmatic engineer who genuinely understands the local culture and works effectively with the people to make meaningful changes. Unlike many of the American diplomats and officials stationed in Sarkhan, Atkins eschews extravagant lifestyles and conspicuous consumption, earning him the respect of the Sarkhanese people.

Throughout the book, the authors emphasize the importance of understanding the cultural context and nuances of foreign nations to implement successful diplomacy and development programs. They suggest that genuine empathy, humility, and practical knowledge can bridge gaps and foster positive relationships among nations. Overall, *The Ugly American* serves as a cautionary tale, urging Americans to reevaluate the ways in which their country interacts with others and to adopt a more respectful and thoughtful approach to foreign relations.

The novel triggered a national conversation about the effectiveness of American foreign policy and diplomatic efforts, particularly in Southeast

Asia. It led to discussions about the significance of American diplomats, experts, and officials in understanding and engaging with foreign cultures. The book was perceived as a criticism of the US government's handling of international relations, particularly in countries like Vietnam. Many readers felt that the portrayal of American diplomats' ignorance and cultural insensitivity rang true and highlighted the need for reforms.

The Peace Corps in Tanzania outlines the contributions and experiences of Peace Corps volunteers in Tanzania from independence in 1961 to 2022. It evaluates the extent to which the objectives of the Peace Corps program were met or not. Although the Peace Corps program has since 1961 contributed immensely to the development needs of Tanzania in multiple sectors, over the years the Peace Corps program has faced several challenges that call for improvements.

In writing this book I must acknowledge that I have left a lot unsaid, questions unasked or unanswered, and many gaps unfilled. This was largely because I was unable to access early Peace Corps records, most of which I discovered are in private hands rather than at the National Archives and Records Administration (NARA) in Maryland. Those records of the Peace Corps that are with NARA do not seem to be well kept and organized. I was also unable to do fieldwork in Tanzania or visit the John F. Kennedy Presidential Library in Boston due to the COVID-19 pandemic and other logistical problems.

ACKNOWLEDGMENTS

While doing research for this book I accumulated a debt of gratitude to many people, who paused their busy lives and gave me the benefit of their thoughts and experiences. I want to acknowledge the returned Peace Corps volunteers who worked in Tanzania, many but not all of whom are quoted by name in this book. I am indebted also to others who helped and furnished leads to informative interview subjects. Among these are John Coyne, who used his website to inform returned volunteers from Tanzania about my research project. I also want to extend my heartfelt gratitude to the interlibrary staff at William Paterson University, M. Judy Matthew and Urooj Khan (now with Montclair University); the reference librarians at the Schomburg Center for Research in Black Culture, Musa Jatta, Troy Belle, A. J. Muhammad, and Maira Liriano were all very helpful. At the Kent State University Press, Susan Wadsworth-Booth, Trevor Perri, and Clara Totten believed in the project, kept me moving, and fitted the book smoothly into their production process. Finally, I thank my wife, Margaret, for her moral support.

INTRODUCTION

It was 2 A.M. on October 14, 1960, while campaigning for president of the United States of America in Michigan, when then senator John F. Kennedy excited the imagination of ten thousand University of Michigan students to serve abroad to help people in developing countries. Later, at a stump speech in California Kennedy pointed out that the United States needed to counter the endeavor by the Soviet Union to send "hundreds of men and women, scientists, physicists, teachers, engineers, doctors, and nurses ... [who were] prepared to spend their lives abroad in the service of world communism."[1]

Kennedy intended to counter the Soviet Union's endeavor with a program named Peace Corps Volunteers (PCVs). Thus, the corollary may have been peace, but the intent was to counter communist campaigning at a grassroots level.[2] However, when on March 1, 1961, President Kennedy signed Executive Order No. 10924 establishing the Peace Corps on a pilot basis, the emphasis had changed. Peace was the intent, propaganda was not. At a news conference after signing the order, President Kennedy stated, "Our Peace Corps is not designed as an instrument of diplomacy or propaganda or ideological conflict. It is designed to permit our people to exercise more fully their responsibilities in the great common cause of world development."[3] American volunteers' contribution to world development was articulated in the Peace Corps Act (Public Law 87–293) as follows:

> Sec. 2. The Congress of the United States declares that it is the policy of the United States and the purpose of this Act to promote world peace and friendship through the Peace Corps, which shall make available to interested countries and areas men and women of the United States qualified for service abroad and willing to serve, under conditions of hardship if necessary, to help the peoples of such countries and areas in meeting their needs for trained manpower, and to help promote a better understanding of the American people on the part of the peoples served and a better understanding of other peoples on the part of the American people.[4]

Despite the lofty ideal about creating a better understanding between Americans and the peoples that hosted the PCVs, the deployment of PCVs inadvertently projected American power and influence in newly independent countries like Tanganyika, which following the union with Zanzibar in 1964 was renamed Tanzania.[5] The American embassy in Dar es Salaam administered the Peace Corps program in Tanzania. This mandate was spelled out in the first agreement signed between the United States government and that of Tanzania. Because the American embassy in Dar es Salaam administered it, the Peace Corps never became a functional part of its host's government infrastructure.[6] As we shall see, this caused lack of communication and other issues that in part contributed to the crisis of 1969 when the government of Tanzania closed the Peace Corps program.

President Kennedy appointed his brother-in-law, Robert Sargent Shriver (1915–2011), as the first director of the Peace Corps. Shriver served in this capacity from March 22, 1961, to February 28, 1966. In early 1961, Shriver embarked on a series of exploratory visits to eight countries in Africa and Asia intended to determine more exactly the extent of the need for Peace Corps activities in these countries. Shriver was accompanied by Harris L. Wofford, a special assistant to President Kennedy; Edwin R. Bayley, Peace Corps public information director; and Franklin H. Williams, Peace Corps advisor on cooperation with the United Nations and international agencies.[7] Harry Belafonte, whom the president had appointed as Peace Corps advisor and goodwill ambassador, did not accompany the team.

According to Shriver, in each country they conferred at length with leading officials, ministers and secretaries directly involved with possible Peace Corps operations, members of US technical assistance missions, embassy staffs, and representatives of the United Nations and voluntary agencies operating in that area: "In most areas we were able to make field trips into areas which Peace Corps volunteers may work, so that we could see at first hand the circumstances of need and the conditions under which volunteers would live and work."[8] Based on their itineraries, Shriver and his team reached a number of conclusions:

> First, the Peace Corps is wanted and is welcome in every country we visited. Prime Minister Nehru of India, President Nkrumah of Ghana, and Prime Minister U Nu of Burma want Peace Corps volunteers and they want them

to succeed.... We learned this not only from prime ministers and presidents, but from the ordinary people in these countries.

Second, the requests for Peace Corps assistance will far exceed the present supply of qualified volunteers. In nearly every case, we shall be able to meet only a small part of the need. In just the eight countries we visited, requests were made for volunteers to fill more than 3500 jobs. So there will be no problem in placing the 500 to 1000 volunteers established as a 1961 goal by President Kennedy.

I am convinced that if, in the future, our country is to meet the unparalleled opportunity to win friends and advance the cause of peace and freedom, thousands of additional Americans will have to step forward and say, "I will serve."

Third, the Peace Corps must expect attacks from communist propagandists or even from ill-informed nationalists. In one country, for example, a pro-communist newspaper demanded during our visit that the government "get Mr. Shriver and his Peace Corps guerrillas" out of the country.

Fourth, the manner, the mode, and the way Peace Corps volunteers carry out their work will be just as important as the quality of their work. Peace Corps volunteers must go in a spirit of humility, seeking to learn as much as to teach.

Fifth, the Peace Corps offers a major opportunity for large numbers of Americans to serve their country overseas in peaceful ways and with great benefit to their own educational, professional, and human development.

Sixth, Peace Corps work will be difficult and demanding. Frequent doubts were expressed about the willingness and ability of Americans—young and old—to give up luxuries like automobiles, air conditioning, and television to take up the challenging life of the average citizen in Africa or Asia.

Seventh, America's greatest challenge is to mobilize our national will behind a major international effort to advance the cause of peace and freedom. In wartime, we were able to harness the full energy of our people to achieve victory. We must do the same thing in the fight for peace. There is a war on—a war against ignorance, poverty, disease, and all forms of oppression. Changes sweeping Asia, Africa, and Latin America demand effective action to solve ancient problems.

Although at the beginning host countries were glad and appreciated the services of the PCVs, the Peace Corps's Second Annual Report indicates that not all was well:

In the first 22 months of the Peace Corps operations abroad, 294 Volunteers did not complete their service. Of these, 65 returned for compassionate reasons, usually family illness or death, 37 others had to resign for medical reasons. In addition, six Volunteers died while in service—four in plane crashes, one in a jeep accident, and one as a result of illness.

Of the total who returned, 186—4.2% of the total overseas—came home because they were unable to adjust to the difficulties, the frustrations, and the uncertainties of Peace Corps duty overseas. While this is a remarkably low figure . . . it nevertheless serves as a constant reminder that the Peace Corps has a responsibility to select carefully, to train thoroughly and to give each Volunteer a realistic and honest picture of what Peace Corps service means.[9]

The objective of the Peace Corps program was to promote peace and friendship between the United States and host countries by volunteers fulfilling the following three goals:

a) to help the host countries (HCs) to meet their need for trained men and women in various sectors of their society and economy,
b) to help promote a better understanding and friendship between the American people and those of the host country, and
c) on returning, the Peace Corps expected volunteers were to share their knowledge of other peoples with the American people.

When the Peace Corps was founded in 1961, the Kennedy administration sought credibility for the fledgling organization. President Kennedy appointed Harry Belafonte one of its advisors. Belafonte accepted the appointment, but with a clear-eyed view of the Peace Corps's third objective. As he put it: "Most people thought the Peace Corps was a chance for America to show how beautiful we were as a people, our great generosity. I viewed the Peace Corps another way. Get enough Americans to go to these countries and live for two years with indigenous peoples in environments where [these volunteers] learned something else altogether and bring them back to America to educate their own communities. To point out that their own humanity was inextricably bound to the humanity of the peoples of the developing world."[10]

However, due to Cold War geopolitics the Peace Corps encountered difficulties in realizing its objectives. This reality dawned on Belafonte when his plan to build a cultural center in Conakry, the capital city of Guinea, which he wanted to be staffed by Peace Corps volunteers, was abandoned because President Sekou Toure cut off diplomatic relations with the United States over the Congo Crisis. In Ghana, Kwame Nkrumah's socialist tendencies stirred anti–Peace Corps sentiments whereby they came to be looked at as "cow-boy imperialist agents."[11] Thus, the manner, the mode, and the way Peace Corps volunteers behaved and performed their work determined relations with their host country. Questionable volunteer behavior resulted in the cancellation or suspension of programs between 1966 and 1997 in several African countries, including Botswana, the Comoros, Eswatini (Swaziland), Ethiopia, Guinea, Kenya, Liberia, Malawi, Rwanda, Sierra Leone, Tanzania, and Uganda.

Nevertheless, at home Shriver succeeded in creating a mystique of the Peace Corps that garnered a litany of praise including then secretary of defense Robert McNamara, British distinguished historian Arnold Toynbee, presidential candidate Barry Goldwater, and former vice president Hubert Humphrey: "In creating a powerful mystique, the founders of the Peace Corps appealed to the hopes and aspirations of millions for peace and at the same time provided an antidote—to the image of the democratic, unselfish volunteer—to the unflattering stereotype of the overseas American publicized in *The Ugly American*."[12] One would expect that the Peace Corps's success in image building would almost have immunized it against public scrutiny and criticism. It did not. To begin with, in 1963 coverage of the Peace Corps by the American press was more favorable than it had been in 1961 and 1962. In 1961, when the Peace Corps was established, there were many critics of the program: "In July 1961, the Louisville, Kentucky, *Star Journal* concluded that the Peace Corps was 'emerging from the role of whipping boy into a healthy adolescent.' In predicting success for the Peace Corps, the *Star Journal* summarized the unfavorable commentary of early 1961 when the Peace Corps had been heralded as a 'Kiddie Korps,' 'an expensive joke,' 'a haven for draft dodgers,' and 'a sequel to the Ugly American.'"[13]

In 1961, columnist Robert Ruark criticized the Peace Corps as a "Crewcut Crusade," a "Kiddie Korps," and a "Brownie troop of do-gooders." In 1963, the *San Diego Union* reported: "The Peace Corps rests on the fundamental error that we are going to advance civilization and world peace by helping a handful of people on the edge of a sea of human want. It's like sending a lone nurse's aide to pull all the teething of the world."[14] In the meantime, the *Times-Union* of Jacksonville, Florida, of June 23, 1963, opined:

> Any lasting contribution by the Corpsmen to the peace of the world remains to be demonstrated. Much has been made of their ... seeking to promote international understanding ... but it is not yet established that the effort planted seeds which will flourish after the Corps is withdrawn.
>
> There is, on the contrary, evidence that the Corps ... was cynically accepted and used while being resented by those it was professed to serve.[15]

Among the more strenuous doubters in 1963 was the Rockford, Illinois, *Star*, which called the Peace Corps "The most over-rated, over-publicized and over-sold travel club in the world."[16] And in Monroe, Louisiana, the *World* said that the "Peace Corps members largely are propagating Kennedy's ideas of socialism and brotherhood of nations, which means one-worldism and the abandonment of American sovereignty."[17] Nevertheless, Shriver managed to steer the Peace Corps program to success, which quieted the doubters.

This book not only outlines the contributions and experiences of Peace Corps volunteers in Tanzania but also evaluates the extent to which the Peace Corps's three objectives were met. The book is composed of fourteen chapters. Chapter 1 examines the contribution of the first group of Peace Corps volunteers in Tanganyika (later: Tanzania), which consisted of surveyors, engineers, and geologists. Just before independence in December 1961, Tanganyika's prime minister elect, Julius Nyerere, had a conversation with Under Secretary of State Chester Bowles. Nyerere told Bowles that the soon-to-be independent nation was about to embark on a national road-building project for which it needed surveyors, engineers, and geologists. Could the Peace Corps provide such assistance? The Peace Corps informed Nyerere that it could provide such assistance. The group of surveyors, engineers, and geologists arrived at Dar es Salaam in November 1961, but it had to wait until after Independence Day, December 9, 1961, before it could commence work.

Chapter 2 examines matters related to race that surfaced as a result of recruitment and training of the first volunteers that the Peace Corps sent to Tanganyika, Ghana, and Colombia. The first group that went to Tanganyika numbered thirty-five men, of which there was one African American, one Japanese American, one Chinese American, and three Jewish Americans. The second group was composed of nurses, all of whom were white. The absence of minority volunteers raised the question about why not many were volunteering.

Chapter 3 is about the volunteer nurses whom the Peace Corps sent to Tanganyika when the country's healthcare system was going through a transitional period that saw many British medical personnel leaving the country. The chapter highlights the difficult conditions that these nurses worked in that not only challenged them physically but also required them to use their ingenuity to improvise and provide the best nursing services they could.

Chapter 4 is about the T-5 volunteer civil engineers (1964–66) who, while working with the Public Works Department, faced an interesting impediment, namely the inability to acquire the labor they needed. Their tour of service happened to coincide with the waning of patriotic voluntarism that had accounted for many self-help projects soon after Tanzania's independence in 1961.

Chapter 5 is about Peace Corps volunteer teachers, one of whom taught me at Chilonwa Middle School in grades seven and eight in 1966 and 1967. The expansion of primary education called for more teachers, and the Peace Corps met part of this demand. Unfortunately, in 1967 Tanzania changed course toward a socialist mode of development, which in turn changed its education policy that questioned the contribution and influence of American Peace Corps teachers.

Chapter 6 examines developments in Tanzania related to the country's evolving foreign policy that subsequently put Tanzania at loggerheads with the United States, leading eventually to the closure of the Peace Corps program in Tanzania in 1969. First, some Tanzania politicians accused some Peace Corps volunteers of being "camouflaged" spies. Then the assassinations of Dr. Martin Luther King and Sen. Robert Kennedy aroused deep anger in high levels of Tanzania's government, including those who were well inclined to the United States. These anti-American sentiments and others led to the closure and interruption of the Peace Corps program in 1969.

Chapter 7 analyzes the conditions and diplomatic negotiations that eventually resulted in the resumption of the Peace Corps program in

Tanzania after its ten-year absence, from 1969 to 1980. The resumption of the program required significant changes in United States and Tanzania relations, as well as a reconstitution of the program that was cognizant of Tanzania's needs rather than what the Peace Corps thought Tanzania needed. After 1970, Tanzania required expertise in particular areas that differed from what previous Peace Corps graduate "generalists" could provide. A volunteer without work experience and "doing things like a volunteer" was no longer tenable.

Chapter 8 highlights what I label as Peace Corps volunteer "mishaps." This included behavior that the Peace Corps was rightly concerned about and that could tarnish its image. The Peace Corps emphasized obedience to host-country laws. This chapter highlights one inadvertent adoption case that led to the termination of the volunteer involved and the mysterious disappearance of a volunteer later presumed to have faked his own death. Another case was the death of Peverley "Peppy" Kinsey, which recently was the subject of Peter Reid's acclaimed book *Every Hill a Burial Place*.

Chapter 9 offers some anecdotes of volunteer life in Tanzania that show that it was not all work for some volunteers. Volunteer social life in Tanzania included dating among volunteers, which led to marriage, as well as socializing between volunteers and nationals. One volunteer's story is about the absurdity of capturing a young giraffe for fun.

Chapter 10 examines early volunteer departures and terminations from service in Tanzania. Although the Peace Corps Act of 1961 stipulated that the president of the United States could terminate the service of a volunteer at any time, the act did specify the reasons that could lead the president to do so. It appears that until 1969, the Peace Corps did not have clear guidelines about termination, with the exception of forbidding volunteers to take firearms, vehicles and motorcycles, pets, and radio transmitters into the host country. Violating such rules could be grounds for dismissal. Early terminations and departures deprived Tanzania of the much-needed services of these volunteers.

Chapter 11 examines the reentry experiences of returning volunteers from Tanzania, including challenges that were of a psychological nature and others that had to do with finding jobs and places to live and entering graduate school. Psychologically, many indicated difficulties readjusting to American life or relating to family and friends. Although the Peace Corps tried to help with career placement and psychological counseling, volunteers indicated that they had not been adequately prepared for reentry before leaving Tanzania.

Chapter 12 is about an organization known as Friends of Tanzania. In the spring of 1991, a small group of returned volunteers from Tanzania living in the Washington, DC, area met to explore the possibility of forming an organization that would collect funds to support development projects in Tanzania. Friends of Tanzania was established on August 3, 1991, during the thirtieth anniversary of the Peace Corps. Ever since, the organization has collected funds that have gone to support numerous grassroots projects in Tanzania, including the construction of classrooms and school latrines and paying school fees for disadvantaged students.

Chapter 13 pays tribute to those volunteers who passed away while serving in Tanzania and describes the circumstances of their demises. The conclusion highlights the contributions of, and setbacks faced by, the volunteers; it also considers whether the various Peace Corps volunteer groups met the three major mandates of the Peace Corps: (a) to help host countries meet their need for trained men and women in various sectors of their society and economy, (b) to help promote a better understanding and stronger friendship between the American people and those of host country, and (c) on returning, for volunteers to share their knowledge of other peoples with the American people.

CHAPTER 1

Tanganyika One (T-1)
Engineers, Surveyors, and Geologists

Introduction

We know very little about Tanganyika's request for Peace Corps Volunteers in 1961. According to Scott Stossel, Chester Bowles, the former ambassador to India and an under secretary of state, had good relations with Julius Nyerere, the Tanganyika prime minister elect: "An ardent Peace Corps supporter, Bowles told Nyere [sic] about the new program, and the prime minister said he was at least provisionally interested; the country was about to embark on a national road-building project, and it needed surveyors, geologists, and engineers, among other technical assistance. Nyere [sic] inquired whether the Peace Corps might be able to provide that help with the project."[1]

Robert Sargent Shriver immediately determined to send a Peace Corps representative to investigate the situation in Tanganyika. Lee St. Lawrence volunteered to go to Tanganyika in early March 1961. When St. Lawrence returned a month later, Franklin Williams recalled that Shriver became "phosphorescent" with pleasure when hearing the stories about Tanganyika that St. Lawrence told. Shriver was thrilled to hear that Nyerere had formerly proffered an invitation to the Peace Corps.[2]

On July 17, 1961, Prime Minister Julius Nyerere visited Washington, DC, to meet with President John F. Kennedy after his appearance before the United Nations Trusteeship Council to update the council about Tanganyika's transition to independence. His meeting with President Kennedy, which was also attended by Henry R. Lebouisse, the director of Interna-

President John F. Kennedy meets Prime Minister Julius Nyerere of Tanganyika, July 17, 1961. West Wing Colonnade, White House, Washington, DC. (Kennedy Library Archives)

tional Cooperation Administration, was brief, lasting only forty-five minutes. When Nyerere was asked after the meeting what had been discussed, he replied: "I have discussed cash. I don't know whether I am successful."[3] It was subsequently learned that the two leaders had in fact discussed a wide range of possible technical assistance projects, although neither the prime minister nor the Kennedy administration would reveal the size, type, or cost of aid proposals being contemplated.

However, a joint communique issued from the White House said President Kennedy made clear the intention of the United States to join in helping Tanganyika to meet the objectives of its three-year development plan. Moreover, according to the *New York Times,* a highly placed International Cooperation Administration (ICA) official said that the East African leader was told that among the newly emerging African states, the administration had given Tanganyika a "high priority" status for technical assistance. The official said that the US aid programs would follow the recommendations of a recently completed economic survey of Tanganyika made by the International Bank for Reconstruction and Development. The bank's survey recommended a broad program of assistance in education to develop skilled manpower, construct feeder and trunk roads, and create a program to expand and upgrade agriculture.[4]

It was during this visit that the governments of the United States and Tanganyika signed their first agreement, which entered into force on July 21, 1961, to send the first group of Peace Corps volunteers to Tanganyika. The volunteers would be charged with the task of surveying and constructing feeder and trunk roads as well as surveying and mapping out the country's mineral resources. Soon American newspapers carried a story calling for volunteers for Tanganyika, framed by a picture of Mount Kilimanjaro with a photograph of a Maasai warrior in full regalia. Those whose applications were accepted started training first at Texas Western College in El Paso on June 25, 1961, and later in Puerto Rico and Tengeru in Tanganyika. They would be known as Tanganyika One (hereafter: T-1).

Members of T-1 have different recollections about their predeparture training, especially the part in Puerto Rico. According to George Johnson, a trainee engineer, the training at El Paso was good and focused on technical skills that the volunteers would use in Tanganyika. However, Johnson has a less favorable memory of their training in Puerto Rico. He characterized the training as "a combination of prep-school rah-rah, sophomoric anti-Communism, and a sort of 'muscular Christianity.'"[5] As Johnson further notes:

> I think the Peace Corps designed the training program in response to a novel called the "Ugly American," very popular at that time, which held that the Communists were winning the all-important battle for hearts and minds in the third world because they spoke the local language flawlessly, gladly ate the local foods sitting on dirt floors, never got malaria or dysentery, and shrugged off the bites from those pesky vermin.
>
> Puerto Rico was designed to toughen us up, so we could meet the challenges those Communists were posing for America out there in the third world.... They had us doing morning runs, running through a Marine-style obstacle course every day and going on long underequipped hikes through the rain forest, soaked to the skin the entire time. It was designed to make us miserable, and it certainly did that.[6]

However, Tom Katus does not think that the Peace Corps designed the training based on the "ugly American": "I just do not believe they were anywhere nearly organized, especially in those early days. Probably like many of my fellow trainees I did read and was influenced by the *Ugly American* when I applied. I am dubious that the training was designed to make us miserable, though it probably did."[7]

According to Katus, President Kennedy and Peace Corps Director Shriver were both World War II veterans and very macho. The T-1 training director was Bill Coffin, a chaplain at Yale University and a civil rights activist alongside Dr. King, who was also a former employee of the Office of Strategic Services (predecessor to the CIA, during World War II). He hired his old friend Sgt. Maj. Freddy Fuller, who trained the British commandos during World War II. Fuller would blow a whistle in the morning to wake up the T-1 trainees for a 5:30 A.M. run down wet mountain trails in the dark, until Parson fractured an ankle. The trainers backed off the morning run in the dark as they probably did not want to injure anyone else prior to heading to Tanganyika.

Katus further notes that approximately one-third of the T-1 group had already served in the military and many of them enjoyed the physical challenges. Katus recalls that during one of the first days of training, members of the international press were snapping photos. Parson, who had served as a paratrooper, swung into the cargo net, scrambled over the top of the net, and was featured the next day in the Cuban press with the caption, "Is Peace Corps preparing for the next invasion of Cuba?"[8]

By late summer, 1961, the training of T-1—an all-male contingent of thirty-five surveyors and geologists—was complete. From Puerto Rico the trainees went to Washington for a quick news event with President Kennedy in the Rose Garden. Kennedy gave an impromptu speech, in which he jokingly said, "I'm going to send all of you up to the Hill to lobby your Congressmen and Senators. If you don't succeed, it will be easy to fire my brother-in-law Sargent Shriver."[9] Kennedy was referring to the turf fighting over who would control the Peace Corps. Would it be the State Department, USAID, or a new agency? Kennedy maintained a hands-off attitude about openly supporting it in Congress. He told Shriver that if he and Moyers could make it happen, then that would be great; however, they were not to create headaches for him with the various constituencies. Between them,

Shriver and Moyers personally met every congressman and senator, in addition to the representatives who were lobbied by the volunteers of T-1. Members of Congress from both the Republican and Democratic Parties overwhelmingly approved the Peace Corps Act on October 1, 1961.

Following their Washington visit, the T-1 volunteers flew to New York for one day and one night. They met with Adlai Stevenson, the US ambassador to the United Nations, and they visited a variety of entertainment venues. Katus remembers seeing Julie Andrews and Richard Burton in the original production of *Camelot* and later hung out with a group of T-1 colleagues with the Dave Brubeck Trio in the village.[10]

The T-1 volunteers then flew from Washington to Tanganyika via Frankfurt, Germany. The Peace Corps was still running in public economy mode, so they hired a little nonsked prop carrier (an air transport carrier that offers service at lower fares than regular carriers) to take them from Frankfurt to Nairobi, Kenya. According to Johnson, "As it turned out, that little carrier somehow hadn't filed an adequate flight plan and didn't maintain contact with the relevant air traffic controllers. For whatever reason, our flight got reported back in the US as 'Peace Corps flight lost over Africa.'"[11] The report was false and the volunteers arrived safely in Nairobi; from there, they proceeded to Tengeru, Arusha, for their Swahili language training under Jim Brain. Besides teaching the volunteers Swahili, Brain also acquainted them with how to get along in Tanzania.

As already noted, T-1 was composed of surveyors, engineers, and geologists. The breakdown was as follows: five geologists, twenty-one surveyors, and nine civil engineers. The task of the five geologists was to map the country for the location of economic minerals. Twenty-one surveyors made an inventory of and built farm-to-market dirt feeder roads. These roads, which Tanganyika vitally needed to transport cash crops to market, were constructed primarily by manual labor. Eight of the nine civil engineers served as resident engineers on construction sites of major trunk roads and bridge crossings. The ninth, Gene Schreiber, taught math, English, and road construction at a technical college in Dar es Salaam, Tanganyika's capital city.[12]

Before independence, Prime Minister Julius K. Nyerere (later president) realized the significance of developing Tanganyika's infrastructure to facilitate the country's economic development. At the time, Tanganyika was an agricultural country whose people were in real need of access to markets to sell whatever they could. The problem was that most areas, especially during the rainy season, were inaccessible to regional, territorial, and external markets.

At the time of independence, the lack of good roads in Tanganyika was so severe such that out of the 362,000 square miles in the country—an area equivalent to the size of France, Germany, and Belgium combined—there were fewer than eight hundred miles of paved roads. In some parts of the country, roads did not exist at all. Where roads existed, many were impassable after heavy rains. Therefore, the work that the engineers and surveyors of T-1 were expected to accomplish was of significance. The engineers, together with the geologists, were posted to Njombe, Mtwara, Bukoba, Tabora, Dodoma, and Morogoro, all nodal points in areas where their expertise was most needed.

Besides their education qualifications, the T-1 volunteers were expected to be physically capable of withstanding hardships and continually changing circumstances. Peace Corps told them that patience, perseverance, tolerance, self-sufficiency, and flexibility were essential qualities.[13] Moreover, the volunteers were expected to have "strong leadership qualities and high communication skills" to be able to communicate effectively and work with local laborers. As one T-1 volunteer put it: "We do not have any beatniks or pseudo-intellectuals in our group. This group seems to have an unconscious feeling of adaptability. Whatever comes along we'll play by the ear, and we'll make it. We're here to a [sic] do a job of working, not talking."[14]

T-1 Surveyors and Civil Engineers

In July 1961, the governments of the United Kingdom and Tanganyika jointly applied to the International Development Association (IDA), a World Bank affiliate, for a credit of about £3 million for a road program.[15] The program included the further development of the main network of roads and the construction of feeder roads over a three-year period, from 1961 to 1964. This application followed the submission in November 1960 of a report prepared by the General Survey Mission to Tanganyika.

Shortly after the application was submitted, additional technical information was received, which indicated that Tanganyika's government was considering the use of contractor financing as a means of securing part of the funds it needed to carry out the project. An IDA appraisal mission that visited Tanganyika in February 1962 found that (1) the project consisted mainly of widely scattered betterment works, (2) the selection of design standards had been based on financial rather than technical considerations, and (3) general agreements had already been signed with two contractors to provide financing for most of the larger works.

Tanganyika's government undertook to revise its proposal considering the findings of the mission and submitted a second application in August 1962. Although this application was more carefully prepared than the first, several technical problems, particularly those relating to the fragmentation of the work, remained unresolved. These were discussed with the Tanganyika delegation at the IDA annual meeting in September 1962.

A third application was then submitted in February 1963 and was appraised by an IDA mission, which visited Tanganyika the following May. Action was delayed because of the mission's request for more accurate cost estimates and the incorporation of its suggestions as to improvements in the planned works. This report was based on the revised proposal received in October 1963.

Meanwhile, the number of motor vehicles licensed in the country increased between 1956 and 1961 at an average rate of 8 percent per annum, totaling some thirty-eight thousand automobiles. Traffic densities ranged from about fifty to over one thousand vehicles per day on different sections of the territorial and local main roads. By 1961, the selection of roads to be tarmacked or graveled was based primarily on traffic densities recorded by occasional counts. This criterion led to the paving of short, scattered road sections approaching the main urban centers, the graveling of immediately joining sections, and the leaving of long central stretches between the towns with dirt surfaces. In 1961 many of these latter sections were still little more than graded tracks with little or no drainage. One effect of this policy was the rapid generation of local private automobile traffic around the main towns and a disincentive to long-distance road and bus transport between major centers.

However, the General Survey Mission encouraged a change of policy by recommending the early completion of three territorial main road links. Two of these territorial roads were soon under construction with funds secured in part through contractor finance arrangements. The IDA's rejection of the earlier fragmented projects that had been submitted to it also focused attention on the desirability of eliminating gaps in the existing road system. The projected construction of an interconnected highway system was a step in the right direction.

Roadworks came under the Department of Communications, Power, and Works. While the Public Works Division (PWD) in the department was responsible for all public works, including the maintenance and construction of roads, the Electrical and Mechanical Division was responsible for the maintenance of road equipment. These two divisions established centers in all the provinces and the more important districts were under the control of provincial or district engineers. Because of the distances involved, however, and the country's generally poor communications system, these local officers enjoyed of necessity a considerable degree of autonomy.

The PWD had no separate road branch. Its equipment and personnel could be used on all types of public works, although in practice certain types of equipment and particular personnel were assigned almost entirely to roadworks. The chief engineer of Roads and Aerodromes had direct authority over the provincial and district organizations on matters pertaining to his branch. While from a purely technical point of view a separate road organization with its own facilities, equipment, and staff was desirable, it was difficult to justify in Tanganyika's current stage of development.

Other than the permanent secretary post, expatriates held all the senior posts in the PWD. Most of the staff responsible for roadworks had served in Tanganyika for many years. While one regional engineer, one district engineer, and one district officer were all competent civil servants, the vast majority of the PWD staff had attained only an eighth-grade education and had fought in World War II. According to Katus, most behaved like pompous aristocrats. Because Tanganyika was a United Nations' trusteeship territory, it received the dregs of the colonial service because the best-educated British volunteers wanted to go to the crown jewel colonies, namely, India and Kenya.

Prior to independence, resignations were infrequent since colonial service was considered a career. After independence, however, about one-third of the experienced senior staff concerned with roads retired while others contemplated departure. Although PWD was successful in obtaining replacements, they were generally younger and less experienced engineers. Any government action that adversely affected the status of the remaining expatriate staff likely led to further resignations and further reduced the capacity of the PWD to carry out routine maintenance and new construction. The PWD began to employ consultants on roadworks to make up for some of its staff shortages.

The PWD instituted a training program for Tanzanians who were increasingly filling lower-level jobs, such as supervisors and mechanics, but only a few had reached higher posts as surveyors and junior engineers. The pressure to Africanize government departments was increasing, giving rise to some concern over the rate at which Africans were promoted over non-African employees with more experience. Thus, for the near future, the PWD was dependent on expatriate administrative and technical personnel.[16] Some of the expatriates were American Peace Corps volunteers.

The minister for communications and works reiterated the continued significance of the PWD in his budget speech for the fiscal year 1964/65. He noted that,

> without the existing system of communications the cotton and the coffee growers would not get any money for their crops; and that without the present Works Division there would be no schools for the children to attend for their education, and no hospitals to go to for treatment.
>
> The existence Mr. Speaker, of the Public Works Department... has enabled the United Republic effectively to bridge the gap between time and space separating producer and consumer.[17]

As already noted, bridging the gap between time and space separating producer and consumer was the central objective of T-1 volunteers. The United States Agency for International Development (USAID) provided the funding for projects staffed by PCVs. While the minister for communications and works acknowledged USAID's financial assistance, and how crucial such funding was, he lamented about USAID's rigorous procedures through which applicants for financial assistance had wade before their applications could be considered.[18] However, the ministry's road program for fiscal year 1964/65 was estimated to cost just over £3.5 million, of which £2.5 million was already assured from the World Bank, USAID, and Commonwealth Assistance loan resources.[19]

Fiscal year 1964/65 was the beginning of Tanzania's Five-Year Development Plan, which included the establishment of pilot development settlements under the government's community development ("villagization") program.[20] One of these pilot settlements was Kitete in Mbulu District, Northern Province. Kitete was more than one hundred seventy miles southwest of Arusha on the road to the Ngorongoro Crater. According to Aaron Segal, off to the right side of the road to the Ngorongoro Crater and after the junction to Lake Manyara Hotel, there was what must have been just about the worst road: "a cart-track studded with stones of assorted shapes and sizes, rutted, obscured by tall grass, in short scarcely passable."[21]

The five hundred adult men admitted to the Kitete pilot settlement were chosen principally for their willingness to try something new, namely, to engage in commercial agriculture. Because of the location of Kitete, their success depended in part on the village being connected with local and regional markets, especially on the marketing of its major product—wheat. There was a flour mill at Arusha, and with an improved road the trip was now easy, and wheat prices were attractive. Besides collectively working on their wheat farm, the settlement's farmers grew vegetables on their individual plots, including tomatoes, carrots, peas, lettuce, and the like—all from seeds provided free of charge. Their vegetables found ready a market at nearby Lake Manyara Hotel. The market for vegetables at Lake Manyara Hotel was accessible because of the construction of an all-weather road. The work was done as a local self-help project with American Peace Corps surveyors assisting: "What used to be a nightmarish two-hour trip [could] now be accomplished in less than an hour without risk of breaking one's spine."[22]

Although road construction facilitated the connection of peasant farmers to markets for their produce, the construction of roads soon after independence was also beneficial to large-scale agribusiness. One of these was the Kilombero Sugar Company (KSC), whose significance is best understood in the context of the development of the sugar industry in Tanzania. The first sugar company in Tanzania was the Tanganyika Planting Company (TPC), established in 1930. It was located at Arusha-Chini in what was then the Northern Province near the border with Kenya.

The second sugar company in Tanzania was the Kagera Sugar Mills Company, established in 1958 as a subsidiary of the Madhvani Group of Companies. The plantation and sugar factory were in the Kagera region in northwestern Tanzania near the border with Uganda. Thus, at the time of independence, these were the only two sugar factories in Tanzania, and their sugar production fell far short of satisfying local demand. Therefore, the shortfall in local sugar production was covered by imported sugar.

Before independence, the colonial government had planned to promote the local production of sugar by encouraging the large-scale production of sugar cane and locally processing the cane for the local market. This strategy, later known as the strategy of "import-substitution" was meant to save foreign exchange and alleviate Tanzania's dependence on imported consumer goods.

In March 1962, the third sugar factory, the KSC, was inaugurated at Kilombero in the Morogoro region. However, the location of the sugar plantation and the sugar-processing factory was from the beginning beset with transportation obstacles. The location of both the plantation and the factory necessitated the construction of an all-weather road between Mikumi and Kilombero. Arthur Young supervised the surveying of the road, which was constructed by the Mowlem Construction Company.

The Mikumi-to-Kilombero road was a government contract awarded by the Tanganyika authorities via a public bid process. Young's job, as assistant resident engineer (acting as a Tanganyika agent), was to ensure that Mowlem built the road in accordance with the plans and specifications. According to Young, the Mikumi-to-Kilombero road had several low-level "drifts," which flooded frequently during the rainy season. The construction of high bridges made the road passable all year round. However, these new bridges were only one-lane wide and therefore quite dangerous.

Katus and his colleague Parson surveyed another road from Ifakara to Mahenge, under the supervision of Young. According to Katus, the survey crew buried two-and-one-half-foot concrete beacons with brass caps on them, which they placed on every curve and every five hundred yards on the straightaway. Unfortunately, before the road was constructed the local people, not understanding the significance of the engineering markings, dug them all out, erasing physical evidence of a six-month-long, full field survey and design.

Before the Ifakara-to-Mahenge road project, Katus was involved in rural market surveys intended to guide the development of Tanganyika's feeder-road system in what was then the Eastern Province. In this endeavor, Katus utilized his skills in transportation market analysis and field surveying. According to Katus, the volunteers had an excellent British regional engineer who assigned them to conduct rural marketing feeder road surveys during their first year of service. This resulted in a publication titled *Long-Range Economic and Engineering Plan for Eastern Region's Feeder Road System*.[23] While stationed at Morogoro, Katus conducted a full field survey for the College of Agriculture that was later constructed at Morogoro (today's Sokoine University of Agriculture). He also surveyed a field for Boeing 707 specs; the field subsequently became the national air force headquarters at Morogoro.

Other T-1 volunteers whose work left a mark include Peter Salvatore De Simone,[24] John "Jack" McPhee, George Johnson, and Robert "Bob" Milhous. As civil engineer, De Simone surveyed the route for the construction of the all-weather trunk road connecting Chalinze and Segera on the Tanga-Moshi trunk road. He also taught engineering at Dar es Salaam's technical college. George Johnson was field supervisor and chief surveyor of a section of what is now the Eastern Trunk Road. Johnson and two other volunteers worked out of Mtwara, then the headquarters of the Southern Province. Johnson is proud of what he accomplished, as indicated in one of his responses to a questionnaire: "I got a segment of an important road built. I think I am remembered there fondly." There is no reason to doubt Johnson's contribution given that until the building of the Eastern Trunk Road the Southern Province was very isolated from the rest of the country. This road provided essential transport services for goods and passengers.

McPhee, who graduated with a bachelor's in physics and was working at the Astro-Electronics Division of the Radio Corporation of America near Princeton, New Jersey, before he joined the Peace Corps, learned surveying techniques during his predeparture training at Texas Western College, El Paso, and at Tengeru, Arusha. In Tanganyika, he was based in Dodoma but traveled extensively throughout the Central Province surveying roads, bridges, and building sites, whose measurements he took back to the PWD for Jim O'Hara, a T-1 engineer, to use in drawing up plans for the construction. According to McPhee, he worked with a team of Tanganyikans and passed on to them surveying skills. One of them, Gerald Kigahe, in turn, became a surveyor in his own right.

According to Bob Milhous, he volunteered to work in Tanganyika to contribute to the development of Tanganyika:

> I think much of what I did contributed to development. Unfortunately, I did not really work with Tanganyikans as peers. This contrasts to what I did is

Ghana where I did work with Ghanaians as peers. I did not really get to know Tanganyikans mostly because on the job I worked mostly with the British engineers. This contrasts with my work in Ghana where I did work directly with Ghanaians.

First assignment was working on the Mwanza-Musoma Road. I designed a concrete bridge deck which had way too much reinforcing. I was a recent civil engineering graduate and some things were not obvious. In January 1962 I was sent to Geita [in Tanzania] because there was a major washout of a culvert—that was the reason I was sent but the true problem was that a water supply dam was about to fail. The designers of the dam may have assumed the laterite at the surface was solid—it was not and the discharge over into the spillway was about to erode a trench into the dam which would have sent a lot of water downstream. Someone had constructed siphon to remove water from the reservoir—the siphon was way too small compared to the water entering the reservoir when it rained. Later after returning to Mwanza, I designed a spillway for the dam and supervised the contractor that built it.

I do not remember what I did after returning to Mwanza from Geita—One task I did was remove a failed bridge across the Simiyu River. It was a tricky project—the people in the Tanganyikan road crew were competent in doing work they had not done before[,] otherwise I would have failed in the task. One other project was resurfacing the runway surface at the Mwanza airdrome. The East African Airways pilots were not shy about telling me what I was doing wrong. The sudden increase in the elevation of Lake Victoria caused many problems with infrastructure around Lake Victoria. One project where I did a design as a sketch was for a new docking facility on Ukerewe Island—at the time the major access to the island was by water.

In October 1962 I moved to Dar es Salaam, my assignment was to do a road condition survey. I did not really get started until January 1963 because of Uhuru na Umoja when Tanganyika became a republic and because of the Christmas period. Doing the survey I made trips from Dar es Salaam and latter from Morogoro. I did write a report that I was told was used by the World Bank. Later I did write a paper on physiographic regions in Tanganyika from the viewpoint of roads—I never published it.

I think what I did in Tanzania did meet the objectives of Julius Nyerere in asking for development of the country. I wish I had learned as much about the people as I did the landscape.[25]

The T-1 Geologists

There were five Peace Corps geologists in T-1, namely, Will Julian, Bill Lounsberry, Allen Tamura, Richard Van Loenen, and M. Peter Wright. The geologists were part of the Peace Corps program to support the field mapping efforts of the Tanganyika Geological Survey Department in Dodoma. The survey department was set up and administered by the British Overseas Survey, whose task was to map the geology of the country not only for academic purposes but also to map and identify areas with mineral resource potential. The Peace Corps geologists were to support this effort, which, given the size of Tanganyika, was a long-term effort by the Overseas Survey.

The program of the survey department was to map out or gather basic information about the geology of the entire country for both academic and economic reasons. At the time, the Peace Corps geologists were at the survey department, and the purpose was to map Tanganyika's geology on a smaller scale to understand geologic trends better and identify possible natural resources that could be developed later for economic purposes.

Each Peace Corps geologist was assigned a region of the country to map during the dry season and, in some cases, during the short rainy season. This amounted to spending six months in the field, or bush, in the dry season and three months during the short, rainy season. During the rainy season each of the geologists and field party members returned to headquarters in Dodoma, where they were to write reports of their findings and plot geologic data onto maps. The maps were eventually published as part of the public record. These maps have been useful for those in academia and international natural resource companies. The rocks collected during the field season were also identified microscopically and catalogued for the public record.

When the Peace Corps geologists conducted surveys, they were responsible for members of the field party, who were employed by the survey department. This support staff consisted of a camp manager, a cook, survey field helpers (who accompanied the field geologist during mapping surveys), and a driver, who was responsible for transportation into the field and Land Rover maintenance. A typical field party consisted of four to six people, depending on the needs of the field geologist.

The survey department had time constraints when it came to mapping the entire country but given the geography and environmental conditions at the time, these goals seemed ambitious to meet. The geologists, Julian, Lounsberry, Wright, and Van Loenen, were assigned to map the igneous and metamorphic rocks of the shield: Julian was assigned the Usambara Mountain region near Tanga; Lounsberry, the Serengeti region; Wright, the granitic rock terrain west and southwest of Dodoma; Van Loenen, the Mbeya region and the greenstone rock trend from Mozambique; and Tamura, the sedimentary rocks along the northeast coast, from Saadani northward to the Kenya border.

Prior to engaging in their separate assignments, the department sent the five geologists to complete an unfinished mapping project in the Chenene Mountains north of Dodoma. To hasten their acclimatization, the survey department sent along P. Stanley (Stan) Bagnall, a renowned field geologist at the survey department and a long-standing member of the British Overseas Survey. Through his mentorship, the experience prepared the geologists for their upcoming life in the bush. The mapping experience was also a nice introduction to Precambrian geology and rocks they customarily would not see in the United States. For example, the granitic rocks in the Chenene Mountains were 1.5 billion years old, and rocks in the Hombolo area to the southeast were 2.3 billion years old and derived from the earth's mantle. One interesting aspect of the Chenene Mountains is the topography having the appearance of a denuded or smoothed sur-

Al Tamura's campsite at Dulu, Chenene Mountains (Allen Tamura)

Looking north at the Shield from Chenene (Allen Tamura)

face. On closer inspection of the rocks, there are suggestions that the Chenene Mountain region was covered by continental glaciers, as indicated by surface striations left by the movement of massive ice sheets over the granitic rocks hundreds of millions of years ago.

As already noted, the objective of mapping the geology of Tanganyika was to discover potential natural resources for commercial development. During one of Lounsberry's field surveys in northern Tanganyika, he helped some private geologists investigate a precious mineral discovery whose value had been undetermined at the time. It turned out that the discovery was a unique precious mineral deposit with an unknown name but was later named Tanzanite.

Tamura's surveys along the coast mapped many limestone rocks, especially in the Tanga area and at Mtwara. Unbeknownst to Tamura, his surveys later enabled the development of cement factories in these areas, and the cement's main ingredient was limestone. Today, Tanzania's major cement factories are in Dar es Salaam, Mtwara, and Tanga, along the coast.

The two plants in Dar es Salaam are Tanzania Portland Cement Company (TPCC) and the Twiga Cement Factory, both located at Wazo Hill on the outskirts of the city of Dar es Salaam. Tanzania Portland Cement Company

Allen Tamura's survey crew parked up and ready to head back to Dodoma after six months living and working together field mapping along the northeast coast of Tanzania. *Left to right:* Samwel, camp manager; Saidi, driver; William, field aide; Kaitani, camp cook; and Henry, field aide (Allen Tamura)

began production in 1966 with the principal activity of manufacturing and selling cement. Twiga Cement is a subsidiary of TPCC, which was founded in 1959. In 2005, Twiga Cement became a part of Heidelberg Cement Africa, of which Scancem of Norway is a subsidiary. The cement factory in Mtwara is owned by Dangote Industries Tanzania Limited, a subsidiary of Dangote Cement, which is owned by the Dangote Group, a Nigerian industrial conglomerate founded by Aliko Dangote. The factory operates a 3.0 Mta plant and is the largest cement factory in the country at present.

The T-1 surveyors, geologists, and engineers were followed by another group of surveyors, geologists, and engineers that were part of T-5 and who enrolled in 1964. Geologist Eleanora "Norrie" Iberall Robbins was the first female sent out in charge of a field party in Tanganyika in spite of the chief geologist having told her, "You'll never go in the field."[26] Her chance to go arose when the chief geologist went on leave, and Robbins's boss sent her into the field. Robbins also notes that although the British men who worked for the Geological Survey of Tanzania (GST), Dodoma, teased her for being female, they still worked together.

Robbins with her field crew. *Left to right:* Unnamed driver; Issa Laibu, tracker; Eleanora Iberall Robbins, geologist; unnamed field assistant; Alfred Ndau, field chief; Simon, field assistant (no last name); John Almasi, cook; and unnamed driver (sitting down) (Eleanora Robbins)

Robbins had just graduated with a BS in geology from Ohio State University before she joined the Peace Corps in 1964. During her service in Tanganyika, she trained two young men and made friends with the first two Tanzanian college-graduate geologists who had been in training abroad. Following her field experience in Tanzania, Robbins wrote three technical reports on mineral prospecting. She says these reports were read and seemed useful because she was later contacted and asked questions about them. At the end of her service, Peace Corps gave her noncompetitive eligibility for a US government job, and she worked for the US Geological Survey (USGS) for thirty-four years.

Civil engineer Eric Ries was also part of T-5. Although a civil engineer, Ries was assigned to work in water development, for which volunteers training at Syracuse University provided a lot of training. Upon arrival in Tanganyika, those few T-5 trained in water development were assigned to the Water Development and Irrigation Division (WD&ID, nicknamed "we are damned if we do; we are damned if we don't"). They were basically filling civil servant positions.

During the first year of his service, Ries was posted at Dar es Salaam, and in his second year, he was assigned at Dodoma. While at Dodoma, he spent most of his time out on survey sites for dams and water wells. Most of the survey sites were over the northern half of the country. His response to the question about how his expertise contributed to the betterment of Tanganyika was: "Not much. I helped a few of the local technicians I worked with to improve their English. Most of the dam sites we surveyed were never built. But I learned a lot, especially the second year working for WD&ID Engineering Geologist in Dodoma. I realized that I did not know much about what I was doing and that I was interested in learning more. So after [the] P[eace]C[orps], I finally went to grad school."[27] The story of other T-5 engineers and surveyors is the subject of Chapter 4.

T-1 The "Tom and Jerry" Duo

Thomas "Tom" M. Katus (white) was born and raised on an Indian reservation in South Dakota. Jeremiah "Jerry" Parson (an African American) was born and raised in Albany, New York. In Tanganyika, Parson and Katus, both of whom had already served as professional surveyors on highway projects in the United States and were enrolled in civil engineering at their respective universities but had not yet graduated, became known as "Tom and Jerry." They lived together in adjoining PWD bachelor quarters in Morogoro and were a team for the first one and a half years of their service. They conducted the rural market surveys together, staying in tents or government whitewashed mud huts in the bush for two to three weeks at a time.

In Tanganyika, Katus and Parson, Black and white, respectively, received much more publicity than they had ever desired, or, as Katus believes, really deserved. Approximately one month after they were in the field, *Life International* featured them with a centerfold photo showing them surveying in the Tanganyika bush. The article was titled, "Tom and Jerry saving the roads of Tanganyika." Many of the British engineers who had spent their careers since World War II working for PWD were not impressed with these "greenhorn Americans" getting all the credit. Even the *Tanganyika Standard* featured them on the front page with the title, "Tom na Jerry: the Safari wonders."

When Katus was working on the Ifakara-to-Mahenge road project, Parson was assigned to supervise the cutting of the first game tracks into what later became the Mikumi National Park, which was established in

A track in Mikumi National Park (Muhammad Mahdi Karim, Wiki Commons)

1964, one year after Parson left to return to the United States. The trails that Parson laid out formed a network of game drives that would make the viewing of a wide assortment of Mikumi's wildlife possible. Today, Mikumi is the fourth-largest national park.

Parson's philosophy was to help people help themselves, rather than give them a handout—something he did in the Peace Corps. The only Black person in T-1, Parson had to deal with segregation during his training in El Paso. A bar owner there refused to serve Parson. In protest, his entire group boycotted the town's businesses. Later, when the El Paso mayor gave the volunteers certificates declaring them honorary citizens, Parson shook the politician's hand, strolled away, and tore up the certificate.

By contrast, Tanganyika Africans treated Parson like royalty.[28] One family even offered him their daughter as a bride. He was the first African American they had ever seen. They thought he was a lost African returning. Parson believed that he made a difference as a volunteer because of the lives he touched. A young man named Gabriel Bakari, one of his surveying assistants, became a regional engineer.[29] Parson's time in Tanganyika provided other rewards. He competed twice in the East African Safari, a premier three-hundred-mile road race, becoming the only African American to do so. However, he failed to finish both times. He also raced with the Kenya Rally Drivers Club and in dozens of regional events, although he never won a race.

Did T-1 Meet the Peace Corps Objectives?

Because T-1 was the Peace Corps's pioneering group, it is understandable that the director, Shriver, was interested in evaluating its performance halfway through its tenure in Tanganyika. Earlier in November 1962, the director, together with a party that accompanied him from Washington, visited a large proportion of the volunteers at their work sites. After this visit, it appears that two overriding questions preoccupied Shriver's mind: Did the volunteers meet the three objectives of the Peace Corps, and to what extent were the volunteers motivated to do their jobs? As already noted, the Peace Corps was guided by the following three objectives:

1. Help the people of Tanganyika meet their needs for trained manpower.
2. Help promote a better understanding of the American people on the part of peoples served.
3. To promote a better understanding of other people on the part of the American people.

After Shriver's visit to Tanganyika, the Peace Corps country representative, E. Robert Hellawell, called a three-day meeting of all T-1 volunteers beginning November 20, 1962. Shriver felt that it would be desirable for a representative of Peace Corps or Washington to participate in the group meeting. Therefore, Joseph G. Colmen, who had accompanied the director to Tanganyika, remained behind and attended the group meeting. The following paraphrased narrative about the objectives and outcome of the meeting comes from Colmen's report of that meeting.

Thirty-one of the thirty-five volunteers attended the meeting. The two who did not attend were either not excused from their work assignments or were on leave. Colmen took the opportunity at the opening session to administer a questionnaire to the group. One of the questions was whether the Peace Corps should replace the present volunteers on the road-building-and-geology project in Tanganyika when their tour was up. According to Colmen: "Sixteen said yes, 11 said no. Two were non-committal. The reasons given for *not* continuing this project included belief that roads were not an urgent need in this country; the importance of other projects with greater priority; the interposition of the British as supervisors whose *perceived* attitude toward both American Volunteers and Africans was less than salutary; and the peripatetic schedule of the Volunteers which severely limited contacts with a substantial number of Africans."[30]

In the questionnaire administered by Colmen, volunteers were also asked the following question: "Does your work bring you into contact with as many Tanganyikans as you would like?"[31] This was an important question, which was meant to determine whether the second Peace Corps mandate cited above had been met by T-1. Therefore, the response of the volunteers to this question was of significance. According to the report, fourteen of the twenty-nine said "No."[32] Whether volunteers came into contact with many Tanganyikans depended upon the nature of their jobs and where they were posted. The *Sun,* a Baltimore newspaper, carried a story on May 18, 1962, about the T-1 volunteers. It was reported that one of them, a Japanese American named Tamura, "spent so much time with the Wagogo tribe that he will become an honorary member when the chief gets around to killing a goat."[33]

Initially, the Peace Corps also entertained a philosophy of the host country conducting a national understudy for each volunteer, "the idea being a sound one in terms of providing for transfer of skills from the Volunteer to the counterpart and the ultimate withdrawal of the Peace Corps in that specific assignment."[34] As events developed, however, it became evident that teachers for the most part could not have counterparts. As Colmen put it at the time: "It seems to me that, if the idea of counterparts is still a valid one, programming must emphasize it wherever it is feasible."[35]

Furthermore, because of the "pioneering" status of T-1, the Peace Corps was also concerned about the morale of the T-1 volunteers. According to Colmen, the Peace Corps was especially concerned "with nadirs in the general morale or mental health curve of the Volunteer during his tour of service."[36] At the time of this meeting, when the questionnaire was administered, T-1 volunteers had been in the field for about fifteen months. The volunteers were asked the following question: "Have you had any low points in terms of morale, anxiety, or depression since you arrived?" Twenty-two of the twenty-nine answered "Yes." It was determined that these symptoms developed from one month after assignment up to one year, with most of the difficulty occurring between the third and the sixth months. The causes were listed variously as isolation and loneliness, boredom, personality conflict with either another volunteer or a coworker, heavy workload, or medical problems. According to the report, the largest proportion of depressive reactions occurred from feelings of frustrations about the work itself.[37]

The question, here, is: How did volunteers handle themselves during these periods? Some did nothing. Some requested a transfer or reassignment, either to live with a different volunteer or to work with different supervisors. Some took leave to get a change of environment. Others attempted to develop new friendships, one prayed, and two sought female "companionship," but a number just endured the best they could under the circumstances.

Largely, two important lessons were learned from the meeting: (1) that the continued success of the Peace Corps was dependent upon the mental health and job satisfaction of the volunteer and (2) that there was a need for companionship in which volunteers could feel the sense of having a warm personal relationship with another person. The first lesson was that training must make clear the potential frustrations, boredom, and even hostility in which volunteers may have to work with host nationals, or as in the case of Tanganyika, a third intervening culture. With respect to the second lesson, the Peace Corps realized that whereas it had expected volunteers to endure physical hardship in host countries, volunteers did not experience physical deprivation so much as intellectual and emotional deprivation, which was harder to endure and required intervention.

According to Colmen, in the case of T-1, the addition of T-2 nurses in the country probably served more to satisfy the need for companionship than the Peace Corps may have realized.[38] In fact, dating between T-1 and T-2 volunteers led to marriage in a number of cases: Mary Briggs married Burt Segall; Ann Quink married Art Young; Annie (Patricia) Holstein married Peter De Simone; Pat Hogan married Dr. John King, a Peace Corps doctor in Tanganyika. Others who dated but did not marry were Tom Katus and Carole Siriani.

Finally, it is important to note that the volunteers did receive some praise in the Tanganyika press. William McAteer, a reporter of the *Tanganyika Standard,* praised Katus and Parson for their work in the "wild country of bush and swamp that lies between the Great Ruaha and Kilombero rivers." Although neither "was . . . an African—[each] has always been the object of polite but intense scrutiny. These Tanganyikans had never heard of the Peace Corps, never heard of America even, but they knew that the white man and the strange black man had come to work among them, and they were grateful."[39] McAteer also praised the work done by the five Peace Corps geologists who were engaged in geologically mapping much of the country.

CHAPTER 2

Race and Peace Corps Recruitment and Training

Introduction

The Peace Corps intended to be racially inclusive right from its inception. The task force that Robert Sargent Shriver put together to launch the agency reflected this. The task force included the following African Americans: Harry Belafonte, singer and activist; James Robinson, director of Crossroads Africa; Dr. Benjamin Mays, president of Morehouse College; and Dr. Albert Dent, president of Dillard College.[1] African Americans were among the first Peace Corps country directors; they included Franklin H. Williams (Ethiopia), George Carter (Ghana), C. Lucas Payne (Niger), Chester Carter (Cameroon), and Samuel D. Proctor (Nigeria).[2] Shriver's nucleus staff in Washington, DC, included his assistant, William D. Moyers, former press secretary to Vice President Lyndon B. Johnson, and Franklin H. Williams, former legal counsel of the National Association for the Advancement of Colored People (NAACP) in California. As we have noted, Harry Belafonte was appointed as Peace Corps advisor and goodwill ambassador.

Once the Peace Corps was up and running, Shriver worked hard to ensure that racial equality was an integral part of the agency's ideology. Shriver knew that America was a racist society, but he did not want the Peace Corps to be discriminatory. In a press release given on June 1, 1961, Shriver reiterated, "The Peace Corps wants Negroes, and is seeking them . . . The Peace Corps wants people of all races . . . This is also how we see our task abroad—not to work with Africans and Asians as members of a particular race... but as people. Intolerance, racial tension, and mob violence erupt wherever some men see other men in impersonal terms... when will the ugly incidents of Montgomery and Birmingham cease to be? Only when every man becomes a person to every other man."[3]

However, on June 14, 1961, President Kennedy depicted a slightly different scenario about the Peace Corps's recruitment of African Americans and other minorities. The president suggested that in its endeavor to recruit Hispanics and African Americans, the Peace Corps should appeal and harness their "inborn" affinity with their ancestral and cultural homelands: "Chicanos and Puerto Ricans have an obvious affinity for South America, and the same is true of Negroes and Africa."[4] As we shall see, this strategy did not boost Peace Corps recruitment of African Americans because their affinity with Africa was very limited, much more than the president had presumed.

During the first decade of its existence, the Peace Corps was unable to recruit African Americans in great numbers. We do not have numbers for the early 1960s because Peace Corps recruitment questionnaires did not ask applicants to identify by race. Nevertheless, in the 1960s the Peace Corps failed to recruit many African Americans for several reasons. On the one hand, most African Americans believed that the Peace Corps was an agency for white middle-class Americans.[5] On the other hand, the African American recruitment pool was significantly smaller than that of whites. The Peace Corps recruited volunteers from college campuses. Until the late 1960s, the majority of African Americans attended what are known today as historically Black colleges and universities (HBCUs). These schools were established before the Civil Rights Act of 1964 with the intention of primarily serving the African American community. Notable alumni of one of them, Morehouse College, include Martin Luther King Sr., Martin Luther King Jr., Martin Luther King III, Spike Lee, and Samuel L. Jackson, none of whom volunteered for the Peace Corps.

Besides a small recruitment pool, there were other reasons why not many African Americans volunteered for the Peace Corps. A Louis Harris poll conducted in March 1968 reflected the views of African American seniors toward the Peace Corps. The poll was conducted on thirty-five predominantly African American campuses. According to the Harris poll, on these campuses, the Peace Corps had made little impact. The Harris poll indicated that in 1968 only 9 percent of African American seniors was seriously considering joining the Peace Corps, compared to 13 percent of white seniors polled in December 1967.[6] Of the 9 percent Black seniors who considered the Peace Corps, only 7 percent expected to join after graduation.[7]

According to the 1968 Harris poll, two major conditions kept African American seniors away from the Peace Corps. One was career pressure, and the other was race. However, the two factors intertwined. Because of racial discrimination, African American seniors were concerned about getting good-paying jobs. Thus, 93 percent of African American seniors, compared to 72 percent of white seniors, thought planning immediately for a future career was very important. One-half of African American seniors interviewed in the Harris poll said that they would like to start making money immediately after graduating.

In addition, African American seniors also had to consider family obligations and college debts. The 1968 Harris poll showed that more than 40 percent of African American seniors indicated they had financial burdens and could not afford to spend two years in the Peace Corps. They considered that what Peace Corps offered was not enough for a two-year interlude in their careers after college. On top of this consideration, almost 90 percent of African American seniors, compared to 80 percent of white seniors, thought that foreign financial aid rather than Peace Corps volunteering helped to bolster American foreign policy.[8] Thus, leaving to go work abroad on a humanitarian cause was not easily acceptable or even understandable. More importantly, some African Americans did not volunteer to go to Africa because they had limited affinity with Africa, a factor examined in more depth below.

Moreover, as the civil rights movement gained momentum, most African Americans considered volunteering to serve in the Peace Corps as a diversion from their civil rights activism at home. Recruitment brochures may have contributed to this attitude. A 1965 Peace Corps recruitment brochure carried the following message: "Have you been arrested five times in the last five months for sitting in? Do you think we should ban the bomb, integrate Mississippi into the United States, abolish the State Department, and turn the Met to folksingers? The Peace Corps is just your cup of espresso."[9] Insofar as the Peace Corps originated during the crisis of the racial demonstrations in America, "it just seemed such bad taste to send people abroad for good will when it was so needed at home."[10] However, as we shall see, there were other organizations besides the Peace Corps that offered and recruited African Americans who were politically engaged to volunteer specifically in Africa.

Nevertheless, the Peace Corps continued its endeavor to recruit African Americans so that the Peace Corps could reflect the rich diversity of the United States and, further, to bring diverse perspectives and solutions to development issues in the countries that volunteers served. This endeavor received particular attention by two Peace Corps directors who came after Shriver and who were themselves minorities. These were Dr. Carolyn R. Payton and Mr. Gaddi H. Vasquez. Another Peace Corps official, Dr. Marie Gadsden, preceded their efforts.

Dr. Marie Gadsden was the earliest highly placed African American woman in the Peace Corps in the mid-1960s. She served as director of training under C. Lucas Payne in the African region. She had very strong ties to HBCUs and pushed for engagement with them and the consequent recruitment of students from HBCUs during that era.

In 1966 and 1967, the Peace Corps initiated an advanced training program (ATP). They purposely recruited juniors in college, with a special outreach effort to HBCUs resulting in six African American Peace Corps trainees. The program recruited fifty volunteers, which included six African Americans. With special efforts made over two summers of training, all six African American trainees went on to serve abroad. Upon returning to the United States, they became successful in their post–Peace Corps careers. One of them, Roosevelt Thomas, received his master's and PhD and became a vice president at University of Miami under President Donna Shalala, former secretary of health and human services under President Bill Clinton. Shalala is herself a returned volunteer and congresswoman from Miami, and she is Lebanese American.

President Jimmy Carter nominated Dr. Carolyn R. Payton, a veteran Peace Corps staffer and trained psychologist, to head the volunteer assistance organization in 1977. She began her thirteen-month tenure with an acceptance speech that reaffirmed the Peace Corps's mission of meeting the humanitarian needs of host countries and called for increased funding and a concerted effort to recruit Blacks and other minorities.[11]

Dr. Payton appointed Carol Word, who had volunteered in Tanzania (1964–66), acting Peace Corps country director to the Gambia (1974), and Peace Corps country director, Thailand (1975–77), as her special assistant in the endeavor to recruit more African American volunteers. Dr. Payton managed to get a contract with the Phelps Stokes Fund to finance the recruitment of volunteers from HBCUs. However, according to Word, for some reason it appears that the Peace Corps did not embrace the effort: "It felt like a 'project' that was being conducted apart from the general recruitment process."[12] The Peace Corps discontinued the "project."

Besides the inability to increase African American numbers in the Peace Corps, Dr. Payton's effort, as director, to take the organization in a different direction proved to be a challenge, plagued by interagency infighting and a lack of political influence. Her goals of increasing technical skills training, developing good volunteer assignments, upgrading staff support, and improving language training ran into budget constraints. She clashed with Sam Brown, then director of ACTION, which had been created in 1971 to administer the Peace Corps Volunteers in Service to America, and other volunteer service programs. Dr. Payton resigned in November 1978, citing, in part, policy differences between ACTION and the Peace Corps.[13]

Gaddi H. Vasquez was appointed director of the Peace Corps by President George W. Bush. He served from February 2002 to September 2006 and was the first Hispanic American director. Vasquez placed a high priority on recruiting minorities. During his confirmation hearings, Vasquez said: "We all recognize that the face of America looks vastly different today than 40 years ago—or even 10 years ago. In step with those changes, I consider it a high priority to expand the diversity of the Peace Corps so that it becomes a true reflection of America. Diversity of ethnic backgrounds, life experiences and beliefs has strengthened our country in countless ways. And in doing so we achieve an opportunity to engage a broader segment of the American population in one of our nation's greatest programs."[14]

By the end of Vasquez's tenure, 16 percent of the 7,810 volunteers were minorities—the highest percentage since the agency began collecting data on volunteer diversity. Paradoxically, the appointment of Vasquez raised objections from the *Los Angeles Times, Boston Globe, Washington Post,* and *New York Times.* Former volunteers also criticized Vasquez's appointment for lacking experience with, or previous membership in, the Peace Corps.

The Peace Corps and the Race Factor in the United States

The *New York Times* edition of January 14, 1962, carried this headline: "Peace Corps looks for more Negroes." The *Times* reported that the Peace Corps would like to have more "Negroes" for service in Africa and elsewhere: "But it [the Peace Corps] said that the small proportion of 'Negroes' among its volunteers did not constitute a *problem*" (emphasis added).[15] This denial means that the Peace Corps was trying to recruit African Americans without making an issue of it. William D. Moyers, associate director of the Peace Corps, was quoted as having said, "We are making every effort to see that we have a representation that is reflective of the country. We are not recruiting Negroes just for African projects, any more than we are recruiting Asian-Americans for Asian projects."[16]

As we have noted, Peace Corps efforts to recruit African Americans encountered several obstacles. The pros and cons of joining or not joining the Peace Corps were highlighted in an interview aired by Washington radio station WOL in 1968. A transcript of the interview was published in the July/August edition of the *Peace Corps Volunteer* in 1968. The interviewees were returned volunteer Earl Brown, who served in Tanzania (1964–66); Mrs. Willie Hardy, director of Washington, DC's, Community Action Project; and Oumarou Youssoufou, first secretary at the Niger embassy in Washington, DC.

The question posed to the interviewees was, "Should black Americans join the Peace Corps today, or should they stay at home to work in domestic problems?" Whereas Brown was in favor of volunteering, Hardy was opposed to African American young men volunteering for the Peace Corps. Brown used his own experience to explain what he believed were advantages that could come out of serving in the Peace Corps. As a Peace Corps volunteer in Tanzania, Brown felt that "he had acquired a broader perspective, a broader scope that he knew himself and his values and was prepared to work in domestic problems."[17] In addition, according to Brown, volunteering in the Peace Corps had changed him "from being an American to simply a human being."[18]

However, Hardy believed otherwise. As far as she was concerned, there were so many problems domestically that Black college students ought to have been taking care of "as their own thing." She posed a counter question against African Americans serving in the Peace Corps: What use is serving abroad only to come back to the same situation you were in when you left, "being the low man on the totem pole?"[19] Moreover, Hardy found Peace Corps altruism and African American involvement ironic, and said,

> let's spread a little goodwill here [in the United States]. Then we can more afford to go [abroad]. Any African nation that really knows how its black brothers are treated here would have some real hang-ups if we went over and started telling them how they could best do things.
>
> These developing countries are talking about freedom. They're talking about sustaining themselves. They're talking about being their own masters. We black people in America cannot talk about that, and I don't know what we could possibly give a country that's talking about that kind of thing.[20]

Ambassador Oumarou Youssoufou concurred with Brown. He emphasized the advantage of foreign travel that came with volunteering for the Peace Corps. As he put it, it was good for African American Peace Corps volunteers to go to Africa, to see it, and come back: "It helps to show them their origin is something they can be proud of." The significance of Africa to African Americans is examined below. For now, it suffices to note that Malcolm X and Maya Angelou, both of whom traveled to Africa in the early 1960s, encouraged African Americans to visit their ancestral homeland.

Largely, by 1962, only one hundred twenty volunteers were serving in several African countries. Out of the one hundred twenty volunteers, only four were African Americans. The lack of African American representation in the Peace Corps groups sent to Africa was not only noticeable but also it called for the Peace Corps to explain why. The Peace Corps's explanation was that there were not many African Americans ready to volunteer. However, the Africans suspected that the Peace Corps recruitment process discriminated against African Americans. Their suspicion resulted from what was currently in the news about events involving racism and racial discrimination in the United States. Thus, the brush of discrimination tarred the Peace Corps.[21]

However, whereas the Peace Corps recruitment process did not discriminate against African Americans, they had to deal with racism during training before they left for their assignments abroad. For some African American volunteers, training marked their first prolonged contact with whites. According to Zimmerman, "Sometimes... trainings seethed with [racial] tension. Officials rarely discussed racial animosity among trainees, presuming that white bigots would not opt to serve abroad. The Peace Corps instructed selection and training officers to root out 'those psychologically unsuited to intimate contact with persons of other races,' whether they be fellow volunteers or foreign nationals."[22]

Because trainees were predominantly white, female African American trainees were probably especially susceptible to racial discomfort. A female African American trainee, Patricia Eaton, told Zimmerman how she felt training in "a sea of white faces": "That really scared me, to go out there in the middle of nowhere with all these whites. I was very uncomfortable."[23] A Peace Corps psychologist who vetted Eaton did not make matters any better, especially in regard to interracial sexual taboos of the time. The psychologist asked her what she would do if a white volunteer made a pass at her, which she had already experienced. According to Zimmerman, Eaton demurred and said they all respected her and that such a thing would not happen.

Likewise, African American male trainees experienced racism during training before deployment. The case of Jerry Parson illustrates the reality of racism during training before deployment. Parson was the first African American recruited by the Peace Corps (T-1); T-1 received seven weeks of training beginning June 25, 1961, at Texas Western College (now University of Texas at El Paso). Parson experienced racism while in training from a roommate and from the local community. Unbeknownst to the Peace Corps, Parson's Peace Corps training roommate was a bigot. During a briefing by health officers, he raised his hand and asked, "Is Patrice Lumumba dead?" The medical doctor replied, "I am an MD not a political scientist nor journalist, but I believe the press reported that he had been assassinated earlier this year." The trainee then replied, "Well I think I have him for a roommate."[24] As Parson had a goatee and horn-rimmed glasses, there was some resemblance and as a result some nervous laughter. His roommate was asked to leave the briefing session and was immediately terminated.

During training the volunteers of T-1 patronized local pubs in El Paso. A Tex-Mex bar in El Paso, Texas, where T-1 were receiving their first seven weeks of training concentrating on surveying, engineering, and geology, denied Parson admittance to their bar even though they readily accepted Texans and Mexicans. As soon as T-1 volunteers heard of this, several immediately supported Parson and proposed a boycott of all El Paso businesses until the bar opened its doors to all. Immediately, the entire training group supported the boycott, including not riding on the city trolley buses from the training site to the Mexican border at Juarez. Juarez was only a one-mile walk to the border, and it saved the T-1 trainees the $0.35 bus trolley fee, which they could spend on cheap tequila at $0.10 a shot.

The boycott made national headlines. The *New York Times,* the *Herald Tribune,* and probably the *Washington Post,* as well as the *El Paso Times,* reported it. National media coverage of the T-1 boycott caused concern at the Peace Corps headquarters in Washington, DC. The Peace Corps still needed support from southern senators and congressmen to pass the Peace Corps Act. Thus, the Peace Corps was very concerned that if the boycott was compared to the civil rights boycotts, then it could blow Peace Corps out of the water politically. Shriver sent Franklin H. Williams to El Paso to help defuse the situation.

According to Katus, Williams met individually with Parson and then with all the T-1 volunteers. Katus does not recall that Parson ever shared what he and Williams may have discussed. When Williams met with the entire group, he congratulated them for standing up for Parson. However, he also cautioned them to be very careful what they said to the press. He outlined that Congress was still considering the Peace Corps legislation on Capitol Hill and they did not need further incidents that could derail the Peace Corps program. Nevertheless, the boycott continued quietly as the bar did not immediately integrate.[25]

At the T-1 graduation ceremonies that Shriver attended, all volunteers got to shake the hands of Shriver and the other dignitaries, including the mayor of El Paso, who gave them El Paso honorary citizenship cards. Dressed in their best suits, they all went through the reception line, with the mayor being at the very end of the line giving out the cards. All three major networks, NBC, ABC, and CBS, as well as some of the print media, including the *New York Times* and the *Washington Post,* covered the event. Katus recalls that they went through the line alphabetically. Parson would have been toward the end of the line. After passing through the line and receiving the honorary citizenship card from the mayor, Parson lifted it up so all the networks could focus on him and tore it in half.

Meanwhile, Williams lobbied for and became the first Peace Corps director in Ethiopia and the first African American director overseas anywhere in the world. During his tenure, Ethiopia received 415 Peace Corps volunteers, thirty of whom were African Americans. Still later, President Johnson nominated Williams as ambassador to Ghana. Kwame Nkrumah protested and challenged Johnson saying, "I need a senior white ambassador."[26] Johnson apparently called Nkrumah directly and emphasized that Williams had to be even better than any of the other whites he could assign to such an important country as Ghana.

What Johnson did not know is that Nkrumah and Williams had been fellow undergraduate students at Lincoln University in Pennsylvania. Williams was from an upscale Harlem family and according to his university roommate, Bobby Freeman, he could be quite arrogant and would frequently throw a tray of food back at the Lincoln student wait staff. According to Katus, Nkrumah was one of the wait staff working on the food line for extra money. It is likely Nkrumah remembered Williams's obnoxious behavior, which may have been the reason he objected to Williams's appointment as ambassador to Ghana. Interestingly, Nkrumah was deposed in a coup while Williams was ambassador.

Besides Parson, there were two other minority T-1 volunteers. These were Francis Lum, a Chinese American, and Allen Tamura, a Japanese American. Lum grew up in Chinatown, San Francisco, a block away from the cable car line. I would consider the setting a subculture of America. Everyone he dealt with was Asian and spoke a combination of English and Cantonese. Social interactions in such a closed community usually involved achievement, expectations, and competitiveness. Although the high school he attended was integrated, his friends remained only Chinese. San Francisco was a large and diverse city. Yet, Lum lived in a Chinese American insular community.

Lum's college experience was no different. Although University of California, Berkeley, was famous worldwide, the international aspect did not change things. He settled for a Chinese fraternity to join and did not develop friendships with any non-Chinese students. After graduating from Berkeley, Lum joined the Peace Corps for training at El Paso, Texas. This was the first opportunity he had to interact closely with non-Chinese people. The volunteers at El Paso caused his world to open up widely. Never had he been with such an articulate group. There were many strong opinions held, but never at a loss of humor. Lum told me that he never experienced racist behavior from his fellow volunteers. If anything, he learned from the group how to be empathetic to those who are different.

However, Lum remembers one racist incident at El Paso during training. One of the instructors told him to do something and then followed the command with "Chop-Chop." To Chinese Americans the phrase "chop-chop" is offensive. The etymology of the phrase is the Canton or Guangzhou word *kap*, which spawned the pidgin English phrase "chop-chop." Its Chinese usage means to "make haste." However, when it evolved into pidgin English it acquired a different connotation and came to reflect differences of status between the speaker and the person addressed. When a "coolie" was sent on an errand requiring haste, he was told to go "chop-chop." In this regard, Europeans in Canton who used the term were considered obnoxious and condescending. Hence, when Lum's commander used the phrase it had the same effect as the *n*-word to an African American. Lum reacted by giving him "the stare."

Allen Tamura was a third-generation Japanese American born and raised in California. He did not speak Japanese and did not adhere to many of the traditional values of his Japanese heritage, to the dismay, especially, of his grandparents. After World War II, the family moved back to the Los Angeles area and settled in Pasadena, like many Japanese American families coming from American internment camps, which almost all Japanese American families living on the West Coast were sent to at the outbreak of World War II. Like many minority families, the Tamura family moved to Southern California as it provided economic opportunity. In Southern California, it was common to live in diverse communities with people who were Black, Mexican, white, Asian, Jewish, Eastern European, and more. As his parents worked diligently to find their way back into the community, they encountered much bigotry, remnants of the war's aftermath. His parents tried to protect him and his brothers from prejudice, but being so young during the 1950s, they learned not to pay attention to racism and just carried on with their lives.

During the early years of school, Tamura and his brothers were active in school sports and other social events. It was mainly through these activities that they learned how to interact with other kids with differing backgrounds. Participating in sports was a way for them as minority kids to be recognized and, maybe, to gain notoriety and respect. In return, they gained the importance of team play, sportsmanship, a great deal of humility, and, importantly, how to get along with others who were different from them. In retrospect, Tamura says, these experiences became part of his foundation.

When Tamura went to college and eventually to graduate school, he was still one of few Japanese Americans in geology. For some reason, he was not deterred, although his father and some of his professors wondered about his pursuing a career in petroleum and mining, a field that, at the time, was mainly white: "But, looking back, I managed to survive and had a wonderful career working in various geologic basins worldwide. The path was non-linear [and] even included time spent at the Tanganyika Geological Survey, one of the early highlights."[27]

During the seven weeks Tamura was training with the rest of T-1, his roommate was from the Deep South. According to Tamura: "It was a good time as we got to know much about each other. He had never met an Asian, much less of Japanese descent, and I had never met a Southerner. The time spent was brief, but it was a chance to meet another person from a different background, which was probably by design. It was a good experience for both of us."[28]

The Peace Corps and the Race Factor in Africa

In 1982, Loretta Ann Helms was among eighty Americans sworn in as Peace Corps volunteers (PCVs) in Nairobi, Kenya, East Africa. She was one of only six African Americans in the group of eighty. According to Helms, her experience in Kenya exposed fundamental flaws in Peace Corps predeparture training, especially the failure to address potential problems that African American volunteers, especially, could expect to encounter in host African countries. Of particular concern was whether African American volunteers would be accepted or rejected by nationals of the host countries. According to Helms, this failure on the part of the Peace Corps left "the African American volunteer ill prepared for service, often arriving in the host country with unrealistic expectations and leaving embittered and hostile towards both the host country nationals and the U.S. Peace Corps as an organization."[29]

The question of why African American Peace Corps volunteers were sometimes accepted and sometimes not cordially accepted in African countries is not just a matter of inadequate predeparture training. African American Peace Corps volunteers' relationships with Africa and Africans reflect a much broader historical trajectory, namely, the slave experience, racism, and racial discrimination against African Americans in the United States. For African Americans, the Middle Passage resulted in a physical as well as psychological rupture with Africa that was for the longest time difficult to bridge. Ever since the ancestors of African Americans arrived in the United States, a process of distancing them from Africa had ensued. First, their physical characteristics were stigmatized to dehumanize them. For the longest time, being Black has been so stigmatized that a lucrative business in cosmetics has arisen selling skin bleaching creams to those who would like to lighten their complexions. Likewise, so-called "nappy" hair continues to be denigrated, resulting in the use of grease and hot combs to straighten such hair. The stigmatization of African phenotypes contributed to a sense of racial inferiority.

Besides the stigmatization of their physical characteristics, African Americans (designated as "Negroes") were assaulted psychologically by being made to believe they were inferior to whites and that, as a people, they have no history worth telling. Before the late 1950s and early 1960s, African American children were seldom taught about Africa, and when Africa was mentioned at all they were made to be ashamed of it. In his seminal book *The Mis-Education of the Negro,* Carter Godwin Woodson highlights how the American education system enforced the distancing of the "Negro" from his or her African origins. According to Woodson, the objective of the American education system was to make African Americans subservient to people of European descent: "For example, the philosophy and ethics resulting from our educational system have justified slavery, peonage, segregation, and lynching... Negroes daily educated in the tenets of such a religion of the strong have accepted the status of the weak as divinely ordained."[30]

The separate but equal school policy relegated African American children to schools that lacked resources and provided poor quality education. According to Woodson, what students learned was skewed in favor of European contributions to humanity. Woodson notes: "From the teaching of science, the Negro was ... eliminated. The beginnings of science in various parts of the Orient were mentioned, but the Africans' early advancement in this field was omitted. Students were not told that ancient Africans of the interior knew sufficient science to concoct poisons for arrowheads, to mix durable colors for paintings, to extract metals from nature and refine them for development in the industrial arts. Very little was said about the chemistry in the method of Egyptian embalming."[31]

Likewise, the history that African American students learned emphasized European history to the detriment of African history. The history of Africa and Africans in the New World was either omitted or taught in reference to the exploits of Europeans in Africa. This is because African history was considered inconsequential despite Africa being home to the first domesticated sheep, goat, and cow; the first to engage in iron working; and the first to produce stringed instruments.[32] Alternatively, when Africa and African history could not be denied, the image of Africa was that of a continent characterized by savagery and barbarism. Such a portrayal discouraged African Americans from identifying with their places of origin.

Furthermore, in some American circles, it was asserted that African Americans were "really" Africans, and therefore had no claim to full citizenship in America. Presidents Jefferson, Madison, and Lincoln were in favor of African Americans returning to settle somewhere in Africa. This was also the idea behind the American Colonization Society. Some African Americans supported the idea while others vehemently opposed it, preferring integration into mainstream American society.

Besides the American school system, the American mass media has also propagated the distancing of African Americans from Africa and African people. As James Baldwin recalls:

> At the time that I was growing up, Negroes in this country were taught to be ashamed of Africa. They were taught it bluntly by being told, for example, that Africa had never contributed "anything" to civilization. Or one was taught the same lesson more obliquely, and even more effectively, by watching nearly naked, dancing, comic-opera cannibalistic savages in the movies ... The women were forever straightening and curling their hair, and using bleaching creams. And yet it was clear that none of this effort would release one from the stigma and danger of being a Negro; the effort merely increased the shame and rage.[33]

Baldwin was describing the lived experience of African Americans in the 1940s and 1950s. This generation also witnessed changes that were taking place in colonial Africa, especially the specter of African independence from European colonial rule, beginning with Ghana in 1957. African Americans reacted to African independence from European colonial rule in two ways. A minority, which had followed developments in colonial Africa closely, reacted positively by identifying with independent Africa as their ancestral homeland. Some ventured to visit and see things for themselves. The latter included novelist Maya Angelou.

Angelou visited Ghana in the early sixties. In her novel *All God's Children Need Traveling Shoes,* Angelou highlights her sojourn to Ghana, described as a return to her African roots. Over a few years spent in Ghana, she transformed herself by learning Fanti, dressing in Ghanaian style, and engaging in local politics. However, after encountering prejudice and losing her son to an automobile accident, she returned to the United States.

However, many African Americans remained ambivalent about Africa. Their ambivalence, as well as a lack of financial means to travel to and visit Africa, perpetuated disbelief that independence from European colonial rule transformed Africans into being the equal of the rest of humankind. When those who were doubtful had occasion to visit the continent, they had difficulty shaking off their negative feelings about Africa and looked to identify some discreditable aspects of African cultures.[34]

To some African American Peace Corps volunteers, living in Africa brought sorrow as well as joy. As David Peterson del Mar notes: "Africa confronted volunteers with communities they could not join, privileges they could not shed, and tragedies they could not fix."[35] In 1962, Ed Smith arrived in Ghana as a Peace Corps volunteer teacher. When he arrived at the school he was assigned to teach, a Ghanaian villager welcomed him and dubbed him "a child of Africa, returning." However, Smith soon found himself at sharp odds with his newfound African kin. African teachers and others mocked him for his Pan-African pretensions. In dismay, Smith concluded that he had little affinity with Ghanaians. An entry in his diary sums up how he felt: "I am not one of them, and never can be."[36] Smith's encounter with Malcolm X when he visited Ghana further disillusioned him because Malcolm X disparaged his volunteer service.

In 1964, Malcolm X visited Egypt, where he attended the Conference of the Organization of African Unity (OAU). After the OAU conference, Malcolm X visited Kenya, Tanzania, Nigeria, and Ghana.[37] While in Tanzania, Malcolm X gave an interview to the *Tanganyika Standard,* a local English daily newspaper. The following is an excerpt from that interview; in reference to the presence of "Negroes" in Africa, Malcolm X had this to say: "The right type of Negro can make a great contribution in Africa. But the type that is being sent here now by the American Government is not designed to make a contribution to things African. They are designed to create an image that will make the African feel repulsive. It is my contention that they make Africans hate American Negroes."[38]

Wesley Lynch, an African American volunteer who had barely been in Tanzania for six months before Malcolm X gave the above interview, took exception to Malcolm X's comment: "My training and experience in agriculture and administration compelled me to accept the challenge to come to Tanganyika, not as a 'tool' of the American Government to brainwash people [about] the intelligence of Africans, but to share my knowledge as a professional in my field and to help people ... to develop and expand and progress."[39] Lynch further accused Malcolm X of engaging in a "selfish cause of personal acclaim and efforts to promote one's self." Lynch also thought that Malcolm X's comments were "thoughtless provocations" and an "affront to the cause of education, need for world progress and development, and international relief from human want and suffering."[40]

Other African American volunteers who went to Africa keenly felt the onus of their peculiarity in Africa.[41] In 1962, Willie Mae Watson, from Virginia, was a volunteer teacher in Nigeria. One day she asked her students to write short descriptions of her. The following are some of the descriptions: "She is moderate of height. She has white skin. She is beautiful. Her nose is like an African nose. She is tall, of white colour, well built. She packs her hair neatly at the back."[42] When she braided her hair her students applauded her, saying she was the first "European" they had seen wearing an African hairstyle. To her students, Watson, who was light-complexioned, was either white or European. She may have identified herself at the time as a Negro, but her students did not find anything that suggested she had any affinity with them racially.

Carol Word, a T-6 African American volunteer from 1964 to 1966, was posted at Kifungilo Upper Primary School in Tanzania. The school's history is interesting. It was established to cater to the education needs of children of mixed race, most of whom, before independence, were the progeny of European fathers and African mothers. Although Word is herself of mixed race, her students considered her as a "curiosity." According to Word, she sensed that the students had not known a Black American before: "I looked somewhat like them, but I was not African. They had questions about where my parents were from. It was just an initial reaction. Remember, this was long before TV was widely available. They knew of American singers like Jimmy Dean, but never spoke about any black performers, so I assumed they didn't know much about . . . black Americans or our culture."[43]

Before Word arrived in Tanzania, she had some trepidation. She expected a life of deprivation such as living in a house without indoor plumbing and electricity. The "culture shock" she expected did not happen. When she arrived at Kifungilo, her accommodations and surroundings amazed her. In a letter to her mother dated January 7, 1965, she wrote: "You just wouldn't believe how pretty this place is, especially when you've seen other parts of the country. The school is located on one of the highest peaks of the Usambara Mts. (about 6500 ft.) . . . The buildings are very nice and unusual because they are two and three story high, which is not common at all in the country. They have their own electric generator here, so we have electricity until 9 O'clock at night."[44]

At Kifungilo, Word and the other two (white) Peace Corps volunteers lived in a separate house apart from the African teachers. Word describes the amenities as follows: "We each have our own bedroom (there are four). There are three basins right outside my room in another room where my wardrobe is and three in the same place on their side of the house. In between, at the top of the stairs, there are lounge chairs and a table and a bathroom is there, too. Downstairs there's a living room with a fireplace, a kitchen (large), and a washroom with a shower. It's a pretty large house."[45]

Unlike the Peace Corps volunteers' residence, the Tanzanian teachers' houses at Kifungilo were more rudimentary. According to Word, this arrangement bothered her the entire two years but, "realistically, I wonder whether I would have been up to the challenge of rustic facilities. At age 21, I probably would have viewed it as part of the adventure of P[eace] C[orps] living." However, Word says that she did regret not having gotten to know the Tanzanian teachers up close because of this separation.

According to Word, the housing arrangement at Kifungilo was likely made with their comfort in mind. Be that as it may, Word notes that living with her two white roommates (four different ones over the two years) did not present any challenges or, as an African American, the need to adjust. She explains why this was the case:

> I had roomed with 2 white PCVs [Peace Corps volunteers] during the 3 months of training at Syracuse. My college was 99% white, and though I did not live on campus, I was accustomed to being in a "white environment."
>
> My housemates and I got along very well. In fact, one of them is Candy Warner who has headed up Friends of Tanzania for many years. We have remained in touch over the years—I visited her when she and her family lived in Switzerland—and we get together with our spouses regularly here in [Washington,] DC. At Kifungilo, the three of us shared cooking responsibilities, socialized together on weekends, and occasionally traveled together. I did not have to make any adjustments on racial grounds to ensure amicable relations. I can't even imagine what adjustments those might have been.[46]

In Tanzania, some volunteers experienced a profound sense of community—being "let in and becoming part of the family." However, unbeknownst to them "becoming part of the family" came with expectations and obligations that were alien to American culture. Norrie Robbins, a (white) T-5 geologist, was stationed at the Geological Survey Tanzania (GST) headquarters at Dodoma (1964–66). Her best friend in Dodoma was the healthcare worker at GST, Mary Chibaya. Robbins recalls that, "She always said she would send her children to me. We kept in contact by Christmas cards. And indeed, in 1997 her youngest son, Frank Ngalabutu showed up on my doorstep. He stayed for a month, and then joined friends in Los Angeles. Now he is a builder, working in the Los Angeles area, living with his wife and two children."[47]

While in Tanganyika, Tamura had the impression the locals cared less about ethnicity and more about the reasons for the volunteers' presence. Since the timing of the Peace Corps projects coincided with the independence of the country, T-1 volunteers became associated, for better or worse, as part of the nation-building effort. For that, volunteers were graciously welcomed. When working in the Dodoma region, the Wagogo elders welcomed Tamura as their guest, as was their custom. They gave him full cooperation in performing his fieldwork. "In some ways," he says, "I felt quite at home, still living as an ethnic minority far away from home."[48] The

Wagogo supposedly intended to make him an honorary member of their ethnic group.

Earl Brown was a T-6 African American volunteer teacher in Tanzania. Whereas Ed Smith's experience in Ghana disillusioned him about Africa, Brown's experience in Tanzania created deep bonds with Africa and African people. In Tanzania, Brown was posted at Nyegina, Musoma, where he taught upper–primary school students English, math, science, and physical education. Like many volunteers, Brown joined the Peace Corps as an idealist driven to serve his country by helping others in need. According to his wife, Mary Ann, he particularly wanted to serve in Africa and was very excited about going to Tanzania.[49] When the plane arrived at Dar es Salaam, Brown asked that he be the first to disembark so he could kiss the soil of "the land of his ancestors."[50]

Brown learned Swahili and became a fluent speaker, which helped him to cultivate close relationships with his students and become part of the village community at Nyegina. Toward the end of his service, Brown invited Mary Ann to visit him. On November 5, 1966, they were married in the Cathedral Church, Musoma. About four hundred people, including several volunteers, attended the wedding and the reception. The cost of the reception was a whopping $300!

Newlyweds Earl and Mary Ann Brown at Nyegina (Mary Ann Brown)

While the Peace Corps was a "people-to-people" program, intended to create friendship between Americans and the nationals of the host countries volunteers served, this objective was sometimes undermined by subtle racial differences and prejudices. Elizabeth Platt, a T-6 teacher at Morogoro Girls Upper Primary School, did not adequately understand the teenage girls she was teaching: "I was probably more prejudiced than I thought I was about Black people.... For the first year I didn't want to eat the food. I ate only peanut butter and marshmallow fluff for lunch and drank coke. About Xmas time at the end of the first year I became very ill and lost a lot of weight. I was so hungry for decent food that I began eating with the girls (beans, rice, ugali, a little meat and fish, a few vegetables)."

Unlike Platt, Lowel Winkelman and Dwight Yates (T-7), who taught at Tabora Boys Secondary School, socialized with their students while maintaining the expected boundaries between teachers and students. They visited with the African headmaster, Reuben Seme, and socialized with other teachers at the Tabora Club, whose membership included African professionals in town. The Tabora Club gave the volunteers membership at a reduced subscription. As Boy Scouts master, Winkelman went camping on weekends with his school troop. Later, he escorted four of the scouts to the Outward-Bound Mountain School at Loitokitok, Kenya.

In Tanzania, as elsewhere in Africa, Latin America, and Asia, racial boundaries among Peace Corps volunteers dissolved such that volunteers formed bonds of friendship that may otherwise have been uncommon in the United States. In Tanzania, the working relationship between Katus (white) and Parson (Black) evolved into a friendship that would last a lifetime. As we noted in chapter 1, *Life* magazine, an American magazine published weekly until 1972, dubbed them "Tom and Jerry," after the American animated franchise of the same name and a series of comedy films created in 1940 by William Hanna and Joseph Barbera.[51]

Sometimes friendship between volunteers led to interracial dating and marriage. Far from home, "either race [Black and white] of Americans [felt] truly safe to love the other."[52] While in Tanzania, or later after they had left the Peace Corps, some volunteers socialized and engaged in interracial liaisons, some of which led to marriage. After he left the Peace Corps the late James "Jim" Belisle (T-1) worked in Vietnam where he met and married Nga. Alex Veech, also a T-1 volunteer, later married Linda, a Chinese American. William "Will" Julian, a T-1 geologist, married a Goan woman who had been born in Tanzania. These interracial relationships and marriages say something about the Peace Corps volunteers' exposure to foreign cultures and detachment from the American racist milieu during their service. The Peace Corps not only offered volunteers the opportunity to serve abroad but also to experience exposure to different peoples and cultures. They came to understand, appreciate, and feel some affinity with non-Americans (including in matters of love). Love, as the song by Gaither Vocal Band goes, can indeed turn the world. In Tanzania, T-1 volunteers—probably more than other Peace Corps cohorts—came close to Shriver's Peace Corps's goal: "to see people as people."

However, those who considered marriage had to reckon with antimiscegenation laws when they returned to the United States. Before 1967, mixed-race couples needed to check with the embassy legal counsel if their marriage would contravene antimiscegenation laws in their states of residence. Besides antimiscegenation laws, returning mixed-race couples also faced strong racial prejudices against interracial marriage.

In the United States, widespread prejudices against miscegenation were remnants of purulent antimiscegenation, expressed by the likes of Congressman Seaborn Anderson Roddenberry (1870–1913, D-GA) when, in December 1912 and January 1913, he introduced a proposal in the House of Representatives to insert a prohibition of miscegenation into the US Constitution and thus create a nationwide ban on interracial marriage. Roddenberry's proposed amendment was also a direct reaction to African American heavyweight champion Jack Johnson's marriages to white women, first to Etta Duryea and then to Lucille Cameron. In his speech introducing his bill before the US Congress, Roddenberry compared the marriage of Johnson and Cameron to the enslavement of white women, and warned of a future civil war that would ensue if interracial marriage was not made illegal nationwide:

> No brutality, no infamy, no degradation in all the years of southern slavery, possessed such villainous character and such atrocious qualities as the provision of the laws of Illinois, Massachusetts, and other states which allow the marriage of the negro, Jack Johnson, to a woman of Caucasian strain. [Applause]. Gentlemen, I offer this resolution . . . that the States of the Union may have an opportunity to ratify it. . . .

Intermarriage between whites and blacks is repulsive and averse to every sentiment of pure American spirit. It is abhorrent and repugnant to the very principles of Saxon government. It is subversive of social peace. It is destructive of moral supremacy, and ultimately this slavery of white women to black beasts will bring this nation a conflict as fatal as ever reddened the soil of Virginia or crimsoned the mountain paths of Pennsylvania.

... Let us uproot and exterminate now this debasing, ultra-demoralizing, un-American and inhuman leprosy.[53]

Subsequently, antimiscegenation laws were enacted in many states.

The United States' antimiscegenation laws may have indirectly influenced the Peace Corps's unofficial policy that discouraged interracial marriage. In Africa, the first Peace Corps interracial marriage was between Yvette Burgess, an African American from New York, and Charles Polcyn, a white volunteer from Wisconsin. They were married in January 1962, while both were serving in Nigeria. According to Zimmerman, before they could wed, they were required to consult with a US embassy lawyer about marriage laws in America. The lawyer permitted them to marry because in both New York and Wisconsin Black-white unions were legal.[54]

Brenda Brown, an African American who volunteered in the Philippines from 1961 to 1963, served in Dar es Salaam as Peace Corps associate director, where she met her future husband, Richard "Dick" Schoonover. Schoonover was a foreign service officer with the United States Information Agency (now known as Public Diplomacy and Public Affairs) at the American embassy. Brown and Schoonover dated while in Dar es Salaam together, and they married in Washington, DC, in 1968, even though Brown is from Baltimore, Maryland. One of the reasons they selected Washington was that they had many mutual friends there.[55] The other reason was that Brown's African American stepfather did not approve of their marrying.[56] Brown and Schoonover attracted occasional stares from a few nosy folks in Washington. However, for much of their forty-year marriage, they lived overseas.

Thus, in respect of personal interracial relationships, the Peace Corps yielded an important dividend. For some white volunteers the two-year experience would be their first opportunity to know a Black American on a close, personal basis. The chance to meet outside the pressures of US society furnished white and African American volunteers with a basis for a reevaluation of the stereotypes that persisted in the land from which they had come.

African American Volunteer Alternatives to the Peace Corps

African Americans had various options to volunteer besides the Peace Corps. There were many nonprofit organizations and volunteer programs that allowed African Americans to contribute their skills and time to various projects. Some examples include Operation Crossroads Africa (OCA), the Student Nonviolent Coordinating Committee (SNCC), the College for Black Education in Washington, DC, and the Pan-African Skills Project came up with strategies of transnational alliances through which African Americans could offer their technical expertise to Tanzania and other Black nations.

In 1958, Rev. Dr. James Herman Robinson embarked on the first OAC venture with sixty students, which was an interracial and interdenominational group. Two years later, in 1960, one hundred and eighty Crossroaders volunteered in various African countries. The group, which included students from Canada, consisted of twenty-five Southern whites, thirty-five African Americans, two Native Americans, and two Chinese Americans.[57] In 1962, OCA sent two hundred sixty student volunteers to nineteen African countries, where they lived and worked with African students in construction projects for two summer months.[58] Between 1963 and 1968, OCA's peak years, three hundred and fifty American students went each summer to anywhere from fifteen to twenty African countries.[59]

It is to be noted that OCA volunteers mostly engaged in menial construction projects. For instance, they pushed wheelbarrows around or broke rocks for gravel—tasks requiring no specialized skills that the American students could transfer to their local counterparts. However, there was another vital arm of the organization: its medical program. Each year OCA sent physicians, nurses, and medical technicians to work in African countries that had asked for their services: "The program began in 1962 after Crossroads had received numerous requests from African health ministries and other government officials for dedicated, capable medical personnel to help tackle some of the continent's myriad health problems. In 1962 one doctor, five registered nurses and three medical students went to Tanzania in the first Crossroads response to these requests."⁶⁰ One of OCA's success stories was its campaign against measles in Enugu, the capital of Eastern Nigeria. In the summer of 1965, a Crossroads team—one doctor, Samuel Basch, three nurses, and one social worker—carried out a massive campaign that saw fifteen thousand children inoculated.⁶¹

In the history of American foreign volunteerism, the OCA was not only a precursor of the Peace Corps program but also its model. The two shared the same mission, namely the expectation that American volunteers serving in developing countries would create a deep and lasting friendship and understanding between the American people and theirs. OCA achievements helped to convince government officials in the United States that a venture in international cooperation at the grassroots level could be a success.⁶² President John F. Kennedy himself acknowledged that OCA volunteers were the progenitors of the Peace Corps.⁶³ When President Kennedy received a group of Crossroaders at the White House in June 1962, this is what he told them:

> This group and this effort really were the progenitors of the Peace Corps. What this organization has been doing for a number of years led to the establishment of what I consider to be the most encouraging indication of the desire for service, not only in this country, but all around the world, that we have seen in recent years . . . So I want you to know that in going to Africa you represent the best of our country. I know they will welcome you, and I think that you will have the feeling of having served this country and, in a broader sense, the free community of people in a very crucial time.⁶⁴

Besides the OCA, some SNCC members became involved in helping newly independent African nations to meet their needs for skilled manpower. In the summer of 1967, James Forman, a member of SNCC, and Harold Moore, one of SNCC's lawyers, visited Tanzania and Zambia at the invitation of their respective governments. According to Forman, in both countries they talked to very high government officials: "We told them there were many black people in the United States who were willing to come and work in Africa. All these government officials . . . said they wanted us to send as many skilled people that we could contact."⁶⁵ Forman notes that SNCC's initial suggestion to recruit and send technicians to Tanzania and Zambia did not come to fruition but he does not know the exact reasons for the failure. He thinks that the United States put the squeeze on these countries, "for such a program directed by SNCC would have been too dangerous to the international prestige of the U.S. It is also possible that some wild statements by some black leader frightened the Africans."[66]

During their stay in Dar es Salaam, Forman learned of the accusations that directly associated the African American presence in Africa with the CIA. These were the claims he believed to be valid: "In Africa today, there is a great suspicion of black people in this country. This is a correct suspicion since most of the Negroes who have left the States for work in Africa usually work for the Central Intelligence Agency (CIA) or the State Department."[67] In 1964 Malcolm X made similar remarks while on his tour of Tanzania and Ghana.

The SNCC's idea to recruit skilled African Americans eventuated in the Pan-African Skills Project (PASP), which became operational in January 1970, with one office in Dar es Salaam, Tanzania, and another at 475 Riverside Drive in New York City. The purpose and objectives of PASP was to mobilize the much-needed technical skills of African Americans to assist in the economic development of newly independent African countries, and to help bridge the gap, "brought about through years of deliberation [*sic*] misinformation on the part of others, between Afro-Americans and our African Brothers and Sisters."[68]

However, according to Brenda Gayle Plummer, PASP recruited more people than it could place, since Tanzania made the placement decisions and proceeded cautiously.[69] The first batch of recruits consisted of sixteen people with vocations viewed as best suited for the needs of the host country; such occupations included a veterinarian, printer, electrician, biochemist, and engineer.[70] Moreover, PASP organizers strived to prevent recruits from falling into conventional expatriate lifestyles, and PASP workers received their salaries on an African pay scale. In addition to directing PASP recruits, the PASP office in Dar es Salaam served as a gathering place for a diverse collection of radicals and dissidents and functioned as a point of orientation for African American tourists.

In 1968, several African American professors at Federal City College in Washington, DC, left the college following a dispute about the curriculum for Black studies. Among them were Courtland Cox, Charles Cobb, and James P. Garrett. They went on to form the Center for Black Education

(CBE), which opened on September 14, 1969, in Washington, DC. Its curriculum included courses such as Pan-African World History, African People and World Reality, and Skills and Training for Black Communicators. The later course, according to Garrett, initially addressed neighborhood residential renovation efforts.[71]

The goals of CBE were inspired by President Nyerere's policy of Education for Self- Reliance, whose objectives were to (a) instill values and worldviews that reflect the needs, aspirations, and culture of the society and to (b) obtain social and technical skills so that one may serve as a productive member in the development of society. According to Garrett, President Nyerere was insistent on being practical in terms of whatever assistance African Americans could provide to Tanzania to replace the Peace Corps volunteers.[72] The CBE's main contribution was in Tanzania's education sector. Garrett was among CBE's volunteer teachers and worked in Morogoro, about one hundred twenty miles west of Dar es Salaam, the then-capital of Tanzania.

In 1972, Benjamin F. Scott, a graduate in chemistry from Morehouse College and the University of Chicago—who spent twenty-five years in the commercial application of nuclear science with corporations based in Illinois and Massachusetts—published a paper titled "The Technology of Liberation: Proposal for a Pan-African Academy of Science." Scott suggested that the academy would plan the overall rapid development of a business-technology complex among African and Afro-nations. Scott claimed it would be a good and timely institution in that it would address the training and retraining of Black technologists in the application of science and economics for the liberation, rather than the exploitation, of African nations: "In broad outline ... the task of the Academy is to inventory the personnel assets and liabilities of African and Afro-nations, to estimate the monetary resources available for ventures in both single nations and groups of nations, and to create a vehicle for bringing the personnel and money together in an efficient way which promotes the greatest impetus to further growth of competence."[73]

Moreover, Scott underscored the significance of political will for the realization of his proposed academy. "Among the states of the African continent," he states, "the impediments to planning for technological development transnationally are political. Which nation shall have which specialties is certain to raise thorny political issues and put a premium on statesmanship. However, if political consideration is deferred, the best distribution of specialties can be decided solely on the basis of scientific inquiry and analysis."[74]

The issue of science and technology was also on the agenda of the Sixth Pan-African Congress, held at the University of Dar es Salaam, Tanzania, in 1974; it was the first congress held in Africa since the inception of the Pan-African Congress Movement in 1900. In 1972, a steering committee consisting of Geri Stark Augusto, Edward Brown, Courtland Cox, Charlie Cobb, James Garrett, and Sylvia Hill began to meet in Washington, DC. The Scientific and Technical Committee was also formed, which began functioning in Spring 1972 and worked in conjunction with various political groups for the next two years. Among those involved were William Douglas (a metallurgist); Fletcher Robinson, James Hobbs, Frances Welsing, and Alyce Gullattee (all doctors); and Neville Parker and Don Coleman (both engineers). The International Secretariat office was organized in 1973 in Dar es Salaam by Courtland Cox serving as secretary general, Geri Stark Augusto as communication liaison, and Edi Wilson and Kathryn Flewellen as administrative support.

After several date changes, the Sixth Pan-African Congress convened at the University of Dar es Salaam, and it was hosted by the Tanganyika African National Union (TANU, the ruling party) from June 19 to June 27, 1974. The congress had two main items on its agenda, namely, the liberation of Angola, Mozambique, Southern Rhodesia, and South Africa from white minority regimes, and the establishment of a Pan-African Center for Science and Technology.

The two-hundred-plus delegates from the United States included members of the Scientific and Technology Committee mentioned above whose intent was to propose to the conference the idea of establishing a continent-wide African Center for Science and Technology. Paradoxically, "in the prevailing atmosphere, the proposal for a Center for Science and Technology was attacked on the grounds that it represented 'bourgeois science.'"[75] Dr. Fletcher Robinson, a member of the committee, notes, "our reception at a formal level was a terrific blow... We were not accepted in the kinship of Pan Africanism. There could not be discussion of science and technology in terms of how we could use our expertise and training for African interest wherever we were in the world, because the discussion was completely politicized."[76] Delegates from Guinea, Somalia, and Congo-Brazzaville accused the Science and Technology Committee of being pawns of the imperialists who came to bring forth whatever their doctrine was of imperialism. Others expressed fear that such an organization would be a breeding ground for CIA-type infiltration. Thus, the imperative of science and technology in the transformation and empowerment of African countries and societies was maligned and ignored by the Sixth Pan-African Congress.

Nevertheless, before they left Tanzania, five members of the Science and Technology Committee from Howard University in Washington, DC, were invited to a private audience with President Nyerere at his residence at Msasani, Dar es Salaam. These were Dr. Don Coleman, Dr. Neville Parker, Dr. Fletcher Robinson, Dr. Alyce Gullattee, and Dr. William Douglas (a Howard-trained metallurgist). They told the president that they were ready to "get it on" with an international, multidisciplinary organization to provide technical assistance to Africa. President Nyerere responded without hesitation: "If you people can organize to that end, I am not going to wait until Africa makes up its mind to make my mind."[77] Evidently, President Nyerere was not only trying to find out what he could do but also give the team confidence in its mission.

During the visit, Dr. Neville Parker, the committee's vice chairperson and an assistant professor of civil engineering at Howard University, gave President Nyerere a copy of his address to the congress titled "The Pan African Imperative for Increased Emphasis on Science and Technology." Besides outlining the nature of the science and technology envisioned for the purposes of harnessing Africa's enormous natural resources, Dr. Parker notes: "One cannot speak of the scientific and technological needs of the Pan African world without dealing with technological adaptation—not merely technology transplantation, but the need to copy, adapt and improve upon any given item of technology, be it equipment or a precedure [sic]. The impact of this will be felt in a reduction in [the] cost of numerous commodities and services—hence an effective increase in personal income—a stimulation of light industry, and the use of indigenous materials as substitutes."[78]

In his address, Dr. Parker also notes that the United States and the Caribbean are the largest sources of trained Black scientific and technological manpower: "America is a potential resource of Black scientists and technologists whose skills are never fully utilized or developed because of racist policies, job competition, relatively low salaries, and just plain lack of opportunity to be of service or be involved in development processes."[79]

It is important to note that Dr. Parker, who graduated from City College of New York in 1965 with a bachelor's degree in civil engineering and a master's and PhD in systems engineering from Cornell University in 1971, in 1976 went to the University of Dar es Salaam as a Fulbright senior scholar, and a year later, he was appointed head of the Department of Civil Engineering. Parker remained at the University of Dar es Salaam until 1988. Likewise, Dr. Fletcher Robinson joined the Peace Corps one year after graduating from medical school and volunteered in Tanzania from 1966 to 1968. Thus, what the Science and Technology Committee was proposing was akin to the Peace Corps's objective of utilizing volunteers' technical skills in the development of their host countries.

Furthermore, Dr. Parker reiterated that the committee's strategy for Pan-African development was aimed at arresting prevailing conditions and moving on to brighter tomorrows. The committee proposed the establishment of the Pan African Center of Science and Technology (PACST), and that, "This center [would] serve as an effective tool in bringing about self-reliance and self-sufficiency in the Pan African community as regards material needs ... because it will facilitate the sharing of scientific and technological talents in the Pan African community on both an applied and research basis. It will utilize the skills and knowledge of brothers and sisters on a learning-partner basis, whether these skills and knowledge come from practical living, formal education, or a combination thereof."[80]

Specifically, the Pan African Center of Science and Technology would have the main purpose of providing:

1. The development of an ever-increasing pool of Africans skilled in science and technology.
2. Research leading to sensibly applied technology for rapidly meeting the material needs of the Pan-African community.
3. A pool of skilled talent and pertinent scientific information for the use of Pan-African nations.
4. A place where Africans can share both their knowledge and skills related to science and technology.

5. The dissemination of this shared information to the Pan-African community.
6. A central repository for scientific and technological information.[81]

Dr. Parker further states in his address that the program of the PACST would be defined by the following four functional areas: learning, applied research and implementation, applied analysis, and information dissemination. The PACST should be a Pan-African supported, directed, and staffed institution; headquartered in Africa; and dedicated primarily to the solution of client-initiated problems.[82] In the long run, perhaps even in the short run, the PACST amounted to a mammoth undertaking requiring a worldwide organization of skilled manpower upon which to draw for expertise in carrying out various projects. Unfortunately, as we have noted, in the prevailing atmosphere of the Sixth Pan African Congress the proposal for a Center for Science and Technology was attacked on the grounds that it represented "bourgeois science." Therefore, plans for a continentwide Science and Technology Center were not adopted.

Lastly, although the Harvard Tanganyika Project (HTP) was not an African American initiative, like OCA, its activities in Tanzania preceded those of the Peace Corps program. The HTP was conceived by Peter C. Goldmark Jr., a junior at Harvard who was the well-off son of the inventor of the LP vinyl record.[83] The HTP sent its first cohort of volunteers in the summer of 1961, just before Tanganyika gained independence from Britain. The cohort consisted of twenty-six students who taught English in various schools. In 1962, the HTP began offering a yearlong option in addition to its original summer program.[84] After 1962 some HTP volunteers taught at the Kurasini school near Dar es Salaam, whose students were mostly exiles from southern Africa. The African American Institute, a US foundation, helped to finance the Kurasini school. The foundation, whose representative in Dar es Salaam was an African American named Ed Anderson, was later exposed as CIA-funded.[85] There were suspicions and allegations that some volunteers involved in the HTP during the 1960s might have had connections or ties to the CIA. However, concrete evidence supporting these suspicions is limited, and the true extent of CIA involvement remains uncertain.[86]

CHAPTER 3

Tanganyika Two (T-2)
Volunteer Nurses

Introduction

At the time of independence in 1961, Tanzania's health-service system was rudimentary; there were 119 hospitals, 22 rural health centers, and 825 dispensaries—in a country with a population of about 10 million.[1] Thus, the ratios of population to health facilities were extremely high: 78,992 for hospitals; 427,273 for rural health centers; and 11,394 for dispensaries.[2] Between 1961 and 1968, the government endeavored to expand the health-service system, with a goal of one provincial (central) hospital, one district hospital, and at least one dispensary in each chiefdom, depending on population density.[3]

At the time of independence, Tanzania also faced a severe shortage of medical staff. In 1961, there were 400 medical doctors (MDs) and 580 medical assistants (MAs) and rural medical aids (RMAs). The population ratio per MD was 24,819 and 7,759 per MA and RMA. The population per MD dropped from 24,819 in 1961 to 18,135 in 1971. However, this rose again from 19,053 in 1981 to 21,462 in 1987 because of a shortage of MDs. By 1989, the population to MD ratio had risen to 24,374.[4] In 1961, there were only 791 nurses (of all grades). The population ratio per nurse was 11,890. However, the number of nurses increased to 9,598 by 1984, bringing down the population ratio per nurse to 2,095.[5]

Based on this background, this chapter examines the performance of T-2, a Peace Corps project that sent an all-female contingent of twenty-five nurses and two laboratory technologists to Tanzania in September 1962.[6] The T-2 project was negotiated by Derek Bryceson, minister for health and labor, just before independence. He recognized the serious inadequacy of the country's health delivery system: "He foresaw the departure of many highly trained European personnel. And he was well aware of the heavy political pressure for 'Africanization' of the country's administrative and social services—despite the critical shortage of trained Africans to look after the needs of ten million Tanganyikans in such fields as medicine, nursing, and public health. Bryceson therefore welcomed the prospect of using a contingent of Peace Corps nurses to help stabilize the situation in Tanganyika's hospitals."[7]

However, there was a cabinet reshuffle before the Peace Corps nurses arrived in Tanzania. In the reshuffle, Bryceson was replaced by Said Maswanya as the new minister for health and labor.[8] According to Friedland, although Maswanya was favorable to the project, he was also less enthusiastic:

> Even had Mr. Bryceson remained, however, this would not have guaranteed effective cooperation at the working administrative level. In Tanganyika, as doubtless quite generally in . . . developing countries, enthusiasm at the policy level does not necessarily mean enthusiasm at the working level. And it is important to remember that at this time the Tanganyikan civil service was undergoing substantial change and was deeply preoccupied with serious problems of internal organization and stability—while at the same time attempting to maintain the normal work of government administration. It is not surprising, therefore, that the Tanganyika Two did not receive the kind of enthusiastic welcome or administrative cooperation that would be likely to lead to effective communication.[9]

In the United States, those selected for the T-2 program attended an eight-week training program at Syracuse University from July 2, 1962, to August 25, 1962. The schedule was built around several areas of concentration. In most instances, the educational pattern was centered on group instruction and discussion. In some cases, individual study and laboratory experience were added as major elements. The main areas and the total number of hours assigned to each were as follows:

1. Swahili Language Training .... 68 hrs.
2. Area Studies... 137 hrs.
3. American Studies and World Affairs .... 105 hrs.
   (including Communist Movement)
4. Nursing Procedures and Techniques......................... 57 hrs.
5. Medical Studies and Personal Hygiene...................... 54 hrs.
6. Physical Conditioning and Recreation .... 50 hrs.
7. Peace Corps Orientation..................................... 9 hrs.

The objective of the Swahili language training was to provide each trainee with an introduction to the basic components of audio-lingual skills in the language of the host country which, when coupled with the additional intensive Swahili training to be conducted in Tanzania, would allow each volunteer to communicate effectively with the Tanzanian people they would meet and work with.[10] Although the core of the training was classroom-based, it was supplemented by language laboratory sessions together with extracurricular conversational experience for the trainees through informal contact with two Tanzanian graduate students at Syracuse University.

According to Susan Proctor (née TonsKemper), who was one of the trainees, the language training was superb. She notes that Kamau Mwangi, a doctoral student from Kenya, was their primary classroom instructor. Mary Jo Kasindi, a Tanzanian from Dodoma, lived with the nurses in their dormitory; Kasindi taught the nurses Swahili songs and dancing in the Tanzanian style. Proctor notes that much dancing was done in the dormitory after hours.[11,]

The objective of the Area Studies course was "to provide the most thorough introduction possible" to the Tanzanian culture and society in which volunteers would live and work for two years. This introduction was made up of two components. The first consisted of the basic facts about Tanzania's institutions and practices and its "way of life." The second was a general and supposedly comprehensive framework within which basic information could be structured and interpreted. In this way, it was anticipated that the volunteers would be adequately equipped not only to begin their tour of duty but also to continue learning about the country and "maturing as inhabitants in a particular cultural setting."[12]

It is interesting to note that the instructors of the Area Studies program included Eduardo Mondlane (future president of FRELIMO, the Mozambican liberation movement, who was also assistant professor of sociology and anthropology at Syracuse University), Agehananda Bharati (assistant professor of anthropology and director of the Research Committee on East African Studies at Syracuse University), and Anthony Rweyemamu, (a Tanzanian doctoral candidate in political science at Syracuse University).[13] The consultants for the Area Studies program included Professor Margaret Bates, Associate Professor Gus Liebenow, and Sam Ntiro, who was Tanzania's high commissioner to the United Kingdom.

The primary objective of the American Studies and World Affairs course was "to turn out Volunteers who [were] knowledgeable and informed representatives of the United States": "As Americans working for a lengthy period in a foreign land, the Peace Corps members [would] be faced with many questions about a number of different facets of American life and society. They [had to] be prepared to answer such queries and to discuss various subjects in a sophisticated and intelligent manner. This [required] some systematic attention to basic features of American life and the role of the United States in the international political arena."

Instruction in the American Studies and World Affairs course involved selected readings, formal presentations, and group discussions. The volunteers were introduced to this section by exploring the problems and issues facing contemporary America and the Americans working in other countries. As we have noted, at the time, the image of overseas American was tainted by the publication of Burdick and Lederer's *The Ugly American* (1958), which was an indictment of American foreign policy and cultural ignorance.

The Nursing Procedures and Techniques program at Syracuse was oriented specifically toward the immediate job the volunteers would be called upon to perform in Tanzania. Largely, they would be expected to serve as general duty nurses in government hospitals; a few could be tapped as supervisors or instructors. To perform these roles effectively and competently, the volunteers would have to have an especially firm understanding of the nursing procedures and techniques they would be most likely called upon to use to meet unfamiliar health needs and medical situations and conditions of a new land.[14]

The Nursing Procedures and Techniques program for T-2 had one serious drawback. According to one of the nurses involved,

> This was the weakest part of the Syracuse training program. The nursing professor who taught a good portion of this should have journeyed to Tanganyika herself to learn a thing or two. The Dean of the School of Nursing

had visited the three hospitals where we would initially be station[ed], but I don't recall her saying much of any use about what to do, what not to do, how the British Medical and Nursing systems differed so much from American models, both in treatments, medications, but also in expectations of decorum and hierarchy. Most importantly, we could have used some down home advice in what to do when confronted with poor or no equipment and medication shortfalls. That should have come from an experienced Tanganyikan nurse who had also worked in an American hospital.[15]

Moreover, orientation and training in medical studies and personal hygiene was intended to minimize the concerns and anxiety of the volunteers about personal health problems and hazards associated with residency in an underdeveloped and unfamiliar country:

> Specifically, this section will provide a thorough introduction to the most common health problems and hazards in Tanganyika, familiarize the participants with the proper precautionary practices and personal preventative medicine, and stress the various medical facilities and assistance available as workers in the host country. In other words, an accurate picture will be drawn presenting a straightforward account of important health concerns while, at the same time, emphasizing that knowledge, consciousness, and available medical assistance can reduce potential hazards to a minimum and manageable risks.[16]

Furthermore, trainees were acquainted with specific diseases (water-borne, insect-borne, zoonotic, and respiratory), and their transmission and prevention; parasitology and entomology; hematology in the African setting; mental health and psychiatric considerations; first aid; personal tropical hygiene; new immunizing agents; and nutrition.[17]

Lastly, trainees were given a Peace Corps orientation intended to give them an overview of the agency they would be representing. The orientation involved introducing the participants to the agency and the total Peace Corps effort so that each volunteer finally chosen would serve with a full understanding of her role in this new venture in American international relations with newly independent countries.[18]

T-2: What They Did and the Challenges They Faced

On Wednesday, September 5, 1962, twenty-three nurses and two medical technologists of what came to be known as T-2 left New York City for Dar es Salaam via London, Rome, Tunis, Khartoum, and Nairobi.[19] After what must have been a very tiring twenty-two hours of flying, they arrived at Dar es Salaam on Friday, September 7. At the airport they were welcomed by Robert Hellawell, Peace Corps country director, and Dr. Charles Mtawali, principal secretary of the Ministry of Health.

In Dar es Salaam, the nurses and medical technologists commenced the second part of their training, which consisted almost solely of intense Swahili language instruction, six hours per day for seven weeks (September 12–October 26, 1962). The Mgulani Salvation Army Camp just south of Dar es Salaam served as both a housing site and a venue for the in-country language instruction. After their seven-week period of instruction, the volunteers were assigned to one of three hospitals in the country, as indicated in Table 1.

Table 1: Initial Hospital Assignments—Year One: n= 27/26**

City & Hospital	# T2s	Names—Registered Nurses (Alphabetical by first name)	# RNs	Names—Medical Technologists	# MTs
Dar es Salaam Princess Margaret Hospital*	16	Ann Quick * Carole Siriani Diane Sievert * Donna Abner Ethel Brown * Fran Hartery Georgia Mumford * Jean Read Mary Briggs * Mary Stafford Pat Hogan * Patsy Mason Sally Lazar * Susan Tonskemper	14	Becky Davis Lee Overstreet	2
Tanga Tanga Gov't Hospital	8/7	Annie Hohlstein * Barb Lyman Claire Linsmayer * Gail Croy Jo Snyder * Marlys Bralic Rita Lauderbaugh * Ruth Dygert	8/7**		0
Moshi: Moshi Gov't Hospital	3	Bev Russom * Mary Gibbons * Ruth Fulton	3		0

* Renamed Muhimbili Hospital in 1963.
** One member of this group resigned after only two months in the country.
Source: Susan Proctor, ed., *Bio Sketches & Life Stories*, 2nd ed. (Placerville, CA: 2015), ix. In author's possession.

The three hospitals to which members of T-2 were posted differed in terms of setting, size, staffing, and facilities. Dar es Salaam and Tanga are located along the Indian Ocean coastline of Tanzania, while Moshi is in the interior, on the foothills of Mount Kilimanjaro, Africa's highest mountain. Being on the Indian Ocean coastline, Dar es Salaam and Tanga are characterized by hot and humid weather, whereas Moshi is less humid. Dar es Salaam, being the capital, was more urbanized than the other two towns. Tanga, the second seaport in the country, was also the second-biggest town after Dar es Salaam in size and population.

Regardless of where they were posted, the T-2 nurses faced similar challenges professionally, culturally, and emotionally. Professionally, the challenges they faced included dealing with insufficient medications, equipment, and therapy options. To understand the severity of these challenges one needs to understand the array of afflicted patients who were thrust into their care.

In 1961 and 1962, the African Medical and Research Foundation conducted studies about the health services of the newly independent country and presented a report to the new government. The report indicated that the pattern of morbidity and mortality was the result of a variety of diseases: smallpox, typhoid, whooping cough, measles, cerebrospinal meningitis, and poliomyelitis, which were widespread; plague, trypanosomiasis, typhus, and rabies, which were localized; influenza, malaria, and the newly identified Chikungunya and O'nyong nyong fevers.[20]

According to the above report, whooping cough and measles were significant contributors to child mortality. At independence in 1961, nearly half the country's population of nine-and-a-half million were children under 15, and by far the largest group was that of infants. High mortality in infancy continued into early childhood and resulted in the death of 30 to 40 percent of children before they reached maturity.[21]

Treatment of diseases that afflicted infants, children, and adults depended on the availability of medical personnel, their training, and skills as well as on the availability of medications and medical equipment. As already noted above, the difficulties faced by T-2 nurses in the course of their duties included insufficient medications and medical equipment, which called upon the nurses to improvise and be flexible and creative. According to Susan Proctor, who was stationed at Princess Margaret Hospital (Muhimbili), and later at Mwanza Hospital, she had to improvise in several ways:

> I learned to take blood pressure without a stereoscope by palpating the brachial artery. It gave me a *gross* measure of the systolic reading. In the leprosy clinic in Mwanza, I learned how to use a 5cc syringe filled with procaine penicillin to administer five 1 cc doses to five patients without retracting the plunger on the syringe—as I had been taught to do—so as not to contaminate it—and my patients. It was the only syringe I had. I kept boiling the ten needles I had as an attempt at some kind of sterility and used them over and over again. The tips were full of ragged burrs. It never occurred to me to write to someone in the states [sic] asking for a good supply of syringes and needles. I was too young and naïve.[22]

Furthermore, when Proctor worked at Mwanza Hospital, she continued to face even more serious challenges, including the most difficult delivery of a baby she had ever experienced. The following is her description of the delivery of an unusually big baby:

> This baby's mother was in the "Grade 1" ward or the "paying" ward at Mwanza Hospital which suggests she had enough money to not only deliver her infant in an environment with supposedly better medical and nursing care but also presumes she had access to prenatal care and took advantage of it.
>
> To my knowledge, widespread use of sonograms or ultrasound in medicine wasn't available until the mid to late 1960s and then only in the wealthier countries of the world. I never saw or heard of any sonogram services anywhere in Tanzania when I was there, including at Muhimbili Hospital.
>
> During a prenatal exam, a vaginal exam late in pregnancy would have ascertained something called cephalo-pelvic disproportion, that is that the "inlet pelvis", the bony opening through which the baby passes during labor, was smaller than the circumference of the infant's head. This is most undesirable. However, this mother likely passed that "test" assuring the examiner that she could have a normal vaginal delivery since the vaginal exam would have confirmed that the inlet pelvis was of adequate size for a vaginal delivery.
>
> What was likely unknown here however, was that the infant's shoulder circumference was greater than the circumference of the infant's skull, a very

unusual development. Almost always the girth of the skull is larger than the combined girth of the shoulders. There would be no way to know that without an X-ray, or these days, a sonogram. Radiation is and was judiciously avoided to prevent unnecessary X-Ray exposure to both mother and fetus.

So not knowing the shoulders were larger than the head, the doctor allowed labor to progress. The head was in the vaginal canal but there was "shoulder dystocia", that is, the shoulders were too large to pass through the inlet pelvis. This is truly an emergency because there can be umbilical cord compression when the cervix clamps down on the cord resulting in the baby not getting enough oxygen to its brain. Labor cannot progress because the baby is "stuck."

With the head almost delivered, the doctor could not push the head back up into the uterus in order to do a Cesarian section—too risky—and setting up for a C Section takes precious minutes and seconds further endangering the lives of both mother and infant. He had to act quickly. This development in labor would be excruciatingly painful to the mother as well.

So fracturing the clavicle allowed for the shoulders and the rest of the body to be delivered using the power of the very strong uterine contractions typical of the end of labor and likely saved the infant's life.[23]

Another T-2 nurse, Ruth Elizabeth Dygert Shiers, who was stationed at Tanga Hospital, says that besides all of her nursing education, she put to good use all of the flexibility, creativity, and improvising skills she had learned while growing up and working on a small subsistence-level dairy farm until she left home to start college. At Tanga, she found the level of access to every aspect of good hospital care a huge challenge: very few medications, short supply of clean linens such as bed sheets and others, and inadequate auxiliary supplies (syringes, needles, etc.). Regardless, she and her T-2 colleagues believed that they showed a level of concern for and attention to "compassionate care" that was not expected and was sometimes an issue of dismay to the existing administration of the hospital.[24]

Besides their professional challenges, the T-2 nurses faced social and cultural challenges that were part of living in a completely different social-cultural setting. Evidently, their training at Syracuse in the Area Studies course did not include cultural nuances and etiquette that would have prepared them for what to expect and how to navigate their way around their host communities. Most T-2 nurses were in their early twenties and fresh out of college and some, as Proctor notes, were unprepared about how to respond to male attention in a different cultural setting. This was, however, attenuated by their living arrangements, which, as Proctor says, helped to insulate them more than male Peace Corps volunteers in Tanzania.

The T-2 nurses' tour of duty was from 1962 to 1964. Their stay in Tanzania was eventful in several ways. In July 1963, President Julius Nyerere visited Washington, DC, as a guest of President John F. Kennedy. The two men had met briefly in 1960 prior to Tanzania's becoming independent, when both had yet to assume the reins of their respective nations' governments. According to William R. Duggan, Kennedy and Nyerere had a candid conversation when they met in 1963:

> The essentials of the conversation between the two leaders were, of course, highly classified. Press reports indicated that they *discussed* the inception of the OAU [Organization of African Unity], problems of southern Africa, global race problems, and matters of aid. Nyerere ... questioned the American president closely as to the rationale behind American foreign-aid generosity. Nyerere said the president responded that such aid was not primarily for altruistic motives but for reasons of national self-interest. When Nyerere asked the president to elucidate this point, President Kennedy is reported by Nyerere as saying that the self-interest lay principally in building a national and international defense against the encroachments of Communism.[25]

Although 1963 was relatively calm in Tanzania, it was followed by a more sensational year of 1964. First, the army mutiny in the early hours of January 20, 1964, created an unsettled situation especially in the places where the three battalions were stationed, namely, Dar es Salaam, Nachingwea, and Tabora. The Peace Corps volunteers who were stationed at Dar es Salaam and Tabora were especially in imminent danger. At Tabora, it is said that soldiers there went around looking for *wazungu* (white people) to kill.

Second, the escalation of the Vietnam War (1955–75) particularly created tension between the United States and Tanzania, as the later became vocal in opposing the war. The politics of the Vietnam War affected the lived experience of T-2 nurses and those who followed them. As Proctor notes:

> The emotional challenges largely involved politics and my slowly growing awareness that the US was not all "pure" as I had been taught. I saw my country from the outside with all her triumphs but also her foibles. This awakening is perhaps not unusual for any early twenty-something, and is in fact, a normal developmental phenomenon. However, to have it occur while living in a different culture was particularly unsettling. I began questioning my faith and my country. And the war in Vietnam didn't help. When President Johnson escalated the bombing of Hanoi in January 1965, I told new people I met that I was an Mcanada—a Canadian—because the Canadians always come off so squeaky clean.[26]

Apparently, the training and orientation offered in the World Affairs course did not prepare Proctor to see her country from the outside "with all her triumphs but also her foibles."

Likewise, the Area Studies course did not prepare T-2 nurses for navigating Tanzania's cultural landscape such as how to deal with (nonwhite) male attention and other things, often small, to do or not do to prevent cultural faux pas.[27] This is of significance because most of the nurses were young (ages twenty-one to twenty-four), while the oldest four were ages thirty-five, thirty-seven, thirty-eight, and forty-two. Youth, as they say, is fraught with naïveté.

T-2 Nurses and the Peace Corps Mandate

At the time of independence, medical facilities, physicians, and nurses were in short supply. In 1961, there was one hospital for each 78,992 inhabitants; one doctor for each 24,819 inhabitants; and one nurse for each 11,890 inhabitants. In recognition of these deficiencies, the government requested a contingent of Peace Corps nurses who would supplement the work of local and expatriate nurses. The latter were British, and following Tanzania's independence, many of them opted to return to the United Kingdom. As we have noted, the initial assignments of T-2 nurses concentrated them at three hospitals at Dar es Salaam, Tanga, and Moshi. Princess Margaret Hospital (Muhimbili) in Dar es Salaam received the biggest number of volunteers.[28] Since friendships with the local people and integration into the local community are among the Peace Corps's most cherished goals, it is pertinent to examine the extent to which the T-2 nurses advanced these goals.

William H. Friedland, a sociologist, was director of Area Studies for T-2. In mid-1963, Friedland carried out three intensive weeks of field work in Tanzania, "during which he was able to see almost all members of T-2 in action."[29] In 1966, Friedland published a chapter titled "Nurses in Tanganyika" in *Cultural Frontiers of the Peace Corps,* edited by Robert B. Textor and Lambros Comitas.[30] His objective was to examine the experiences of T-2, paying particular attention to the negative aspects of the program "in order to glean lessons that might be of general value."[31]

According to Friedland, the T-2 nurses were excellent American goodwill ambassadors because their patients appreciated the attention and the care rendered to them.[32] However, Friedland notes: "Volunteers were housed together in single housing units and assigned their own mess area which was rapidly converted into a 'Little America.' When I visited the groups midway through their tour, the prevailing atmosphere was almost entirely American with a few Tanganyikan overtones—rather than vice versa. This was hardly conducive to high morale, since in the training program much emphasis had been placed for integration with Tanganyika society."[33] The nurses' lack of interaction with Africans outside the confines of a hospital was a hindrance to the Peace Corps mission, namely the creation of enduring social relationships between volunteers and local people for the purpose of facilitating good relations between the people of the United States and the people of Tanzania.

Moreover, Friedland points out that although the T-2 nurses came into contact with many Africans at all levels in the hospital hierarchy,[34] there was a lack of social interaction between the volunteers and their Tanzanian colleagues off the job. Furthermore, Friedland notes that one of the reasons for such a lack of interaction off the job was the heavy stress placed on social distance among various strata of the hospital hierarchy.[35] However, one of the T-2 nurses offers a different perspective on this lack of informal, off-the-job interaction.

According to Proctor, T-2 nurses in Dar es Salaam did not develop close relationships with Tanzanian staff nurses because many, if not most, of the nursing staff at the Princess Margaret Hospital (Muhimbili) were male and married. She points out that this situation did not lend itself to close personal relationships outside the work setting. She further notes: "Indeed, the male nurses with whom we worked were in most cases our supervisors and ... various strata of nursing personnel [just did] not socialize." It is interesting to note that when Proctor was transferred to Mwanza, on the shores of Lake Victoria, the Black South African nurses with whom she worked were not only there as exiles from apartheid South Africa but also inured of the British nursing system as she was, and they were also the same rank as she. Thus, they became good friends.[36]

By and large, Friedland notes that measured by most standards T-2 was a success.[37] However, in his three intensive weeks of fieldwork and interviews with members of T-2, Friedland was unable to discern how the nurses cared for their patients, which in their view made a big difference and was professionally satisfying. Instead, Friedland believed that T-2 nurses exhibited serious morale problems, which, in turn, he suggests, contributed to what he determined to be a high attrition rate of the group or the number of departures from Tanzania of group members prior to the completion of their two-year tour of service. Table 2 indicates the number of T-2 members who left before the completion of their two-year tour of duty.

Table 2: Group Longevity versus Attrition (n=27)

# Completed Entire Tour	# Left Very Early in Tour	# Left Due to Marriage	# Left Due to Adoption of Child	# Left Due to Illness	Attrition
19 (70.3%)	1	5 (all after 1 full year)	1 (after 1 full year)	1 (near end of year 2)	8 (29.7%)

Source: Susan Proctor, ed., *Bio Sketches & Life Stories,* 2nd ed. (Placerville, CA: 2015). In author's possession.

From Table 2, we see that only one nurse left the program very early after the group arrived in Tanzania, most likely before the close of 1962. According to Proctor,

> It is true ... that with marriage, T-2 PCVs did begin to depart, beginning in April or May of 1963. In and around that time period, there were five marriages, all of them to T-1 PCVs or to other Peace Corps or TEA [Teachers of East Africa] personnel who had completed their tours of duty and were headed back to the states [sic]. A bit later that year, the Peace Corps sent another nurse home because she had quietly adopted a toddler. Peace Corps in-country staff found that unacceptable. Of interest, that child, now about

55 years old, was our guest at our most recent T I-T II reunion in October 2018. She resides in Colorado.[38]

Proctor strongly disagrees with Friedland that the T-2 group's attrition was due to frustration with their work environment. She says:

That seems to be skewed thinking. This was 1963. Most American women expected—in fact wished to be married—and there was a reciprocal cultural expectation that they do so. During this era, the US was barely out of the 50s, the decade of the ideal housewife and mother who was expected to spun [sic] a career in favor of marriage and family only. It was not uncommon for college to be seen as something "to fall back on" should marriage not come one's way. Indeed, this was very much my experience despite an intense, rigorous, five year baccalaureate program in nursing. Careers were something to be engaged in until marriage came along. With all due respect to Dr. Friedland, his interpretation that workplace stress was the impetus for marrying suggests to me a lack of awareness of the cultural norms of the time governing the behavior of young American women. A young woman in love would have married for love's sake, not out of work related frustration.[39]

To conclude, during the early years of Tanzania's independence, the likelihood is that the services of Peace Corps volunteers were very much appreciated. However, as the reality of independence set in, some Africans may have exhibited sensitivity toward what they believed were overbearing *wazungu* (white) foreigners, which included the American Peace Corps volunteers. Soon after independence most Africans became apprehensive of being photographed by *wazungu*. After his visit in mid-1963, Friedland notes that there was an incident that greatly soured relations between Tanzania and the Peace Corps. The incident involved some T-5 nurses who, due to their lack of cultural sensitivity, took photographs of an African woman in a delivery room. The two nurses involved in this incident were summarily sent out of the country.[40]

CHAPTER 4

Tanganyika Five (T-5)
Civil Engineers, 1964–1966

Introduction

The work of the T-1 engineers, highlighted in chapter 1, was continued by civil engineers who were part of the T-5 contingent that included agriculturalists. Like the T-1 engineers, the T-5 civil engineers worked in the Public Works Department (PWD) and provided much-needed expertise, especially in the construction of roads and dams. However, completion of these construction projects hinged on the availability of communal labor. Beginning in 1962, the Tanzanian government mobilized people to provide voluntary labor under the policy known as "self-help." At first glance, self-help or voluntary labor projects seemed an obvious solution to the economic problems facing the newly independent country. As Joseph Nye points out, capital was scarce but labor was plentiful, and there was a strong spirit of nationalism among the people.[1]

The January 1963 edition of the *Tanganyika News Review* reported that by the end of 1962, "the people of Tanganyika had by self-help built 9,725 miles of new roads, repaired 4,397 miles of old roads, made 308 dams and undertaken many other projects."[2] As a result, through self-help schemes the government was able to save £500,000. These savings were estimates of what the PWD would have had to spend if labor had not been voluntary.[3] Nevertheless, the enthusiasm for self-help schemes soon declined. This was due in part to the fact that self-help was competing for labor with other work, especially farming during the rainy season.

T-5 Civil Engineers in Musoma

Bill Crosby and Neil Christianson were posted to the PWD in Musoma, where they were engaged in the construction of dams and roads. In the course of their work, they were frustrated by the lack of labor. One evening they were heard venting their frustrations in a bar in Musoma: "PWD wants to construct culverts and bridges but won't pay for labor," griped a normally amiable Crosby. "And we need at least thirty guys just to do the bridge on the Ikizu-Ikoma road,"[4] added his colleague, Christianson. Glumly, Crosby took another swig of Tusker beer.

"Ehh, I hear you," replied the dignified African sharing their table, "President Nyerere expects Tanzanians to volunteer labor for the good of the country. But of course, they do not. Therefore, little is accomplished. This hurts our district." Then he mentioned a problem of his own. The district council for which he worked had difficulty collecting taxes because the people were so poor. "And if we took their cows as taxes they would make war on us," he declared.[5]

Silently, the three men pondered their respective situations. But then the eyes of the dignified African brightened. Leaning across the table, he grinned. "*Sikia* [hear me]," he said, "the district council will provide funds to hire laborers if you withhold half their salaries to pay their taxes. Then our district will get culverts and bridges as well as tax revenue." The spirits of the two volunteers abruptly improved. Their new friend, they thought, must be more than a mere employee of the district council. "Have another beer," they chorused.[6]

When next the call for hired laborers went out, over a hundred men showed up. Christianson and Crosby only needed thirty but when the taxes of the first group of men were paid, they hired new people. Never again did the two engineers have trouble finding laborers.

In Musoma, the T-5 surveyors and engineers worked with the PWD and Water Development and Irrigation Division (WD&ID). Volunteers working for PWD constructed culverts and bridges on secondary roads, most of which were unsurfaced dirt and, therefore, often impassible during the rainy season (which kept farmers from getting their produce to market). They established work camps, ensured supplies were hauled, expedited the acquisition of trucks and bulldozers, hired laborers, and supervised construction. They also trained young Tanzanians to continue the work

Traffic halted by high water flowing over a drift between Musoma and Mwanza. A drift is a layer of concrete placed across a seasonally dry streambed to allow better traction for vehicles and prevent the road from washing out during the rainy season. (Neil Christianson)

after the volunteers returned to the United States. Work areas were large, about two hundred miles (322 km) of roadwork in the case of Christianson and Crosby.

Volunteers working for WD&ID carried out surveys. These included geophysical surveys to find potential well sites, core drilling to determine if soils were strong and dense enough to support dams without leaking, and topographic surveys to identify where to place dams and how to distribute water from wells, dams, and rivers to users. Water development was especially important in Tanzania because large areas of the country are arid and semiarid, with high temperatures and rates of evaporation, and erratic, unreliable rainfall. Many streams are seasonally dry.

Some volunteer engineers were assigned Tanzanians to train. Christianson and Crosby were impressed, not only by them but also by the ingenuity and teamwork displayed by the other members of their African crews. In some cases, a "trainee" had already been better trained for certain jobs than the volunteer had been. In such cases, the African crew could do most of the work without supervision.

Time spent in the field varied. For instance, Christianson and Crosby spent their first six months living in tents, choosing sites to upgrade, and establishing work camps before moving to Musoma, from which they visited each work site once a week to monitor progress. Water Development and Irrigation Division (WD&ID) engineer Bob Ferris, based in Mwanza, made one-to-two-week-long safaris to sites of interest within his district. Eric Ries, also with WD&ID, was away so much that he seldom used his apartment in Dodoma.

When in the field, the engineers and surveyors lived in tents, caravans, and small huts. Those working in teams generally hired an African *mpishi* (cook). Ferris, with no teammate, cooked for himself. They boiled their drinking water or mixed it with Clorox and then covered up the Clorox taste by drinking it with orange squash. Alternatively, they brought jerry cans of town water, which was safe to drink, on safari but then had to ration its use. Bob Ferris managed on two to three gallons per day for up to two weeks. His baths were just a quick splash once a day with cold water. Whenever Christianson and Crosby saw heavy rain coming their way, they stripped naked and ran out into the rain with a bar of soap to bathe.

Tanzania's official workday ran from 7:00 A.M. to 2:30 P.M. In any case, WD&ID surveyors could not survey on hot afternoons because heat waves

A newly installed culvert. Culverts were adjusted in size to fit the circumstances of a drainage problem. (Tom Meier)

rising off the ground made it impossible to get accurate readings with their transits. Afternoons were spent writing up field notes, reading, and napping (in the shade of a nearby tree on hot days), and evenings were spent drinking beer, orange squash, or gin and tonic, and listening to the radio while insects beat against the brightly lit glass of their Petromax and hurricane lanterns. Sometimes they just sat in the dark wondering at the stars before crawling under mosquito nets to fall asleep to the whine of mosquitoes, or, if deep in the bush, to the mournful whoop of a prowling hyena.

However, even volunteers who spent most of their time in the bush periodically got into town for at least short periods. Ferris's idea of heaven was returning to Mwanza from a long safari and soaking in a tub of hot water while sipping an ice-cold drink, listening to Johnny Mathis, and reading his mail. Never again, he says, will he take flush toilets for granted. Ferris fondly remembers Liberty Cinema in Mwanza, which showed Elvis Presley and old Western films. The cinema in Musoma was named the Diamond Talkies, and the Fourways Grocery Store let volunteers pay when they could. The Barclays Bank manager in Mwanza once let Ferris overdraw his account before going on vacation.

Since leaving Tanzania over half a century ago, T-5 engineers have periodically posed the question: Did Tanzania benefit from our presence? The

Bob Ferris and his crew (Bob Ferris)

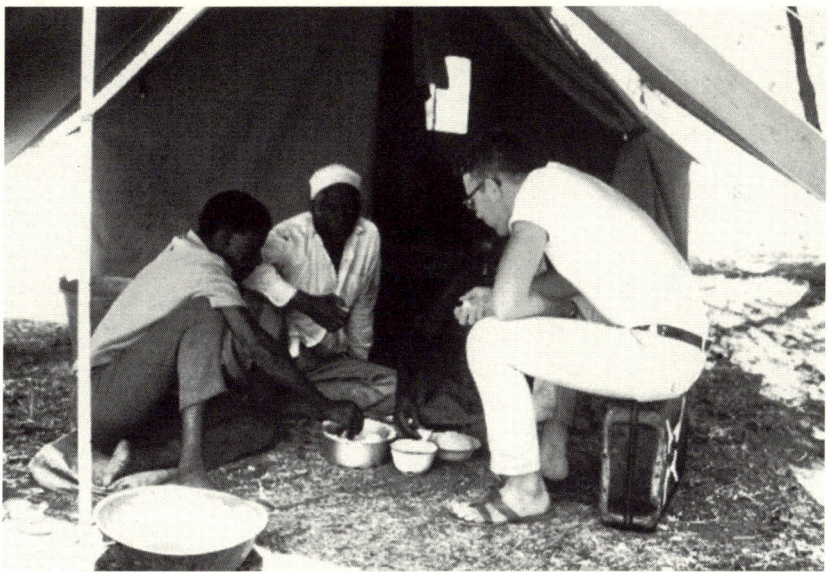

Eating ugali, maize flour cooked with water to a porridge-like consistency and served with a sauce. Bob Ferris's crew insisted that it wasn't proper for a white person to sit on the ground like them. (Bob Ferris)

PWD engineers think so because they were able to see their efforts bear visible fruit in the form of new dams and culverts, not to mention trained Tanzanians capable of carrying out engineering duties. For instance, Christianson and Crosby completed over 90 percent of the culvert and bridge construction to which they were assigned. Furthermore, they trained five young Africans who proved capable of continuing the work after the two volunteers left. Consequently, Christianson and Crosby feel good about their impact on the country. Using Google Maps, Christianson recently discovered that at least one of the bridges that he, Crosby, and their crew constructed still exists.

Ries and the other WD&ID surveyors and engineers, Richard Russell, Jeff Gabiou, and George Frame, are less positive, probably because their outputs, being in the form of maps and tables, were less strikingly visible. Furthermore, they suspect that few of the dams, which they surveyed, were ever constructed. Consequently, other than training two assistants to take on his duties, Ries feels he did not do much for Tanzania. He thinks his major contribution may have been in showing Tanzanians that not all whites felt superior to them.

CHAPTER 5

Tanzania Six (T-6)
Volunteer Teachers, 1964–1969

Introduction

In 1961, when Tanzania became independent, the country did not possess the financial or other resources necessary to provide even four years of schooling for all children. Of those children who were fortunate enough to attend primary school, the majority had no opportunity to proceed beyond grade Standard IV. In 1961, Tanzania had 89,564 students in Standard IV who took the national examination to enter Standard V. Out of 89,564 only 17,623 went on to Standard V. Tanzania also had 13,033 students who sat the Standard VIII General Entrance Examination (used to qualify and select students for secondary and tertiary education), and 6,180 were selected for secondary schools, teacher training, and trade schools.[1]

After independence, the government drew up a Three-Year Development Plan (1962–64), which gave priority to the expansion of secondary education and provided for the opening of seventeen more secondary streams in rural areas and seventeen in urban areas. Although the emphasis was on secondary school expansion, the Ministry of Education also tried, within the limits of available financial resources, to increase the number of school places after Standard VI. The plan provided for government assistance toward almost two hundred additional classrooms in urban areas and twelve hundred in rural areas during the next three years.[2] Table 3, on the next page, shows the growth of the education sector between 1961 and 1966.

Table 3: Growth of Education, 1961–1966

Level	1961	1966	%
Primary School	486,470	740,991	52%
Secondary School	11,832	23,836	101%
Teacher Training	909	2,560	182%
Technical Education	2,697	2,095	-22%
University Education	811	1,719	112%
Total	502,219	771,201	53%

Source: Karim Hirji, "School Education and Underdevelopment in Tanzania," *Maji Maji* 12 (1973): 1–22.

Table 3 indicates that teacher training did not grow in tandem with the expansion of primary and secondary education. The expansion of primary and secondary education created a demand for more teachers than were available. If the goals of providing education to more children were to be met, then the additional teachers would have to come from outside the country until Tanzania could train all their teachers locally. After independence, the majority of American Peace Corps teachers alleviated the shortage of teachers, especially at the primary school level. By 1969, when the Peace Corps program closed, three cohorts of Peace Corps volunteer teachers had served in Tanzania. However, another group of American teachers preceded the Peace Corps under a program known as Teachers for East Africa (TEA), mainly for secondary schools. Teachers for East Africa also included British teachers.

The Teachers for East Africa (TEA) Program

In December 1960, a conference was held in Princeton, Massachusetts, to consider the educational problems of East Africa, namely Kenya, Uganda, Tanganyika, and Zanzibar. The conference, sponsored by the American Liaison Committee of the American Council of Education, was attended by representatives of the pre-independence governments of East Africa, representatives of the United States and the United Kingdom, and representatives of voluntary agencies concerned with education in East Africa. The East African governments' representatives stressed that their most pressing problem was the expansion of secondary education, as Table 4 indicates. The conference proposed and recommended that the United States should undertake to meet this shortage—not eventually but immediately. Thus, the TEA program was born.[3]

Table 4: Secondary School Enrollment, East Africa, 1952 and 1960

	1952			1960		
	Boys	Girls	Total	Boys	Girls	Total
Kenya	1,160	64	1,224	4,623	786	5,409
Uganda	4,410	645	5,055	21,113	4,311	25,424
Tanganyika	2,726	91	2,817	4,163	482	4,645
Zanzibar	672	148	820	944	410	1,354
Total	8,968	948	9,916	30,843	5,989	36,832

Note: Figures are for African education.
Source: P. C. C. Evans, "American Teachers for East Africa," *Comparative Education Review* 6, no. 1 (June 1962): 70.

Teachers College at Columbia University sought American college graduates to prepare for teaching service in secondary schools in East Africa. The college undertook the recruitment, selection, and training of the candidates at the request of the Agency for International Development of the State Department. Those interested were urged to apply immediately, and applicants had to be US citizens. Arts and science graduates and graduating seniors with no teaching experience (but who had been professionally trained), certified graduates with no teaching experience, and experienced teachers were all eligible to apply for the program.

Upon completion of training at Teachers College or Makerere University, Kampala, Uganda, or at both institutions, the teachers would receive two-year appointments as salaried education officers in East Africa. Although preference in selection was given to applicants who were single, married people could apply and, if chosen, would receive travel allowances for dependents. However, it was not possible for both husband and wife to be employed with the program.

In 1961, 145 teachers were sent to East Africa. Their categories and numbers were as follows: A (57), B (38), and C (50). In 1962, 108 teachers were sent to East Africa in categories A (33), B (43), and C (32). Table 5 shows their assignments by country, as of March 21, 1963.

As Table 5 indicates, Tanganyika received the largest number of Teachers for East Africa—totaling 135 by March 21, 1963. This number would rise with the arrival of more teachers under waves three and four. For 1964, the aim was to recruit 125 teachers, distributed among Groups A, B, and

Table 5: TEA Assignments by Country, as of March 21, 1963

	Kenya	Tanganyika	Uganda	Zanzibar	Total
1961 Wave 1	32	69	41	3	145
1962 Wave 2	22	66	19	1	108
Total	54	135	60	4	253

C in about the same proportion as the previous contingents. This contingent would consist of teachers in the fields of biology, chemistry, English, geography, history, mathematics, and physics, who would commence their tour of duty in the fall of 1964.

The Peace Corps Teachers

After the formation of the Peace Corps, Robert Sargent Shriver, the director of Peace Corps, began to argue that Peace Corps should replace TEA in East Africa. However, the East African countries did not agree. According to R. Freeman Butts, director of International Studies of the TEA, the East African countries were so satisfied with Teachers College's selection and training of TEA instructors that they would not accept the usual Peace Corps volunteers who only had liberal arts education and no professional preparation for teaching. However, eventually new training officers at the Peace Corps were able to work out an agreement with Teachers College for a modified training program for Peace Corps teachers.[4] In 1964, Peace Corps training for secondary school teachers in East Africa began at Teachers College at Columbia University, while Peace Corps teachers for upper-primary schools trained at Syracuse University.

The first group of Peace Corps volunteers that trained at Syracuse University was named Tanganyika Three (hereafter: T-3). The following is an excerpt from a letter that was sent to those selected for training in the T-3 program by Dean Alexander N. Charters, University College, Adult Education Division, Syracuse University: "A rigorous and accelerated program of academic instruction and physical conditioning has been programmed to prepare you for your assignment as Peace Corps volunteer in Tanganyika. The training you will receive will be professional, practical and purposive. It has been carefully structured to develop the skills you will need to operate with maximum effectiveness under the specific conditions imposed by your respective assignment."[5]

The training began on September 1, 1963, and continued for an eight-week period, ending October 26, 1963. The program had eight instructional components, and the total number of hours assigned to each were as follows:

1. Technical Studies...130
2. Area Studies..64
3. American Studies and World Affairs 64
4. Philosophy, Strategy, Tactics, and Menace of Communism........ 20
5. Health and Medical Training 20
6. Physical Education and Recreation (including 10 hrs. of first aid)...70
7. Swahili Language Training 96
8. Peace Corps Orientation..16
                                  Total Instructional Hours   480

The trainees were preparing to go to Tanganyika at the invitation of the government, whose Three-Year Development Plan targeted the expansion of the primary and secondary education systems. Thus, each trainee would receive tutelage in the cultural foundations of both Tanganyikan and American education, the psychological foundations of human development and learning, the purposes and skills in testing and measuring student progress, and the methodology of teaching.

The T-3 program, through the Area Studies component, emphasized the significance of trainees being knowledgeable in the historical, political, and cultural aspects of Tanganyika; contemporary international problems; the role of the United States in world affairs; and the nature of the Communist Movement. Equally emphasized was the role of a Peace Corps volunteer. The trainees were told: "Underlying all of the instructional activities is the singular objective of emphasizing upon you the need to understand your role as an outsider in the society of your host country. It is hoped that the knowledge you gain will enable you to know the bounds you cannot overstep; be able to recognize the impact your presence and innovations may have on the Tanganyikan people; and be able to recognize the methods, attitudes and approaches that will be effective or ineffective."[6]

Peace Corps expected T-3 trainees to represent the United States in a positive manner. In this regard, under the American Studies and World

Affairs component, the program provided trainees with an understanding of: (1) the civilization they would be representing abroad and (2) the objectives and mechanisms of international relations.[7] Likewise, for the sake of their wellbeing, trainees were given information about the health problems and diseases prevalent in Tanganyika, and the steps that could be taken to avoid contracting them.[8]

Other cohorts of volunteers for upper–primary school teachers and secondary school teachers followed until the Peace Corps program closed in 1969. A T-6 Volunteer, Thomas "Tom" Houlihan, taught me at Chilonwa Middle School from 1966 to 1967. Regardless of the cohorts they belonged to, all volunteers faced the same challenges in the course of their service. To begin with, they had to adjust to a British curriculum (based on rote learning) that was still in place in Tanzania after independence.[9] After 1967, they had to adjust to a new system known as Education for Self-Reliance, which had come into force after the decision to turn Tanzania into a socialist country. The name *Tanzania* was adopted after the union of Tanganyika and Zanzibar in April 1964.

Like their counterparts in Cameroon, some volunteers discovered that assignments included teaching subjects they neither took in college nor prepared for in training.[10] At Chilonwa Middle School, Houlihan taught all subjects, including math (his major in college was physics with a minor in math), English, geography, and science. It was at Syracuse University that, after enrolling in the Peace Corps, he was trained for three months to be a teacher. However, what he really learned about teaching was gained while he was at Chilonwa Middle School. Likewise, Susan Hoffma Rabideau found her teaching job unfulfilling because she was an engineering graduate who was asked to teach math and science at Moshi Technical School. In a similar vein, Mike Goldwasser (1966–68), who was posted at Mpwapwa Secondary School, was assigned to teach physics and advanced math, despite having had very little background in these subjects and graduating with a BA. Nevertheless, the Peace Corps assured him that they had confidence that he could do it!

At Nyakato Boys Secondary School near Bukoba, one of the courses John Ratigan was assigned to teach—in addition to English—was Form 2 History, which covered the history and "civics" of Tanzania, which Ratigan knew very little about. Even more interesting is that Ratigan was asked to officiate at the Bukoba town polling station in the national election held in early 1965. According to Ratigan, he was perturbed when the headmaster asked him to serve as an official in the nationwide election despite being a newly arrived foreigner.

In some places, fulfilling their duties was difficult because the basic tools required for teaching were not available. Aileen Cochrane Dower, who was a member of T-6, was posted together with her husband, Hal, at Ibadakuli Upper Primary School (a middle school) near Shinyanga. She notes that her students had no paper or books, so their responses were oral: "Math problems were worked on individual slates with crumbly chalk. I used the 'blackboard', which was painted concrete. The crumbly chalk did not work well on that. The *New York Times* sent rolls of newsprint and my mother sent boxes of markers and masking tape. I would write the lesson on the paper and tape it to the 'blackboard.'"

Besides primary school teachers, the Peace Corps also sent teachers for secondary schools. Several cohorts from T-5 to T-12 included secondary school volunteer teachers. The thirty-four volunteers who received training at Columbia Teachers College in late September 1964 were told that the Peace Corps had taken particular care in their recruitment and selection. They would be the first Peace Corps teachers responsible for preparing Tanzanian secondary school students for the important Cambridge Overseas "O-Level" (and in some cases, "A-Level") examinations. Therefore, Peace Corps wanted to put its best foot forward. Their orientation included Swahili language training, political and cultural orientation, and teacher methodology. The latter included pedagogical methods, as well as several days of in-class practice teaching at New York City public schools.

During the three months of orientation, Peace Corps and Columbia Teachers College staff regularly tested and evaluated the trainees to ensure that those sent to Tanzania were capable of living and functioning effectively far from home in a culture quite different from that of the United States. When they arrived in Dar es Salaam in late December 1964, the volunteers stayed at the Mgulani scout camp, today known as Mgulani Hostel and Conference Center, which was operated by the Salvation Army. They remained several days at Mgulani, during which time they got to know the Peace Corps–Tanzania leadership and staff. They also met with Tanzanian Ministry of Education staff, who had been given information about each of them and now informed them which secondary schools they had been assigned.

Those assigned to schools located at a significant distance from Dar es Salaam began to prepare for lengthy train or bus rides that would take them to their schools. Those who were assigned to Bukoba in West Lake province, for example, took the train to Tabora and then on to Mwanza before boarding an overnight lake steamer to Bukoba. Other volunteers traveled to their destinations by bus. The five-hundred-fifty-mile trip from Dar to Mbeya, for example, required two days, including an overnight stay in Iringa.

Whatever means the volunteers used to travel, it provided an instant cultural introduction to Tanzania. First, they had an immediate immersion in Swahili, especially how to use it in everyday life. English was usually available in a pinch; they could speak with another passenger, dining car personnel, or a train conductor. But immersion in Swahili was a great advantage. Second, since many of the schools they were assigned to happened to be relatively distant from the capital, they traveled through a sizeable portion of the country, including going through some of its major towns. They also got a feel of the weather, topography, and more. Third, although the food served on the train was primarily Western, they also saw how other passengers fed themselves, the food they brought with them, or the food they purchased from vendors who eagerly approached the train or bus when it stopped.

When volunteers arrived at their schools, most found that they had inherited houses previously occupied by British or other foreign teachers, which were normally quite functional. Most houses in town had electric power for most if not all day, with a water heater, kerosene stove, and refrigerator. Merchants in most towns were accustomed to selling to British or Western residents and so provided a broad array of processed food and drinks. Local vegetables and meat were available in the market; Western movies, if not shown in the local theatre, were available at the British club; and golf and tennis were available in many communities. Various Christian missionaries ran religiously based secondary schools, and so were an outside source of "here's how we do it" information and ideas. The East African shilling was accepted in all three countries, the EA Common Services Organization was operational, and mail service was regular and reliable.

In January 1966, a second group of secondary teachers arrived. In-country training by Peace Corps and Ministry of Education personnel continued throughout the two years of service. At some point during the first year, Peace Corps and the Ministry of Education conducted a two- to three-day educational conference in Morogoro. Peace Corps also held a predeparture conference in December 1966 in Dar es Salaam to review "lessons learned," develop suggestions for future secondary school teachers, and provide feedback on the entire two-year experience. Representatives of Peace Corps–Washington attended this final conference; their report to Washington concluded that as classroom teachers in well-established schools, this group had not really had "the true Peace Corps experience." The volunteers scoffed at that notion.

Among the secondary school teachers were agriculturalists who intended to introduce agriculture in agricultural secondary schools. From September 1964 to June 1966, Peace Corps volunteer George Cummins was farm manager and substitute agricultural instructor at Galanos Agricultural Secondary School, in Tanga,[11] a school that the author taught at from 1977 to 1979. Cummins held a bachelor of science in agricultural education from Iowa State University. According to Cummins, agricultural biology was the only agriculture course taught at Galanos when he arrived. All teaching was to prepare students for their final exams rather than the practical application of the material on the syllabus after graduating.

Cummins endeavored to change agricultural instruction at Galanos. To begin with, as farm manager, he constructed buildings including an eighteen-hundred-head poultry barn, a brooder, a machine storage shed, repair shop, and farm office. The brooder is where day-old chicks brought in from Nairobi were held until they were ready to enter the laying houses or to be distributed to farmers in the area who were starting household poultry projects. Each of the two laying sheds had a capacity of twelve hundred birds. The school cafeteria served some of the eggs and the rest were sold to the local community.

Cummins also laid out individual garden plots for students and a farm for perennial and annual crops for demonstrating practical application of agricultural methods. Regarding applying what he taught, Cummins vaccinated all birds for fowl pox, fowl typhoid, and Newcastle Disease. The latter was known as *kizungu zungu* (Swahili for *dizziness*) because the affected chickens are disorientated, spin in circles, and lose their balance. The legacy that Cummins left endures.

Peace Corps Teachers and the Peace Corps Mandate

Of the three Peace Corps mandates, the transfer of skills was the least applicable to volunteer teachers by virtue of their profession. The interaction between teachers and students is a transfer of knowledge rather than skills. Besides transferring knowledge, Peace Corps teachers served as role models, whether this was intended or not. As the following aphorism states: "What a teacher writes on the blackboard of life can never be erased."[12] Peace Corps volunteer teachers influenced their students by how they carried themselves. As we shall see later, Tanzania viewed Peace Corps teachers negatively when Tanzania chose to become socialist because American teachers came from a capitalist country.

As already noted, I was taught by a Peace Corps teacher, Mr. Houlihan, at Chilonwa Middle School in Standards VII and VIII. When the headmaster, Dennis Nakati, announced the impending arrival of Houlihan, the school community was excited because he would be the first American and white teacher at the school. This was, of course, the height of the Vietnam War. However, as students, the little that we knew about the war still did not prejudice us against our soon-to-be teacher.

I have no recollection of the reception arranged for Houlihan when he arrived at Chilonwa Middle School. However, what I do remember is a tall and slender young man with a radiant smile entering my classroom and saying, "Habari?" The class rose and said, "Nzuri." The ice, as the saying goes, was broken. Houlihan went on to establish a splendid rapport with us that would last for two years until I graduated in 1967. I was one of about ten students who passed the General Entrance Examination and I proceeded to Dodoma Secondary School. The students Houlihan taught who passed and went on to secondary and other tertiary institutions are evidence of his enabling Tanzania to meet its labor needs in a newly independent nation.

In the absence of quantifiable results from teaching, the reminiscence of former students is the only way we can ascertain the difference that Peace Corps teachers made in their lives. The following are testimonies from graduates of Tabora Boys Secondary School, whose Peace Corps teachers included Joe Winkelman and Dwight Yates.

David J. M. Kapya attended Tabora Boys from 1963 to 1968. After graduating from Tabora, he went on to the University of Dar es Salaam where he studied sociology and French. After graduating from the University of Dar es Salaam, Kapya embarked on an illustrious career, including being the United Nations High Commission for Refugees (UNHCR) representative for Conakry, Guinea. He was also the special advisor to the late president of Tanzania, Benjamin Mkapa, in which capacity he facilitated peace talks between conflicting parties in neighboring Burundi. The following is what he says about his American teachers at Tabora:

> As a direct beneficiary at Tabora School, 1963–68, let me say these teachers, both the TEA and what we the pupils used to call "the JFK Boys", were without blemish. We are the products: Ambassadors, Generals, Professors in Law, Engineering, Medicine, Social Sciences, Natural Sciences, etc. We are many, mostly already retired from active service. These teachers, some of whom have passed on, including Reuben Seme, the Headmaster who had returned from the University of Cambridge with an MSc in Chemistry, taught with professionalism and commitment without comparison. We were very young, all in our teens. When today I cast a glance at the past University of Cambridge Examination papers that we did, I wonder how we were able make it. Given today, I wonder how many would have passed. But we managed to pass, some of us with flying colours! The reunion in 2014 at Dar es Salaam and Tabora was memorable, where teacher and pupil of the 60s met and reminisced the glorious days of TS Kichwa cha Tanganyika. The teachers should come back one more time and visit: those who are still full of energy and are able to travel. Stay safe and God bless.

Another Tabora Boys School alumnus is Ali Tawakali Mtanda. He attended Tabora Boys Secondary School from 1963 to 1968. He went on to attend the University of Dar es Salaam Muhimbili Medical School from 1969 to 1974. After graduating, he joined the teaching staff at Muhimbili Medical School. He retired in 1997 as professor of ophthalmology. Professor Mtanda attributes his success to his formative years at Tabora Boys Secondary School. Reflecting about his Peace Corps and TEA (American) teachers, he says, "During 1963–68 I personally grew from age 16 to age 19. . . . All I can say is for me; they excelled because the foundation they laid in my thinking grew me into a very successful medical professor in Ophthalmology. Now at 70+ and partially retired I still consider that foundation as being instrumental in molding me into the person I am."

Jenerali Ulimwengu, a renowned journalist, is also an alumnus of Tabora Boys Secondary School; he attended from 1967 to 1968 (Forms V and VI). He joined the University of Dar es Salaam in 1969 and graduated in 1972. After graduating, he served Tanzania in various capacities, including being the Pan-African Youth Movement representative for Tanzania in Algiers from 1974 to 1985; a member of parliament from 1990 to 1995; and a member of the National Executive Committee of the ruling party Chama cha Mapinduzi (CCM) from 1992 to 1997. Jenerali Ulimwengu is also the owner of a newspaper company. About his two years of high school at Tabora, Ulimwengu has this to say: "Though I only spent two years there (Forms V and VI), yet my memories of the life there have remained vivid and pleasurable all these years. I think we had some great teachers. I retain fond reminiscences of teachers such as Allan York, who happily did come to Dar a few years ago, Malcolm Cooper, Lillistone, and others. For me, TS was brief but memorable, a solid plank in my development as a lover of the Arts and literature all round."

George Lulenga Fumbuka, FCPA, is chief executive officer (CEO) at CORE Securities in Dar es Salaam, Tanzania. He attended Shinyanga Secondary School and was taught by Peace Corps teachers, to whom he attributes his success: "I am who I am because of William Bordas, George Edgington, and John Barcas. I learn[ed] from them formal English, using SVOPT [subject-verb-object-place-time]. We played basketball together and went with them for picnics. Though it was a Mission School, they were not particularly religious or holier-than-though [sic], they were kind and outgoing."

CHAPTER 6

Termination of the Peace Corps Program in Tanzania

Introduction

When the Peace Corps program in Tanzania began in 1961, the relationship between the United States and Tanzania was warm and cordial. However, from 1965 onward US-Tanzania relations became increasingly frosty. With the significant exception of President Nyerere and a few others, some Tanzanians were puzzled as to why Peace Corps volunteers came to their country. John B. Mwakangale, a member of parliament, expressed the earliest anti–Peace Corps sentiments in a parliamentary session in 1962. The *Washington Post,* on June 12, 1962, reported Mwakangale saying that the Peace Corps volunteers were undermining the government and that wherever they are stationed trouble starts. However, Prime Minister Rashidi M. Kawawa rebuked Mwakangale for his anti–Peace Corps comments.

Nevertheless, suspicion about the Peace Corps continued and became stronger, especially with the escalation of the Vietnam War. A small segment of the population that was politically aware viewed the US role in the world with growing disquiet. In addition, there was concern about racial violence in the United States and US support of the minority racist regimes in Southern Africa. Finally, the assassination of Martin Luther King Jr. and Senator Robert Kennedy aroused deep anger and, on the part of those well inclined toward the United States, despair. Added to these feelings was a profound fear on the part of some Tanzanians that the

United States would not allow Tanzania to succeed as a socialist country and would use its Central Intelligence Agency (CIA) to do so.

The *New York Times* first reported the impending closure of the program in its edition of February 3, 1969, which carried the caption, "Once-Ambitious Plan Is Victim of Harsh Political Climate." The article, by Lawrence Fellows, blamed the diminishing of the program on "overexposure in a harsh and agitated political climate."[1] Fellows implied that the responsibility for the "agitated political climate" rested with Tanzania, exonerating the United States and the Peace Corps of contributing anything, claiming it played only a passive role.[2]

By 1967, President Nyerere, who had enthusiastically asked President Kennedy for Peace Corps volunteers, was complaining that the Peace Corps had changed its character and that some of its idealism had diminished such that it had become a problem. However, as noted in chapter 2, he still entertained the possibility of African Americans volunteering in Tanzania. Paul Bomani, Tanzania's ambassador to the United States and Mexico from 1972 to 1983, cultivated close ties with several African American leaders, relationships that aided generating African American interest in Tanzania. In a 1999 interview with retired President Nyerere, Ikaweba Bunting notes that Nyerere was interested in seeing how African Americans could contribute to Tanzania's development and encouraged the recruitment of volunteers.[3] According to Bunting, Nyerere believed that African Americans who had a psychological need to connect with Africa would be more loyal than white American volunteers.[4]

Besides Nyerere's mistrust of Peace Corps volunteers, several factors contributed to the closure of the Peace Corps program in Tanzania in 1969. These were (a) the nature of US-Tanzania and Sino-Tanzania diplomatic relations, (b) Tanzania's stand against the Vietnam War, (c) Tanzania's anti-CIA sentiments, and (d) Tanzania's new policy of Education for Self-Reliance.

US-Tanzania and Sino-Tanzania Diplomatic Relations, 1960s to 1980s

The United States established diplomatic relations with Tanganyika in 1961. At the time, the diplomatic relationship was one of mutual respect, shared values, and aspirations. Tanganyika/Tanzania opened its embassy in Washington in 1964. However, a series of events and developments subsequently caused the estrangement between Tanzania and the United States, which continued until the administration of President James "Jimmy" Earl Carter (1977–81) endeavored to create better relations.

Relations between Tanzania and the United States first soured in late 1964. Early in November 1964, Andrew Tibandebage, Tanzania's ambassador to the Congo, returned to Dar es Salaam with photocopies of several letters presumed to be from an official of the US embassy in Leopoldville (now Kinshasa) to an unnamed mercenary. In the letters were offers of financial support for him to travel to South Africa to recruit other mercenaries in a Portuguese-supported plot to overthrow Nyerere and his government. Nyerere discussed the letters with Oscar Kambona, his foreign affairs minister, and instructed him to publicize the plot. In an official statement, Kambona accused certain Western countries of plotting to overthrow the government. However, the *Nationalist,* a local daily newspaper, published the full texts of the letters that bore the letterhead of the American Department of State, thus making a direct accusation against the United States.

Consequently, marches and demonstrations took place in Dar es Salaam and in other Tanzanian towns, becoming with each passing day increasingly anti-American. The American ambassador immediately denounced the purported Department of State letters as forgeries. He pointed out the following anomalies: the Department of State had no official named John B. Pac, who had signed the letters; the letterhead had the wrong number of stars over the eagle's head; and the angle of the eagle's beak was wrong. Provided with this evidence, on December 9, 1964, Nyerere publicly announced he had accepted the Americans' statements that the documents were false.[5]

However, another incident immediately followed. On January 15, 1965, Robert Gordon, counselor at the US embassy in Dar es Salaam, and Frank C. Carlucci III, US consul general in Zanzibar, were accused by the government of Tanzania of plotting to overthrow the government and were pronounced *personae non gratae.*[6] When the two diplomats returned to Washington, they explained what "actually" had happened. Based on their explanation, the US government believed that their expulsion from Tanzania was unjustified. The US government conveyed its explanation to the government of Tanzania, which did not believe it and did not accept it.

On February 12, the US government informed the Tanzania government that it was going to expel its counselor in Washington, Herbert Katua. Washington also requested that the government of Tanzania divulge the source of the information claiming that Gordon and Carlucci had engaged in subversive activities. President Nyerere took this as a threat, or as an ultimatum meant to intimidate him into rescinding the expulsion of the US diplomats. He reacted forcefully: "We in this country fought for our independence and won that fight. We are a small country, but we are as much a sovereign state as the United States of America. We have no hostility towards that large and powerful nation. But we are not a vassal state, nor do we intend to become one. We do not bully, and do not like being bullied."[7]

Nevertheless, the US government expelled Herbert Katua, the counselor at Tanzania's embassy in Washington, DC. Tanzania protested against Katua's expulsion and recalled the Tanzania ambassador in Washington, Othman Shariff.[8] In the meantime, the US ambassador, William Leonhart, recalled to Washington for consultation, was expected to return to Dar es Salaam. When Leonhart returned to Dar es Salaam, President Nyerere told him that he believed the two diplomats had acted in their own personal interest and that the evidence in possession by the government showed that neither the ambassador himself nor the government in Washington were involved.

Meanwhile, an evolving close relationship between Tanzania and China did not bode well for an amicable relationship between Tanzania and the United States and strained their relationship, contributing to the disbandment of the Peace Corps program in 1969. In May 1960 Bibi Titi Mohamed and Lucy Lameck, women leaders of the Tanganyika African National Union (TANU), the ruling party, went on a visit to Moscow and Beijing as a cultural delegation. The two women tried to keep their trip a secret. However, the opposition party, the African National Congress (ANC), exposed the trip by publishing a photograph of the two women with Chairman Mao Zedong. Barrington King, an official in the American embassy in Dar es Salaam, cabled Washington about the trip and sent the photograph published by the ANC.[9]

In December 1961 when Tanganyika became an independent state, it also became the tenth African UN member state to recognize the People's Republic of China. Shortly afterward a Chinese embassy and an office of the New China News Agency were opened in Dar es Salaam. At the time, the experience of Tanzanians with anything Chinese was rather scant. In 1961, there was a restaurant and grocery store operated by a Chinese man named Harry Lin; it offered a choice of Chinese cuisine as an alternative to local and British-style restaurants in Dar es Salaam.

Lin's restaurant provided the only real contact that Tanganyikans had with anything Chinese. The two-story restaurant and grocery store building was located on the fringes of the African section of Dar es Salaam. In the restaurant, one could see rotogravure pictures of China, and in the grocery store, one could buy Chinese bowls and chopsticks. In short, if one wanted to learn about China, one could stop by Lin's for a "look-see."[10] At times, the lonely figures of Lin and his family enjoyed the company of sailors, usually from British ships with crews recruited from Hong Kong, who found a little piece of home at the bar of Lin's restaurant.[11]

According to Tom Katus, when the first Peace Corps group (T-1) arrived in Dar es Salaam, the Peace Corps representative Bob Hellawell warned them not to frequent Lin's restaurant in fear of "Red Chinese" influence.[12] He did not want any volunteers possibly being photographed at the restaurant or reported eating at a "Red Chinese" restaurant. Nevertheless, Katus and a few other T-1 volunteers disregarded Hellawell's warning and frequented Lin's restaurant when opportunity availed. Katus recalls about the food: "it was darn good Chinese food and different from other fare you could get in Dar-es-Salaam at European, Indian and African restaurants."[13]

According to Allen Tamura (T-1), because the United States did not recognize China and instead recognized Taiwan, the Peace Corps instructed volunteers not to speak to any Chinese national. Thus, while doing survey work in Tanga, Tamura visited Tanga's town center to buy supplies for his survey crew. He stayed at a hotel in town and while having dinner, a Chinese diplomat and his family came to the same restaurant for dinner. Tamura notes: "They were seated across from me, and we acknowledged our presence with a nod. I'm certain the Diplomat wanted to know about the LA Dodgers baseball team or even the LA Lakers basketball team."[14] Yet, Tamura and the Chinese diplomat did not exchange a word.

Meanwhile, in 1962 China sent a cultural delegation to Tanganyika to negotiate an agreement to establish the framework within which future exchanges of cultural materials and outstanding personalities would take place. The text of the signed agreement was vague in that it was short on specifics: it stipulated no specific number of people that were to be exchanged; no specifics on the administration of such exchanges; and no specifics on how costs were to be allocated. Apparently, what was important to both parties was the agreement's portrayal of friendliness. However, even more significant was that, like many other countries that entered into agreements with China, Tanganyika learned that China scrupulously abided by its international commitments.[15]

Furthermore, in late 1963 several Tanganyika ministers traveled to China. During this visit, plans for Premier Chou Enlai to visit Dar es Salaam in January 1964 and a reciprocal visit by President Nyerere to Beijing in February were made. Both Chou Enlai's visit to Dar es Salaam as well as Nyerere's visit to Beijing were postponed due to Tanganyika's army mutiny and the Zanzibar Revolution in January 1964. It was a year later that Nyerere visited China for the first time.

In June 1964, Tanzania vice president Rashidi Kawawa visited Beijing, where he signed an agreement for about £16 million in development aid. In October 1964, Tanzania opened its embassy in Beijing. On February 15, 1965, President Nyerere left Dar es Salaam for a state visit to China. Nyerere's departure was grand, with a high-profile sendoff by diplomats, government officials, and representatives of liberation movements, which had headquarters in Dar es Salaam. On his trip, a twenty-four-strong party of government and TANU officials accompanied President Nyerere. In Beijing (then known as Peking), the president's delegation was expected to engage in talks with their Chinese hosts on several issues, including trade, economic aid, and "Afro-Asian problems." The latter included the Congo situation, whereby China supported the Congolese nationalists led by Christophe Gbenye against the government of Prime Minister Moise Tshombe, supported by the United States and other Western governments.[16]

During his visit to China, the Chinese press described Tanzania and President Nyerere to be "staunchly anti-imperialist."[17] President Nyerere was strongly opposed to the government of Tshombe, whom the president considered a stooge of Western imperialist powers. The Chinese government also opposed the Tshombe administration. Thus, during the Congo crisis, China and Tanzania were on the same page, standing together in opposition to what they considered imperialist aggression against the people of the Congo.

While in Beijing, President Nyerere met with both Chou Enlai and Liu Shao-chi, and other government officials. On February 19, President Nyerere gave a return banquet in the "People's Great Hall" for his hosts to thank them for their hospitality and to reiterate the friendship between the two countries. He stated, inter alia: "Certainly, we on our side are anxious to learn what we can about China's development, in the hope that we shall by adaptation to our circumstances, be able to benefit from your experience. ... Having achieved our freedom from colonialism, we are now able to reorganize our national life in our own pattern, according to our own traditions and aspirations. By successive political and institutional changes, we have laid the groundwork for our advance to our goal of African Socialism."[18]

President Nyerere went on to ask his Chinese hosts for whatever economic assistance that China could offer Tanzania in its endeavor to transform Tanzania into an "Ujamaa" socialist society. Nyerere's pronouncements during his visit to China about his intent to reorient Tanzania society toward socialism came two years before he officially launched the Arusha Declaration, his blueprint for a socialist transformation of Tanzania's economy and society. Nyerere's declaration to turn Tanzania into a socialist society initiated an ideological rift between Tanzania and the United States that would not bode well for the Peace Corps program, which had started with its "roads-to-market" project to integrate Tanzania farmers into the capitalist global market.

As noted above, President Nyerere discussed with his Chinese hosts issues pertaining to Afro-Asian matters of mutual interests. This likely included the upcoming Asian-African Conference in Algiers beginning on February 24, 1965. The Argentinian revolutionary and Cuban Industry Minister, Ernesto "Che" Guevara, who intended to attend the Algiers conference, arrived in Dar es Salaam on February 11, coming from China.[19] Guevara's visit to Tanzania contributed to the estrangement between Tanzania and the United States because of Guevara's (and Cuba's) involvement in the Congo crisis. Guevara considered the situation in the Congo to be the result of imperial and neocolonial machinations. Guevara specifically blamed the United States and reiterated that, "The reply to attacks by the U.S. against Vietnam or the Congo should be to supply those countries with all the defense equipment they need, and to offer them our full solidarity without any conditions whatsoever."[20]

Guevara spent over four months in Tanzania, between February and November 1965, during which time he entered Tanzania three times, once publicly and twice secretly and in disguise. As we have noted, Guevara arrived at Dar es Salaam from China on February 11, 1965, and stayed until

February 18. Thus, he was in Tanzania as the diplomatic crisis between Tanzania and the United States unfolded. The *New York Times* reported this public visit. The other two times Guevara entered Tanzania secretly and in disguise. In these later entries, he was reconnoitering the possibility to enter the Congo from Tanzania's lake port town of Kigoma, on Lake Tanganyika.

During his visits, Guevara met with Congolese president Laurent Kabila, who was then living in Tanzania. According to Guevara, Kabila impressed him by identifying the United States as the main enemy of the Congo rebel forces. Subsequently, Guevara led a contingent of about one hundred thirty Cuban guerrilla fighters into the Congo and spent seven months fighting against the regime of Moise Tshombe, which was supported by the United States and Belgium.

Meanwhile, Premier Chou Enlai visited Dar es Salaam in June 1965, and in November Kawawa paid another visit to Beijing. Following Kawawa's visit, the Chinese Economic and Commercial Mission opened in Dar es Salaam in 1966. In June 1968, President Nyerere returned to Beijing for a second visit, when Nyerere said that his objective was to learn about the Chinese model of development. Chinese frugality and Chinese leadership's dedication to "serve the people" greatly impressed Nyerere. Hence, as part of his effort to develop a socialist society in Tanzania, Nyerere not only criticized conspicuous materialist consumption but also sought to create a dedicated leadership to the people rather than one of self-seeking elites. As we shall see, this endeavor in part translated into his policy, Education for Self-Reliance, which triggered opposition against Peace Corps teachers in Tanzania.

Besides being on opposing sides during the Congo crisis, Tanzania and the United States were at loggerheads over US support of racist minority regimes in Southern Africa. Whereas the United States supported the white minority regimes in Southern Rhodesia and South Africa as bulwarks against the influence of communism, Tanzania pledged itself to support the liberation of southern Africa and the establishment of majority African rule. In this regard, Tanzania found a dependable ally in China, especially in terms of arms supplies for Tanzania's army as well as for the liberation movements. In January 1964, the first shipment of Chinese arms arrived in Tanzania, by way of Algeria. In August, President Nyerere announced, much to the ire of several Western nations, that he had accepted a Chinese offer of bringing seven instructors to Tanzania to demonstrate the use of the weapons that China had already provided.[21]

During the Cold War, the United States and other Western nations looked at geopolitics differently based on the reasoning "one must be either with us or against us." Thus, countries like Tanzania that endeavored not to support US foreign policies drew its ire. The American press became hostile, mocking and baiting in its limited coverage of events in Tanzania. Ronald "Ron" Sterling Hert, a Peace Corps volunteer who served in Tanzania from 1966 to 1968, notes that American caustic criticism received top billing in the Tanzanian press: "Soon there was rapid growth of acerbity between many Americans in the country and Tanzanians."[22]

Moreover, Malcolm X contributed to the tarnishing of the Peace Corps's reputation in Tanzania. Malcolm X made four trips to Africa. He first visited the continent in late March and early April 1959 and then again two months later. In 1964, Malcolm X made two trips to Africa, one in April and May and the other in November. In May 1964, Malcolm X visited Ghana and had an occasion to address students at the University of Ghana. Among other things, Malcolm X told the students about the welcome he had received in Nigeria:

> When I was in Ibadan at the University of Ibadan last Friday night, the students there gave me a new name, which I go for—meaning I like it. "Omowale," which they say means in Yoruba—if I am pronouncing that correctly, and if I am not pronouncing it correctly it's because I haven't had a chance to pronounce it for four hundred years—which means in that dialect, "The child has returned." It was an honor for me to be referred to as a child who had sense enough to return to the land of his forefathers—to his fatherland and to his motherland. Not sent back here by the State Department, but come back here of my own free will.[23]

In his remarks above, Malcolm X was essentially distancing himself from the African Americans who were in Ghana as US embassy employees or as Peace Corps volunteers.

In July 1964, he visited Cairo, Egypt, when the annual conference of the Organization of African Unity (OAU) was in session (July 17–21). Malcolm X met with Abdulrahman Babu, who was part of the Tanzania delegation led by President Nyerere. Through Babu, Malcolm X was able to have his resolution about the plight of African Americans passed and supported by the OAU. The OAU resolution AHG/Res.15 (1) was titled "Racial Discrimination in the United States." In addition to expressing concerns about racial discrimination in the United States, the resolution called on the government to do all it could to end discrimination based on race, color, and ethnic origin.[24]

While in Cairo, Babu invited Malcolm X to visit Tanzania after the conference, which he did in October 1964, after a two-month stay in Egypt.[25] On October 9, Malcolm X landed at Dar es Salaam. While there, Malcolm X met the African American Pan-Africanist and pacifist Bill Sutherland, who drove him around town for the duration of his stay. On Monday, October 12, a reporter of the *Tanganyika Standard,* an English daily newspaper, interviewed Malcolm X. Among other things, what Malcolm X said about the presence of African Americans in Tanzania and elsewhere in Africa was negative. He especially did not think that those sent by the US government, or its agencies, were out to do any good for Africa.

While many African Americans experience a warm welcome and a sense of connection upon visiting or moving to Africa, there have been instances where some have faced certain levels of hostility or challenges. In some cases, African Americans might face challenges in blending into local cultures due to differences in behavior, language, or customs. This can lead to misunderstandings and occasional hostility. Thus in 1974, ten years after Malcolm X visited Tanzania, a situation arose that caused many African Americans to leave the country.

According to Mwakikagile, in 1974 there were between seven hundred and eight hundred African Americans living and working in Tanzania.[26] However, many left Tanzania following the arrest of two African Americans on charges of illegally importing firearms and ammunition. The incident came to be known as the "Big Bust." James Garrett believes that those involved were not a danger to Tanzania.[27] Nevertheless, Garrett notes that anti-Nyerere and anti-American Tanzanians used the incident to stir up anti-American sentiments. Among those who left Tanzania were African Americans who had come to Tanzania under the Pan-African Skills Project (PASP).

Furthermore, in diplomatic circles, relations between Tanzania and the United States worsened by Tanzania snubbing its nose at the United States by offering refuge to African Americans sought by the US government. Calvin Coolidge Cobb was a prominent North Amityville lawyer and civil rights figure. Cobb was born on March 6, 1925, in Winnsboro, South Carolina. His family fled a lynch mob, to Philadelphia, Pennsylvania, where the family then lived for several years. Later, Cobb attended Haaren High School in Harlem, New York.

A World War II veteran, Cobb subsequently graduated from City College of New York and Brooklyn Law School. In 1949, he married Estelle Young, with whom Cobb had three daughters. Cobb became a prominent lawyer; he practiced law for fifteen years on Long Island and in Greater New York. Besides practicing law, Cobb developed a passionate interest in political and social justice issues. Subsequently, he became affiliated with several fraternal and community organizations, including Alpha Phi Alpha, the Masonic Lodge, the National Association for the Advancement of Colored People (NAACP), the Congress of Racial Equality (CORE), the Suffolk County CORE, and the Organization of Afro-American Unity, which was led by Malcolm X.

In 1966, Cobb was tried and convicted of stealing $25,000 from the Second Baptist Church of Rockville Center. The court placed Cobb on probation and ordered him to return the money. In 1967, Cobb violated his probation, but before the police could arrest him, he fled to Tanzania in September 1967 with his wife and children. Cobb lived in Tanzania for seven years. The US government requested Tanzania to extradite Cobb. Tanzania refused to grant the request by invoking its Extradition Act of 1965, by which it was determined that Cobb was a political refugee.[28]

In December 1974, Cobb and his family returned to the United States. On December 17, he showed up at the district attorney's office in Riverhead, claiming to have returned to clear his name. The court ordered him to be jailed, but on February 18, he was given a three-year prison sentence for his 1966 probation violation. The court released Cobb on March 6 on bail of $10,000, approved by the Nassau County supreme court justice Bertram Harnett in Mineola, over the objections of the district attorney's office. Once out of jail Cobb again fled to Tanzania, arriving in Dar es Salaam on May 4, 1975.

Another African American who sought refuge in Tanzania at the same time that Cobb did was Felix "Pete" O'Neal Jr. Born in 1940, O'Neal was the chair of the Kansas City chapter of the Black Panther Party. On October 30, 1969, the police arrested O'Neal for transporting a gun across state lines, under a law enacted only two weeks prior to his arrest. He fled first to Algeria, and then to Tanzania, where he still lives in exile.[29]

O'Neal's family still resides in the Kansas City area. He has seen neither his ninety-six-year-old mother nor his children (from a previous marriage) since his exile forty-six years ago. O'Neal is a third cousin of US Representative Emmanuel Cleaver. Since 1991, Cleaver and others have unsuccessfully attempted to obtain a pardon for O'Neal. Cleaver took the issue with some urgency to President Barack Obama, but to no avail.[30]

The United States, Tanzania, and the Vietnam War

In early August 1964, President Lyndon Johnson went to Syracuse University to open the Newsome Communications Center on campus. The Peace Corps trainees (T-5) on campus were told to dress up and sit in a particular section, as President Johnson intended to recognize them as ambassadors for peace in his presentation. Newspaper headlines that morning reported that the United States had attacked North Vietnam in retaliation for an attack on two American destroyers in the Gulf of Tonkin. According to one of the trainees, George Cummins, reports that:

> In response to the alleged attack that we learned later "probably didn't occur", Johnson ordered limited air strikes over North Vietnam based on Secretary of Defense Robert McNamara's strategy of applying gradual increasing pressure. The result of this reported attack was a "congressional resolution that, in effect, gave the president carte blanche for the escalation of the war. Johnson wanted such a resolution to protect himself from future congressional attacks on his Vietnam policy." Our Peace Corps group was not recognized or noted in the President's remarks. The escalation of the American involvement in Vietnam was based on a political agenda and not on fact. It disrupted my life for a time indirectly but cost the lives and productive years of thousands of soldiers on both sides and civilians in Vietnam and several neighboring countries.[31]

Hert was in Tanzania from 1966 to 1968. He suggests that no other issue produced a greater solidarity of anti-American sentiment than the escalation of the Vietnam War: "To almost all Tanzanians from house servants to intellectuals ... this seemed clear evidence of a predominantly white belligerent, capitalist America forcing its will upon a small nation of yellow people, socialists on the other side of the globe."[32] As we shall see, the escalation of the Vietnam War contributed to the termination of the Peace Corps program in Tanzania in 1969.

President Nyerere not only championed and pledged support of African countries struggling against Western imperialism but also of other people struggling against dominance by Western powers and the United States. In Tanzania, the Vietnam War provided a platform for student activism and media invective. In October 1967, the general meeting of the TANU[33] Youth League in Arusha passed many resolutions that, among other things, called for the expulsion of all American Peace Corps volunteers from Tanzania. The Youth League accused Peace Corps volunteers of being CIA agents.

According to Karim Hirji, TANU Youth League's call was not an isolated event but a sign of the times. University student groups across Africa in those days tended to adopt a militant anti-imperialist, Pan-African, and, in some cases, socialist stand.[34] At the University of Dar es Salaam, a student organization named University Students African Revolutionary Front (USARF) advocated Pan-African unity and maintained an anti-imperialist stance, especially against the United States.

In August 1968, USARF launched a magazine named *Cheche* (Swahili for *The Spark*). Featuring incisive analyses of key societal issues, it gained national and international recognition in a short while. The first and second issues of *Cheche* included articles by Issa Shivji, Walter Rodney, Yoweri Museveni, Amilcar Cabral, and Dan Nabudere. The government banned *Cheche* after a year's existence because it was independent of the government's authority and spoke without fear or favor. *Cheche* existed from 1969 to 1970. The Marxist orientation and editorial independence of *Cheche* drew the ire of the university and state authorities. The government banned USARF and *Cheche* in November 1970.

Meanwhile, as we have noted, the TANU Youth League considered the Peace Corps's presence unacceptable because it was the face of American imperialism. Tanzanians, especially the young generation, were puzzled as to why Americans came to their country. In the case of Peace Corps volunteers, the bewilderment was particularly great: "Why should educated people from a wealthy country want to live in villages or in the African sections of the larger towns? Why do they speak Swahili? Why do they drink in the local bars, rather than at the European club? For a surprising number, the answer [was] espionage."[35]

In the eyes of radical academics and university students, the United States as a nation and Americans as a people were unreconstructed capitalists: "Young Americans could therefore teach nothing of value to Tanzanians. Moreover, these young Americans [were] representatives of a decadent society. They [were] carriers of a virus which Tanzania should seek to exclude."[36] This attitude was reminiscent of Kwame Nkrumah's suspicions of American goodwill, especially Peace Corps teachers sent to Ghana. In a meeting that Robert Sargent Shriver had had with Nkrumah when he visited Ghana in 1962, Nkrumah told him that he did not want PCVs "indoctrinating our young people. So don't come as social science teachers.... You should come to teach science and mathematics. We don't want you to *affect* them; we just want you to teach them" (italics in the original).[37]

As the Vietnam War escalated, Britain asked Tanzania to endorse the Commonwealth's support of American policy. Tanzania refused. According to President Nyerere, "it was our refusal to do that which caused us to quarrel with the British Government when they proposed that a particular kind of Vietnam peace mission should be sent from the Commonwealth Conference in June 1965. Our refusal to endorse this move also attracted U.S. criticism of us."[38] As relations between the United States and Tanzania deteriorated, the two governments' disagreements eventually, and greatly, slowed discussions about American economic aid.[39]

As tensions between Tanzania and the United States worsened, suspicion of CIA activity in Tanzania grew more acute. In this atmosphere, Tanzania also became suspicious of Peace Corps volunteers. Shriver strove to ensure there was no involvement between the CIA and the Peace Corps. Yet, for Tanzania, a nagging question prevailed: Was it conceivable there were CIA agents who posed as Peace Corps volunteers? We do not know if President Nyerere had such doubts. However, many Tanzanians, including government servants, believed that CIA agents had infiltrated the Peace Corps.

Anti-CIA Sentiment in Tanzania

Through the prism of the Cold War, the Communists viewed the global reach of the Peace Corps with great suspicion and considered it a harbinger of imperialist espionage. "And," according to Stossel, "it was also inevitable that some in the US foreign policy establishment would seek to use the Peace Corps [used] for strategic cold war purposes."[40] Since the Peace Corps was part of the Department of State, the Communists suspected that US embassies abroad would oversee the activities of CIA officers working undercover as Peace Corps volunteers.[41] As we shall see, this was a view that came to prevail in certain circles in Tanzania.

Shriver, the first director of the Peace Corps, realized the detriment that any suspicion of CIA connection with the Peace Corps would have on the Peace Corps's objectives:

> Aware that this sort of suspicion already floated freely through the developing countries, especially in neutral-bloc and Communist countries, Shriver believed it absolutely essential that there be not the slightest hint of imperial or espionage designs associated with the Peace Corps. Even the *appearance* of being an intelligence-gathering operation or a US propaganda machine, Shriver thought, could do irrevocable damage to the Peace Corps' international image, perhaps even undermining its whole reason for being. Thus, he needed at all costs to keep the CIA . . . away from the Peace Corps. [Italics in the original.][42]

Yet Shriver had no way of knowing if CIA operatives could infiltrate the Peace Corps by posing as volunteers. To prevent this from happening, Shriver demanded assurances from President Kennedy that the CIA not use the Peace Corps for espionage purposes. The president agreed. The Peace Corps released an official policy on intelligence on September 6, 1961, which stated, "We do not want the Peace Corps publicly identified in any way with intelligence work, and we do not want the Peace Corps used as a vehicle for intelligence work."[43]

In 1963, Shriver heard rumors that CIA operatives were exploring how to make use of the Peace Corps. According to Stossel, he called President Kennedy immediately: "I'm getting rather suspicious over here that . . . despite your instructions . . . some of our friends over in the Central Intelligence Agency might think they're smarter than anybody else and that they're trying to stick fellows in the Peace Corps."[44] President Kennedy asked Shriver to call Richard Helms, the CIA's deputy director, and tell him that "I don't want anybody in there . . . And if they are there, let's get them out now."[45]

Besides trying to use the Peace Corps, the CIA used embassy staff for intelligence purposes. Ambassador John Howard Burns served in Tanzania from 1965 to 1969. He notes that at the time Tanzania placed a limit on the number of accredited officials each embassy could have, except for the United Kingdom. During his briefings in Washington, before leaving for Dar es Salaam, both the CIA and the Department of Defense made it very clear to Ambassador Burns that increasing the number of their personnel there (CIA) and opening an attaché's office (Defense) were their top priorities in Africa. Although the Department of State never gave Ambassador Burns actual specific instructions to present formal arguments for the removal of the American personnel limitations, it was clear to him that it "was favored by most everyone."[46]

Before leaving, Ambassador Burns had a long, sort of retrospective conversation with President Nyerere while sitting on the terrace of the Government House. The ambassador recalls telling the president, "Mr. President, there is one thing I'd like to say. As long as I have been here I have been urged by my government to try and persuade you to raise, or remove, the limitation on the number of Americans who can be assigned to this Embassy. As you know, I have never mentioned the subject to you and if I can bespeak anything in behalf of my successor, whoever that may be, it is that you never raise it."[47]

According to Ambassador Burns, President Nyerere said, "Of course I won't. What country could have an interest in little Tanzania to justify the diplomatic presence here of more than fifteen persons?"[48] President Nyerere was not being factitious because he was very much aware of the ongoing Cold War politics and America's interest that Tanzania be pro-West and anti-Communist. Was Nyerere limiting US diplomatic personnel to limit US subversive activities in Tanzania?

In 1967, Tanzania was one of several African countries where leaflets were distributed (dropped from the air) in February accusing Peace Corps volunteers of being CIA agents. In other countries, the governments rebutted the charges. However, in Tanzania there was no government reaction. This suggests that the Tanzania government believed in the allegations leveled against PCVs in Tanzania.

At the University College, Dar es Salaam (UCD), there were many rumors about CIA agents and CIA meddling. It turned out that Dr. Stephen Lucas, a lecturer in the Department of Sociology, was a CIA agent. His obituary, posted onsite at the Louisiana State University (LSU), carries the heading "Head of International Programs, Swahili Instructor and Former CIA Agent Stephen Lucas Passes Away."[49] He had also been in the Congo in 1964 at the time of Lumumba's assassination.

Education for Self-Reliance and Peace Corps Teachers

As we noted in chapter 5, after independence, the growth of school enrollment at both primary and secondary levels raised the demand for teachers. Tanzania temporarily met this need by accepting expatriate teachers. Demand for teachers was more acute at the primary school level than at the secondary level. The US and British Teachers for East Africa program aimed at meeting the demand for secondary school teachers. When Peace Corps offered to send teachers to Tanzania, the majority were primary school teachers. By 1966, there were 394 Peace Corps volunteers in Tanzania; teachers totaled 303, out of which 199 were primary school teachers.

In the meantime, while Tanzania accepted expatriate teachers, it endeavored to train teachers locally. In this endeavor, it depended on foreign assistance, including from the United States. Tanzania was one of the recipients of American assistance under the Foreign Assistance Act of 1961, in part passed by President Kennedy's efforts. Tanzania collaborated with USAID to establish the Morogoro College of Agriculture (now Sokoine University of Agriculture), the Institute of Public Administration (now Mzumbe University), and teacher training colleges in both Iringa and Dar es Salaam.

Initially, Tanzania's reception of Peace Corps teachers was warm and friendly because they were meeting a great need for teachers. As President Nyerere said, "It has been necessary for us to use large numbers of teachers from other countries. Without this help none of the expansion we are so proud of would have been possible."[50] However, criticism soon surfaced. The earliest criticism leveled against Peace Corps teachers in Tanzania was that they were not qualified to teach. In November 1963, the secretary of the newly formed East African Teachers' Council, Mr. C. Mwalongo, claimed: "These people are graduates but without proper teacher training. They are learning while they are here.... If the Government wants to get teachers under a scheme like the Peace Corps, they should make sure they get fully trained people."[51]

To what extent was Mwalongo's claim valid? It so happens that, indeed, most Peace Corps teachers had no teaching experience before they joined Peace Corps. Out of 2,538 Peace Corps volunteer teachers in Africa, by December 31, 1965, 55 percent lacked any previous teaching experience, and 21 percent had some experience but not enough to earn a teaching certificate. Only 23 percent held teaching certificates.[52] Most volunteer teachers were liberal arts graduates who were happy to teach but were looking to some other field for their lifetime career.

Peace Corps volunteer teachers received a three-month crash course program in teaching before their departure for Tanzania. Initially, instructors spent much time on introductory theoretical matters, with very little teaching practice. However, instructors later omitted the theoretical material and concentrated on practice teaching. Consequently, this change in training turned highly motivated liberal arts graduates into competent, albeit novice, teachers. According to Stanley Meisler, Reuben Seme, the headmaster of Tabora Boys Secondary School in Tanzania, said that his volunteer teachers were equal to the best of the TEA teachers. Other headmasters echoed his views.[53]

The minister for education, Solomon N. Eliufoo, was equally supportive. He noted that the Peace Corps teachers did not only receive predeparture training at Syracuse University but also attended an in-country training at Mbeya before going to their allocated schools. He told the Peace Corps teachers that Tanzania needed them, especially because of the shortage of teachers for Standards VII and VIII: "These two standards with which you will be concerned are the ones which come just before the secondary stage of education. Thus, you will be participating in the important task of preparing some of our pupils for a just but very competitive selection of pupils into secondary schools."[54] Thus, the training at Mbeya focused on familiarizing the Peace Corps teachers with the new syllabus for Standards VII and VIII that the ministry had just introduced. Eliufoo emphasized the significance of the new syllabus and urged the Peace Corps teachers to become thoroughly familiar with it because it was the basis of the class schedules and textbooks used to teach.

Despite the support of the minister for education, President Nyerere's view of the Peace Corps subsequently changed, especially after 1967. According to the *New York Times* edition of March 5, 1967, President Nyerere increasingly believed that people whose motives were no good to Tanzania had infiltrated the Peace Corps. At a news conference on March 5, 1967, he said that the character of Peace Corps had changed and much of its idealism had gone. The president was answering a question about how Peace Corps teachers fit into the new education policy, Education for Self-Reliance. Nyerere replied that they did not fit at all.[55]

After declaring Tanzania's objective to become socialist, Tanzanians at the behest of President Nyerere questioned the wisdom of allowing Peace Corps teachers to shape and influence the minds of Tanzania's youth. However, it was not only from the classroom that negative, antisocialist influences emanated. During the 1960s, soul music became popular in Tanzania. James Brown's 1968 hit "Say it Loud—I'm Black and Proud" became the craze on school campuses. Soul "digging" even influenced the manner of walking of some young people.

The message of soul music was about Black upward social mobility. James Brown's glitz was testimony to the American Dream, that a Black person could rise from a humble background to a life of affluence. The popular *Nipsey Russell Show* complimented soul's message of African American affluence in America. Russell's favorite back-to-Africa joke was "I don't wanna trade my Cadillac for no elephant."[56] This myth of African American affluence caught the imagination of Tanzania's youth at a time when President Nyerere was reorienting Tanzania toward socialism. It is no surprise that in November 1969, the government banned the playing of soul music in Tanzania. The ban coincided with the departure of the last remaining Peace Corps volunteers from Tanzania.

The Peace Corps compounded Tanzania's climate of mistrust, which eroded its ability to survive. First, it was its tendency to remain a separate American institution outside the Tanzania government structure:

> Despite its long tenure in Tanzania, the Peace Corps never became a functional part of its host.... Peace Corps' responsibility was primarily either to itself or to the American embassy. Directors attended weekly embassy-team meetings alongside *all* the heads of State Department agencies. Many staff families' social lives, and consequently their standards of living, revolved around those of the other United States government employees. The Peace Corps in the capital was just another element in the American community; and when tensions developed between the two governments, the Peace Corps' pleas that it was different lacked credibility.[57]

Second, was the Peace Corps's attitude that "it does not matter what job a Volunteer does, as long as he [sic] does it like a volunteer." The Peace Corps's emphasis on recruiting liberal arts graduates as teachers and lack of diversified programs reduced the feasibility of the program in Tanzania: "Therefore, barring the introduction of new, diversified programs, the Peace Corps would probably have been reduced by about 75 per cent between 1966 and the end of 1968."[58] Although the Peace Corps tried to suggest new programs to the Tanzanian government, by then it was already too late. As we shall see, when Tanzania invited the Peace Corps back ten years later, it took the diversity of programs into account.

CHAPTER 7

Return of the Peace Corps Program to Tanzania

Introduction

The first Peace Corps group sent to Tanganyika in 1961 numbered thirty-five volunteers and consisted of engineers, surveyors, and geologists. The group provided Tanganyika with technically skilled experts, which were scarce, that the government of Tanganyika had specifically requested from the US government. The second group sent to Tanganyika consisted of an all-female contingent of nurses and medical technologists. Again, the Tanganyika government had specifically requested the nurses due to the shortage of nurses following the departure of British nurses after independence.

In 1966, there were 366 Peace Corps volunteers working in Tanzania, the most since the first group arrived in 1961. However, after 1966 the number of volunteers working in Tanzania began to decline. From 366 volunteers in 1966, the numbers dropped sharply to 143 volunteers in 1968. In September 1969, the once robust and ambitious Peace Corps program had shrunk to fewer than ten volunteers. And the Peace Corps headquarters in Washington, DC, was not expected to be asked to supply more. As we noted in chapter 6, several factors contributed to the closure of the Peace Corps program in 1969. At the time, the consensus through termination reports was that it was futile for the Peace Corps to endeavor to revive the program.[1] Following the departure of the last volunteers at the end of 1969, the program remained closed until January 1979 when negotiations began that led to its reopening.

Pathway to the Agreement to Reopen the Peace Corps Program in Tanzania

The reopening of the Peace Corps program in Tanzania required significant changes in US-Tanzania relations as well as a reconstitution of the program that was cognizant of Tanzania's needs rather than what Peace Corps thought Tanzania required. As Ron Hert, a returned volunteer notes, after 1970 Tanzania's needs no longer required volunteers that were fresh out of college who wanted to test their ability to do whatever a situation required them to do. "Doing it like a volunteer" would just not suffice.

As noted in chapter 6, during the 1960s and 1970s much of the relationship between Tanzania and the United States was framed first by the Cold War, and later by the context of US policies toward the minority white regimes in Southern Africa, which contributed toward the closing of the Peace Corps program in Tanzania. However, the election of James "Jimmy" Earl Carter Jr. as the thirty-ninth president of the United States (1977–81) facilitated the thawing of the frosty relationship between the United States and Tanzania. The attitude of Carter's administration was a sharp contrast to that of the Johnson, Nixon, and Ford administrations. Previous US administrations had shunned overtures by President Nyerere to visit Washington. In October 1969, President Nyerere visited Canada. He made it known that he would like to visit Washington but was told that President Nixon would be too busy.[2] In 1970, President Nyerere came to New York to address the UN General Assembly on southern Africa. No effort was made to see President Nixon. In 1975, according to Mann, Boston University invited President Nyerere to deliver the commencement address. Nyerere thought he could use the trip to visit President Ford for a brief meeting and he asked for just such a meeting. The Ford administration rebuffed him, and President Nyerere later declined the Boston invitation.[3]

President Carter invited President Nyerere to visit the United States in August 1977 (see photo on the following page). He was the first president from sub-Saharan Africa to be invited by President Carter. More significantly, President Nyerere was at the time the chair of a council of the presidents of the so-called front-line states in the liberation of Southern Africa. These were Angola, Botswana, Mozambique, Zambia, and Tanzania. As spokesperson of the front-line states, President Nyerere discussed with President Carter the liberation struggles in Rhodesia and Southwest Africa. According

First Lady Rosalynn Carter, President Nyerere, and President Jimmy Carter at the White House, August 1977 (Photograph by Karl H. Schumacher, National Archives and Records Administration)

to President Carter, they had reached an "almost complete agreement" about the diplomatic course to be followed in trying to bring majority rule and legal independence to Rhodesia and Southwest Africa, or Namibia.[4]

However, the liberation of southern Africa was not the only issue that engaged President Nyerere's attention on this visit. Jacqueline Trescott of the *Washington Post* reported on August 9, 1977, that on the fifth day of his visit to the United States, President Nyerere turned from the political questions of southern Africa to the question of his own country's basic agricultural development needs: "Fertilizer and rural electrification were uppermost on his mind during his one-day tour of Tennessee. At a briefing by Tennessee Valley Authority (TVA) officials here [at Tullahoma], Nyerere listened thoughtfully to a rundown of TVA agricultural projects." Eight miles north of Tullahoma on the Duck River, President Nyerere visited Normandy Dam, TVA's newest. An earthen dam, the Normandy Dam was chosen for the Nyerere visit because of its similarity to projects in developing countries like Tanzania. At the time of his visit, Tanzania was developing ideas for the Rufiji Basin Development Authority, a seventy-two-thousand-square-mile project, similar to the Normandy Dam, which was designed mainly for recreation and did not produce electricity. The Rufiji project, however, aimed at irrigation, flood control, and power generation.

From Tennessee, President Nyerere and his entourage flew to Atlanta, Georgia. President Nyerere was scheduled to visit several farms in rural Georgia. Previously, on his way to California from Washington, DC, President Nyerere stopped for two hours at Sioux City, Iowa, to visit the farm of Lyle Scheelhaas. In Georgia, he also visited the Abraham Baldwin Agricultural College (ABAC) in Tifton. The college is named after Abraham Baldwin, a signer of the US Constitution from Georgia and the first president of the University of Georgia. Established in 1908, the four-hundred-acre ABAC campus is used as an open-air classroom for students in the School of Agriculture and Natural Resources due to the large number of trees, plants, shrubs, and fields on campus.

Finally, Jacqueline Trescott reported in the *Washington Post* on August 11, 1977, that before leaving the United States, President Nyerere initiated discussions with American officials aimed at reactivating the Peace Corps program in Tanzania. According to Trescott, at his request, President Nyerere met in Atlanta with Sam Brown, the director of ACTION, the umbrella group for the Peace Corps and domestic volunteer programs. After their meeting President Nyerere invited Brown to Dar es Salaam for further discussions.

In October 1977, the American embassy in Dar es Salaam cabled the State Department about the prevailing situation in Tanzania. This cable referenced the impending visit to Tanzania by ACTION director Sam Brown and Peace Corps director Carolyn Payton, a visit that the embassy considered of major importance. The ambassador suggested that the State Department make sure that President Nyerere was personally involved in the details, timing, and itinerary of the visit. The ambassador referred to having a copy of a letter from ACTION director Brown to President Nyerere dated August 15, 1977, and asked if there had been a reply. If there had been a reply, the ambassador requested to know the contents of the reply. He further intimated that if there had been no reply, then he could take the matter up with the president. These cautions grew out of experience that the Tanzania embassy in Washington, even with the best of intentions, was often unable to "to nail [down] specifics in Tanzania, and that on a matter of this kind nothing but what the President says personally should really be relied upon."[5]

In the above cable, Ambassador James W. Spain reiterated that at a meeting he had attended in Atlanta, Georgia, which had been addressed by

President Nyerere, the president had intimated that he was prepared to consider a return of the Peace Corps to Tanzania if the climate was right. The president had invited Brown to Tanzania to see for himself and judge whether Peace Corps activities were possible in such a climate, and if they were, to talk about possibilities in rural development. The embassy suggested that Peace Corps consider other possibilities such as small farm grain storage, range management, maternal care, childcare, nutrition, and water supply. President Nyerere expected that the visit by Brown and Payton would result in Peace Corps proposals that the government of Tanzania would consider.[6] The ambassador also raised the question of how Peace Corps would be administered depending on what it would do. He offered to assist as much as he could, especially in the early negotiating and political stages. Finally, the ambassador suggested that Brown and Payton visit in January 1978 instead of December 1977.

On January 16, 1978, the American embassy in Dar es Salaam cabled the State Department to inform them that President Nyerere had agreed to receive Brown on January 23 at Butiama, his home village in northern Tanzania. Others invited to attend were Mr. Walker, the American Charge d'Affairs, and Dora Danieli, director for the Americas in the Foreign Ministry. The embassy had been trying to have Carolyn Payton included in the group to Butiama, but to no avail. Instead, Payton and Peace Corps African Regional Director Gaymon met with USAID officials to discuss Tanzania's development scene. Besides meeting with President Nyerere, Brown and his entourage also met with the minister of foreign affairs, the minister of finance and planning, the minister of manpower development, the minister of health, the minister of education, the minister of natural resources and tourism, and Principal Secretary of Agriculture Madallali. The team also visited Zanzibar, where they met with Vice President Jumbe and senior Zanzibari officials, including the ministers of health and education.

As Peace Corps Washington went through the process of negotiating the renewal of the program in Tanzania, the skills that volunteers would need to possess before departure to Tanzania loomed large. As we have noted, the old notion of "doing things like a volunteer" was no longer tenable. In an embassy cable to the State Department dated August 15, 1978, Ambassador Spain noted that having technical knowledge in the areas that volunteers would work in Tanzania was very important. Any doubts indicating that recruited volunteers lacked background training would be unacceptable to Tanzania.[7]

In preparing to renew the Peace Corps program in Tanzania, the Peace Corps appointed Jacques Wilmore to direct the program. An embassy officer met with a ministry of manpower development officer, Mr. Ndukeki, to inform him of the appointment. Ndukeki appeared quite positive in his attitude toward the Peace Corps program, saying that there were quite a few additional areas in which the Peace Corps could help meet Tanzania's need for technical expertise. Specifically, he asked whether trained surveyors could be provided. The embassy officer did not encourage Ndukeki to expect that surveyors would be part of the initial Peace Corps contingent. He suggested, however, that a broader program could be considered once the initial program had begun.[8]

On November 21, 1978, an American embassy officer met with a manpower development team, headed by Director of Training and Manpower Jackson Nyakirangani together with a representative of the Ministry of Finance, Mr. Kibwana, to discuss the status of the Peace Corps agreement. The transfer of responsibility from the Ministry of Finance to Manpower Development had opened renewed negotiation on the draft text of the agreement. Ministry of Manpower Development requested some changes, including the deletion of reference to volunteer leaders. Tanzania's government did not want to create a separate stratum of volunteers. Since all volunteers would be responsible to Tanzania's government officials for carrying out program activities, the government saw no need to create a hierarchy among volunteers. At the same time, Nyakirangani recognized that where volunteers served in clusters, one of the volunteers could become the informal spokesperson of the group on matters of mutual interest.[9]

Nyakirangani also requested the deletion of all references to personnel of private US organizations. The embassy officer argued that such personnel could be needed for short-term assignments. For example, they could work with ministries to develop detailed reports or proposals on areas for utilization by Peace Corps volunteers in Tanzanian development programs, or they could provide technical training to in-country volunteers in the event that unforeseen technical problems arose while implementing any Peace Corps project. Nyakirangani listened but did not change his position, namely that the agreement should delete all references to such class of persons. He felt that the Peace Corps should recruit volunteers with skills such that no additional technical training would be required other than that those available from Tanzania government ministries, thus tailoring programs to Tanzania's own needs and circumstances.[10]

Furthermore, Nyakirangani also raised several other important issues that he agreed did not have to be dealt with specifically in the text of the agreement. On staffing, he said that to begin the program, only the Peace Corps representative and a secretary should suffice, and that Tanzanian employees could be hired as needed. The embassy officer noted the Peace Corps's preference to operate with a lean staff but made the point that the agreement should permit flexibility to deal with future growth and unforeseen needs. Concerning the initial number of volunteers that would launch the program, Nyakirangani thought fifty-four Peace Corps volunteers would be difficult for the Tanzania government to absorb—especially since conflict with Uganda precluded assignment of volunteers to several regions including West Lake, Bukoba, Shinyanga, Mwanza, and Kigoma. He proposed the program to reopen with about twenty Peace Corps volunteers. The embassy officer said it was not clear what number of Peace Corps volunteers was necessary to create a "critical mass" but agreed to seek the Peace Corps's input.[11]

In addition, Nyakirangani raised the issue of the duration of service. He indicated the desire of the Tanzania government that Peace Corps volunteers serve for a minimum of three years. The embassy officer informed Nyakirangani that US law provided for two-year enlistments, though extensions could be encouraged once volunteers were recruited and working. On the recruitment of Peace Corps volunteers, Nyakirangani indicated Tanzania government's wish to participate in the selection process, perhaps by obtaining substantive ministry concurrence based on a review of credentials prior to arrival of Peace Corps volunteers in Tanzania. He referred to the past problems of poor qualifications of Peace Corps volunteers as having undermined the initial Peace Corps program. He added that once Tanzania's government agreement regarding recruitment was given, there would be no basis for recrimination over the caliber of volunteers. He did not know whether the Tanzanian government could send officials to the United States to speed the process of joint selection.[12]

It is significant to note that the US General Accounting Office (GAO) in its 1979 report had also raised some of the same issues voiced by Nyakirangani about Peace Corps programs. The report highlighted changes needed for a better Peace Corps. The GAO's review identified the following among many conditions warranting attention and corrective measures:

- Some programs and projects were of questionable value and lacked accord with Peace Corps goals and objectives.
- There was need to strengthen and periodically review host-country commitments to provide supervision and financial and material support to projects.
- There were some shortcomings in volunteer recruitment and placement.
- Many volunteers lacked commitment and terminated service before their scheduled completion.

The GAO regarded the provision of adequate host-country supervision, support, and contributions as important indications of host-country interest and commitment. In addition, GAO noted weaknesses in recruitment and placement of Peace Corps volunteers. As a result, many volunteers were entering Peace Corps inadequately screened for suitability and poorly informed about the conditions under which they would serve.[13]

Finally, the embassy officer asked Nyakirangani when it would be appropriate for the new Peace Corps representative, Jacques Wilmore, to arrive in Dar es Salaam to take up the handling of Peace Corps matters. Nyakirangani said he would take this up with the minister or principal secretary of manpower development and would provide an answer when he could. Nyakirangani indicated that Minister Mwanga was very anxious to have the agreement signed soon. The two governments eventually signed an agreement on January 9, 1979, in Dar es Salaam, Tanzania. The United States would furnish Peace Corps volunteers as requested by the government of Tanzania to perform mutually agreed-upon tasks in Tanzania. The volunteers would work under the immediate supervision of organizations designated by the two governments. The government of the United States would provide training to enable the volunteers to perform these agreed-upon tasks more efficiently.[14]

Media Coverage of the Peace Corps Agreement

On January 10, 1979, the government-owned daily newspaper, the *Daily News*, reported on the signing of the agreement in a prominent two-column article on page three. The article, titled "Peace Corps to Work Here," featured extracts from Minister Abel Mwanga's statement at the signing ceremony; according to the article, he said that Tanzania "welcomes the reestablishment of the Peace Corps Programme in Tanzania not only to gain the technical know-how but also help to bridge communication gaps between different cultures and promote international understanding."[15] He further reiterated that Peace Corps volunteers "are known for their commitment to forego monetary gains in favour of serving and helping people while at the same time learning from those they help. This is really doing good for humanity, and we feel it is a good opportunity to allow them to serve in our various productive and service sectors where the number of qualified and skilled Tanzanians are not yet adequate." Mwanga also noted that "it is true Tanzania receives experts from time to time through other bilateral aid agreements from the US, but it is necessary to supplement these with volunteers to satisfy our manpower needs." These needs were especially felt, the minister noted, in agriculture, natural resources, engineering, small-scale industrial development, land surveying, urban and rural development, health, and education. Spain, the US ambassador, praised Tanzania for accepting the Peace Corps program and expressed the hope that it would help to speed up the social and economic development of the country.

On January 11, the *Daily News* carried a long front-page editorial that justified the reestablishment of the Peace Corps program. The editorial began with a rhetorical question: "Does our pursuit of socialist objectives preclude cooperation with capitalist countries or stop us from making use of capitalist-minded people?"[16] The question was posed in relation to the reasons that had led to the closure of the program in 1969, namely, suspicions about Peace Corps volunteers from capitalist America sabotaging Tanzania's socialist objectives. Answering the question with "an obvious no," the editor noted:

> In the world as it really is today, it would be the height of folly to try to eliminate cooperation with capitalist countries or capitalist-minded people on the grounds that Tanzania was seeking a socialist future.
>
> Building socialism is a process that will take a long time and will succeed only after we are able to produce enough wealth and have accumulated enough knowledge to eliminate poverty, ignorance and disease.
>
> In the process, we need all the support and assistance we can get. So long as we remain in control of the process, we need not bother about the source

of the assistance we are getting or the ideological persuasion of those who are ready and willing to help us.

We are saying this because of the fears some of our people are bound to have over the decision by the Government to re-establish a United States Peace Corps programme in Tanzania....

Tanzania today is not the same country as it was a decade ago. It is true we are still a young [and] underdeveloped country, but we have now regained our confidence and have the capacity to pursue an independent socialist path of development.

Under the circumstances, it would simply be dogmatic to refuse volunteers from the United States on the basis of their suspected ideology or worse still, the past performance of other volunteers.

The important thing for us is to make sure that volunteers or experts who come to work here do so to achieve our objectives. [Emphasis added.]

In a communique to Washington, Ambassador Spain said that he believed that strong support from Tanzania's government for the resumption of the Peace Corps program reflected in the *Daily News* story and editorial above would effectively head off, for the time being, criticism of resumption of the Peace Corps program. Spain went on to say, "It is noteworthy, however, that [the] Tanzania[n] government felt this editorial was necessary, referring to residual 'fears some of our people are bound to have' about alleged past sins of Peace Corps regarding neo-political activities and undesirable cultural influence of Peace Corps Volunteers on Tanzania youth."[17] The ambassador went on to implore caution as the new Peace Corps program proceeded to evolve.

Nevertheless, one B. Omu-Mura, a resident of Dar es Salaam, in a long letter published in the *Daily News* of January 15, 1979, under "People's Forum" still raised suspicions of Peace Corps. He began his letter by noting that he had been prompted to write to the column "due to the suspect nature of the editorial appearing in the 'Daily News' of January 11, concerning the newly signed agreement re-establishing a United States Peace Corps Programme in Tanzania after a decade."[18] He went on to note that:

Mention ought to be made that the agreement marks a watershed in American-Tanzania relations, though precisely, I don't think [that] means a change of opinion either that of their public or the incumbent Senators who have gone to great lengths to strifle [sic] even financial assistance from International Organizations towards Tanzania just because of our socialist-oriented policies...

As we were told the "volunteers will serve in several of our productive and service sectors like agriculture, natural resources, engineering, small scale industrial development, land surveying, urban and rural development, health and education." This general parameter to which the peace corps have been exposed [sic] raises the very suspicion, premature as it may be[,] which prompted this esteemed paper [*Daily News*] to launch a campaign paving their apparently difficult road ahead clear...

With a very fine phraseology about the building of socialism as being a process that will take a long time and will succeed only after we are able to produce enough wealth and have accumulated enough knowledge to eliminate poverty, ignorance and disease, notwithstand[ing] the support we need, it is obviously an ideological myopicism [sic] to believe that American aid will create a base, a socialist one for that matter, of economic production, with socialized production and accumulation within the general framework of socialist planning, with the purpose of generating wealth for the defeat of our well known three "natural enemies"—capitalism let alone. If this was so, then there wouldn't hence [have] been unemployment, and [an] unequal distribution of wealth, to mention a few ills—in their country.

True as it may be said that Tanzania today is not the same country as it was a decade ago and that we have now regained our confidence and have the capacity to pursue an independent socialist path of development, this should not make us complacent over what the greatest of all imperialist countries in the late twentieth century has in store in its own objective of maintaining oppression.

It has the resources, strength and capability for intrigues to see [that] Africa is rid of those so called pro-Marxist regimes.

It is apparent that Omu-Mura believed that the editor of the *Daily News* was not only complacent about the role of the Peace Corps but also misguided in believing that American foreign policy was friendly to Tanzania. Yet, as we have noted, President Nyerere himself had changed his mind and was more amenable to receive technical assistance that the Peace Corps volunteers could provide to Tanzania. Also, as we shall see, the Tanzanian officials who negotiated the details of the return of the Peace

Corps endeavored to guarantee that Tanzania would stand to gain from the volunteers it would receive.

Project Criteria and General Thrust of Peace Corps Programs after 1979

When Tanzania signed the contract with the Peace Corps in January 1979, the agency had already gone through some changes. Since the first goal of Peace Corps is to provide technical assistance for those nations that request it, from 1961 onward, volunteer jobs evolved as the needs changed. Early programs emphasized education, agriculture, health, and community development, and most volunteers were generalists with little or no work experience.[19] In 1969, Joseph Blatchford succeeded Jack Vaughn as Peace Corps director. Unlike his predecessor, Blatchford emphasized recruiting older, skilled volunteers and dropped the ban on families. He also favored placing volunteers more directly under the auspices of their host countries.[20]

One significant change in the early 1970s was the shift from US-based predeparture training to training conducted in host countries. By 1973, almost 85 percent of all trainees received training in their host country. In 1978, the Peace Corps, under Director Carolyn R. Payton, began anew to recruit generalists. However, Peace Corps trained them in specific skills like disease eradication, maternal and child healthcare, and agriculture.[21] The number of volunteers who were sixty years or older constituted 8 percent of all volunteers, who totaled 7,072 worldwide.[22]

In 1979, when the Peace Corps reestablished its program in Tanzania, ACTION identified eight programs for emphasis: health and nutrition, food and water, knowledge and skills (education), economic development and income, community services, energy and conservation, housing, and legal rights. According to Lihosit, beginning in 1979 the Peace Corps prioritized the first three programs: "The goal was to have 80% of volunteers working in these areas within one year and 100% by 1980–1981. To achieve this goal, training was extended to 16 weeks of which six weeks were for 'skills training' and ten weeks for 'language training.'"[23]

Aquaculture, and specifically fisheries, fell under the food and water category. Thus, the first volunteers who reopened the Peace Corps in Tanzania included fisheries volunteers. As we shall see, aquaculture volunteers whom the Peace Corps posted to Tanzania were not well evaluated or supervised. Rather, the recruitment of the first group that returned to Tanzania after ten years was part of a political package deal by both the US and Tanzanian governments, in which the Peace Corps decided whom to send to Tanzania rather than what Tanzania requested.

Meanwhile, the 1980s saw Peace Corps cooperation with other US agencies, including the USAID. By 1987, the largest single contributor to the Peace Corps's fisheries programs was USAID. With Peace Corps's current focus on basic human needs, it identified fisheries development as an area where volunteers could make significant contributions.[24] However, as we have noted above, fisheries projects in Tanzania encountered difficulties that had been encountered in other African countries such as Togo and Sierra Leone.

CHAPTER 8

Peace Corps Volunteer Mishaps in Tanzania

Introduction

From its beginning, the Peace Corps was very much concerned about the well-being of its volunteers wherever it sent them. It appears that at the top of the list of Peace Corps's concerns was the health of the volunteers, such that preservice training included a segment about hygiene and health risks, especially addressing diseases unfamiliar to Americans and how to take precautions against contracting them. Thus, both before departure and while in their host countries, volunteers had to take prophylactics and periodic inoculations against some of these diseases.

However, whereas the Peace Corps's concerns focused on health-related risks, other risks caused the deaths of volunteers while serving in their host countries. By 1968, forty-nine volunteers and four trainees of twelve hundred in the Peace Corps had died from a variety of causes other than disease. Beginning with the deaths of volunteers in Colombia, those of David Crozier and Lawrence Radley in an airplane crash in April 1962, vehicular accidents, plane crashes, and drownings were the principal causes of volunteers' deaths. Only one volunteer died of disease and another, in Colombia, died of a drug overdose.

In 1968, Dr. John Harkness, director of the Peace Corps medical division, reported that the rate of all causes of death among volunteers was about the same as it was for a comparative age group in the United States. Most volunteers were in their early twenties. The death rate for the fifteen-to-twenty-four age bracket in the 1960s in the United States was one to one for every one thousand persons. Between 1961 and 2015, seven volunteers lost their lives while serving in Tanzania and one died after returning to the United States for health reasons.[1]

Besides being concerned about the physical well-being and safety of volunteers, the Peace Corps was also concerned about volunteers' behavior that was likely to tarnish the image of the organization. According to Eugene Mihaly, Peace Corps deputy director and then director in Tanzania (1966–69), drug use was problematic. Mihaly had to send several volunteers home because they ignored strong warnings that, in Tanzania, drug use would damage the program and offend their hosts.

In this chapter, we examine four mishaps of particular interest. One is the termination of service of Peace Corps volunteer Sally Lazar, a registered nurse (RN), who adopted a mixed-race infant without the permission of the Peace Corps. The second is the death of volunteer Peverley Dennett Kinsey, whose husband William "Bill" Kinsey was accused of killing her. The third is the strange disappearance of volunteer Mark Raymaker, presumed killed by poachers or killed and devoured by lions. The fourth is the fatal hit-and-run case of John M. Peterson.

PCV Sally Lazar, RN: The Adoption that Went Awry

Sally Lazar was thirty-seven years old when she joined the Peace Corps in 1962. She received her nurse's training at St. Joseph's Hospital, Phoenix, Arizona, from 1947 to 1950. Immediately after receiving her RN certificate, she enlisted in the US Army Nurses Corps and served as a first lieutenant until 1954, when she joined the professional staff of St. Agnes Hospital in Fresno, California, as a general duty nurse. She then moved on to the Veterans Hospital in Los Angeles in the same capacity. After promotions leading to the position of assistant head nurse, Lazar left full-time nursing in 1956 to return to university life at Santa Monica City College and UCLA. This academic training resulted in an appointment as nursing instructor at St. Vincent's College of Nursing in Los Angeles, from where she joined the Peace Corps.

According to Lazar, she was motivated to join the Peace Corps to do something for her country besides what she had done as a US Army nurse. She was originally assigned to an island in the Pacific but was told they had canceled their request for volunteers. She asked if she could go to Tanzania instead. She looked on the map and said to herself, "Why not?" She was in her late-thirties and had never been to Africa, so she sent in her acceptance of the assignment. Years later, she said that this was the best decision she had made in her long life.

When Lazar arrived in Tanzania in 1962 as part of the twenty-seven-strong T-2 contingent of nurses and laboratory technologists, she had no idea what awaited her and her colleagues. After arriving in Dar es Salaam, she was assigned to Dar es Salaam's main hospital, formerly the Princess Margaret Hospital and later renamed Muhimbili Hospital. Because she already had some experience teaching nurses in the United States, her supervisor, the matron, assigned her to work with personnel from the World Health Organization (WHO), who were starting a nursing program for local students. However, the matron told her that it would be a while before they could get started because the whole program was not yet set.

With time on their hands, Lazar and other nurses assigned to the WHO program decided to explore their surroundings. While doing so, they came across a Catholic convent where they were greeted by many little children and a group of nuns. According to Lazar, the nuns were tending children who had been left with them "temporarily": "The children (eight months to six years) were dropped off by a family member and would be picked up eventually by another family member, for adoption was not a practice in the extended family culture of the country. We became regulars at the convent and gained the trust of the nuns who eventually allowed us to take the children over 2 years old to the beach."[2] The convent was part of the complex of St. Joseph Cathedral, a Dar es Salaam landmark located on the north side of the Dar es Salaam harbor.

One of the children that Lazar and her colleagues met at the convent was Katrina, whom Lazar describes as "a cute little thing (with a big belly and reddish streaks in her hair)."[3] When Lazar first saw Katrina, she was only eight months old. Her relationship with Katrina grew stronger when she realized that, unlike the other kids at the convent who had families, Katrina had no family to return to. According to Lazar: "She had been left with the nuns permanently by her biological father, an East Indian, who told the nuns her biological mother was an African woman. At that time such a union was not to be tolerated in Tanganyika and the baby would have been shunned."[4]

Katrina was born at Kiomboi on November 13, 1961, to Amirali A. Jetha and Phaibo Matway. Jetha was of East Indian descent and Matway was an African woman. After Katrina was born, her father, of his own free will, handed her over to the care of the Medical Missionaries of Mary Sisters at Makiungu, a hospital located a few miles northeast of Singida, a town in what was then the Central Province. Part of the release document stipulated that Katrina could be transferred later to any Catholic orphanage willing to care for his child.[5] Jetha agreed to pay all expenses for Katrina's care and upkeep at Makiungu. He also offered to pay for travel expenses for Katrina and an accompanying nurse to any other orphanage elsewhere. The fact that Katrina turned out to be at the St. Joseph Cathedral Convent in Dar es Salaam implies that her father paid her travel expenses and upkeep in Dar es Salaam. Jetha also gave permission for his daughter to be baptized and educated in the Catholic faith.

When Lazar decided to adopt Katrina, it took the nuns a while to realize that she was serious, but eventually they relented. The consent of the nuns, as guardians, was required according to the adoption law enforced at the time. According to Lazar, she processed the adoption through the English court in Dar es Salaam. It is to be noted that what Lazar refers to as the English court was the High Court, the only court authorized by law to certify adoptions in Tanzania.

In 1942, the first adoption law was introduced and was known as the "Adoption of Infants Ordinance, No. 5 of 1942, Cap. 14." It came into force on May 8, 1942. Subsequently, it was repealed and reenacted in 1953 as the "Adoption Ordinance, No. 42 of 1953, Cap. 335." The law went through minor amendments in 1962 (Government Notice 478 of 1962) and in 1968 (Children's Homes [Regulation] Act, No.4 of 1968). According to Prof. Balthazar A. Rwezaura, despite the adoption law being in place since 1942 it has remained obscure and by 1988 had received neither judicial interpretation nor scrutiny as a subject of academic discourse.[6]

When Lazar adopted Katrina in 1962, the adoption was one out of only 406 adoption applications approved by the High Court from 1962 to 1985! The question, then, is: Did Lazar meet the adoption requirements accord-

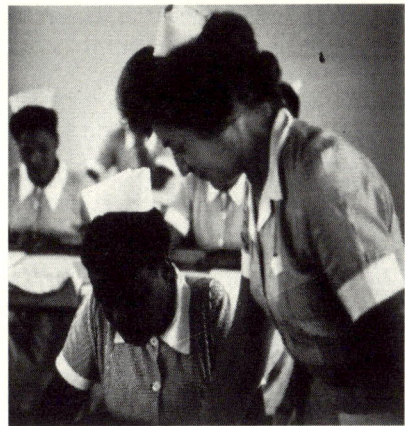

Left: Sally Lazar with baby Katrina (Katrina Lazar)

Above: Sally Lazar instructing African nursing students at Muhimbili Hospital (Katrina Lazar)

ing to the law in force? She certainly met the age requirement, which was set at twenty-five. She also sought the consent of the nuns at the convent as guardians of Katrina, whose consent was required under section 4 (a) of the ordinance. However, she did not meet the requirements regarding residence. According to section 4 (5) of the ordinance, an adoption order shall not be granted to an applicant or applicants who are not residents of Tanzania—residence being interpreted to mean a degree of permanent physical presence in a locality.

After Lazar adopted Katrina, she took her back to the nurses' quarters at Muhimbili Hospital. Soon the English matron heard about Katrina and paid Lazar a visit. The matron told Lazar in no uncertain terms that she could not keep Katrina in her room. The matron contacted the Peace Corps office in Dar es Salaam and Lazar was called in to explain the situation. The Peace Corps director did not approve of the adoption and decided to terminate Lazar's tenure. She and Katrina were sent back to the United States in November 1963. According to an embassy telegram dated November 6, 1963, Peace Corps Tanzania paid Lazar's air ticket at the cost of $714.60, with an itinerary from Dar es Salaam to Washington, DC.[7]

In conclusion, the adoption of Katrina is intriguing and raises questions, which require further scrutiny. Before adopting Katrina, did Lazar consider how she was going to raise a racially mixed child? We do not know if the matter ever crossed her mind. However, since Lazar was white, she very likely raised Katrina in a white social milieu. Nevertheless, in her upbringing, Katrina was likely a victim of prejudice and racial discrimination.

Ever since the Lazar case and others that possibly followed, the Peace Corps had to address the issue of volunteers adopting babies while in service abroad. Today, adopting children during a volunteer's service may still be a complicated process, one that may place an enormous burden on a volunteer, could be incompatible with continued service, and could result in termination of service. The Peace Corps expects that prior to deciding to adopt a child, a volunteer should consult with the appropriate consulate personnel to understand the legal requirements and complications of adoption, both in the host country and the United States, including exit requirements and entry requirements into the United States. In any case, Peace Corps staff will not assist in the adoption process.

The Death of PCV Peverley Dennett Kinsey

On March 27, 1966, Peace Corps volunteer William "Bill" Kinsey was arrested for killing his wife Peverley while they were picnicking near their school. He became the first Peace Corps volunteer ever to be charged with murder. Bill claimed that Peverley had accidentally slipped and fatally injured herself in a twenty-foot fall from a rocky ledge. When Bill was arrested at the picnic site by a Maswa policeman, he was being held captive by one hundred local people who said he had been trying to flee the scene. Nearby, the arresting officer found a rock and metal pipe caked with fresh blood and some threads of human hair. Kinsey's shirt was also bloodied. Bill told the Maswa police that the pipe was part of his camera equipment, and he did not know how the piece had become bloodstained. His clothes, he said, had blood on them because he tried to help his wife after she had fallen.

At approximately 11:30 A.M. on Monday, March 28, 1966, the Peace Corps headquarters in Washington, DC, received a telegram from Dar es Salaam, Tanzania, sent by Peace Corps Country Director Paul Sack. It said that Peverley Kinsey had died as the result of a fall while on a picnic near Shinyanga, Tanzania, the previous day. This first cable contained no information suggesting that any extraordinary circumstances were attendant on Peverley's death.

William C. Canby Jr., acting director of the African Regional Office, immediately convened a meeting of representatives of various other Peace Corps offices with responsibilities in cases of volunteer deaths. By approximately 6 P.M., Peverley's mother, Charlotte Woodall Dennett, and Bill Kinsey's family had been notified, as had the offices of the senators of North Carolina and Connecticut and the representatives of the concerned congressional districts. Also informed were the press and Peace Corps Director Jack Vaughn, who at the time was at a Peace Corps conference in India. Finally, a telegram containing instructions as to the disposition of Peverley's remains was en route to Dar es Salaam.

At 6:55 P.M. on March 28, the Department of State received an immediate telegram saying that Bill was being held by the police in Maswa. The telegram also said that John McPhee, the associate Peace Corps director stationed in Mwanza, the nearest large town and seventy-five miles north of Maswa, was already on the scene. It added that Sack and the Peace Corps's Public Health Service physician in Tanzania, Dr. Charles McHugh, were flying to Bill's aid. The Department of State passed this message to the Peace Corps within the hour, and by 8:30 P.M. William Josephson, general counsel of the Peace Corps, and Anthony F. Essaye, deputy general counsel, were at their offices. They were joined there by two other lawyers on the staff of the general counsel's office to begin a full assessment of the situation. At the same time Dr. W. John Burns, chief of the Special Services Branch in the Peace Corps Division of Volunteer Support, contacted both the Kinsey and Dennett families to apprise them of this serious turn of events. The Peace Corps Director of Public Information, Thomas S. Page, also went to Peace Corps headquarters to assist the lawyers and Dr. Burns in their work.

At 11:28 P.M., after consultation with the acting director Warren W. Wiggins, the general counsel sent a telegram informing Dar es Salaam that Essaye would be arriving on the next international flight. Essaye left for Tanzania from Dulles Airport at 6:30 A.M. on Tuesday, March 29, and arrived in Tanzania at 3 P.M. EST on March 30. At 5:23 A.M. on March 29, the Peace Corps received another immediate telegram from Dar es Salaam giving further details. This telegram informed the Peace Corps that the assistance of a qualified lawyer in Mwanza had been obtained. The lawyer had been recommended by the president of the Tanzania Bar Association. Dr. McHugh and the lawyer were said to be on their way from Mwanza to Maswa by road, at minimum a three-hour trip, because bad weather was preventing aircraft from landing in Maswa.

Another telegram was received by the Peace Corps at 8:40 P.M. on March 29. In that telegram, Sack reported that an autopsy had been performed by a competent pathologist who, the Peace Corps was made to understand, had flown to Mwanza from Nairobi, Kenya, at the request of Kenya Peace Corps country director Robert Poole. In the meantime, upon arriving in Dar es Salaam Essaye conferred with US ambassador John H. Burns and was briefed by the Peace Corps staff. Essaye also talked with attorney general of Tanzania Mark Bomani, the deputy director of the Tanzanian Criminal Investigation Division, and the assistant chief education officer in Dar es Salaam. The telegram also said that Essaye would fly to Mwanza and Maswa the next day along with Sack, and Peace Corps director of African Programs, Thomas H. E. Quimby, who had been in Mogadishu, Somalia, to consult with the Peace Corps director there. When notified about Bill's arrest, Quimby promptly flew to Dar es Salaam and was the senior Peace Corps official on the scene.

On March 31, Dr. Burns called Dr. William Kinsey, Bill's father, in North Carolina to tell him that the developing events would almost certainly require that a highly qualified lawyer be retained to defend Bill. Also, Dr. Burns told Dr. Kinsey of Peace Corps Tanzania's opinion that the defense and related expenses such as expert witnesses would probably be quite costly. The information about the legal expenses was provided to Dr. Kinsey because it was Peace Corps policy not to cover such costs except in court cases abroad involving US military personnel. In other words, the Kinsey family was expected to provide Bill with financial and other assistance.

There was an immediate reaction when it became known in Washington, North Carolina, Bill's hometown, that the Peace Corps would not be covering his legal expenses. The Washington, DC, office of North Carolina Senator Everett Jordan received several telegrams and letters from Washington, North Carolina, residents who opined that they felt it was the duty of the government to provide legal counsel for Bill. Facing reelection in 1966, Senator Jordan promptly acted by asking the director of the Peace Corps, Robert Sargent Shriver, "in the strongest possible terms to provide this young man [Bill Kinsey] with every possible assistance, including legal counsel."⁸ In his recently published book, *Every Hill a Burial Place,* Peter Reid has covered in detail the investigation and Bill's trial for the alleged murder of his wife.

The Disappearance and Presumed Death of Mark Raymaker

Mark Raymaker was twenty-two years old when he applied to and trained with the Peace Corps Tanzania-Ten (T-10) cohort at the Syracuse University Maxwell School. He was from Green Bay, Wisconsin. After graduating from Our Lady of Premontre High in Green Bay, he attended the Naval Academy from 1961 to 1963. Raymaker received a BA in history from St. Norbert College in 1965. He was on the dean's list at college and won a Belcher Scholarship to the Wisconsin Law School. Apparently, Raymaker harbored ambitions to become a professional football player. When he realized he would not play professional football, his life trajectory drastically changed.

In 1965, the Peace Corps posted Raymaker to Malangali Secondary School, in Iringa District. His volunteer service would have ended in November 1967, but he mysteriously disappeared at Kibaya in the Maasai Steppe where he was volunteering for the WHO in a campaign to inoculate the Masai people against smallpox.

The contribution of the Peace Corps volunteers in Tanzania toward the eradication of smallpox is yet to be written. To begin, in the late 1960s and 1970s, Peace Corps volunteers played a role in bringing the final chapter in the global story of smallpox eradication to a close. In 1959, the World Health Assembly (WHA) adopted a resolution proposed by the Soviet Union calling for the global eradication of smallpox under a program to be administered by the WHO. The primary strategy for this program was to vaccinate millions of susceptible people, one person at a time. In May 1965, President Lyndon B. Johnson pledged American support for smallpox eradication. In October 1966, American Dr. D. A. Henderson was called to head the WHO's global eradication effort. As an American, Henderson was familiar with the Peace Corps, which had only been in existence for five years at that point.

Before the global Smallpox Eradication Program began, the Peace Corps sent volunteers to numerous countries to work with the local ministries of health in general immunization programs that included smallpox. As declared in the Peace Corps 1964 annual report just three years after the agency was founded, "in Malaysia, Chile, Honduras, Bolivia, Peru, Colombia, Ecuador and El Salvador, nurses work in rural health programs, some with traveling clinics using the back of a jeep as a consulting-operating room, others in immunization programs fighting smallpox, diphtheria, and polio. Still others staff up-county health centers."[9]

Some of the early efforts of Peace Corps volunteers also occurred through temporary assignments. In August 1967, as part of an immunization project, small groups of volunteers in Tanzania supported teams led by the WHO to vaccinate the Maasai against smallpox. Team members included Peace Corps volunteers Dr. Fletcher Robinson, Eliot Noyes, Susan Morrow (Parkins), Anne Wiggins (Thompson), Donald Wolfensberger, and Mark Raymaker; Robin Dulake, a Voluntary Service Overseas (VSO) volunteer from England; and an interpreter. The groups lived in the bush for one month, eating canned food supplemented by fresh meat from the local game that they hunted.

On August 9, while out hunting, Raymaker went missing. On August 14, three light planes and a helicopter searched the area for Raymaker to no avail. The Peace Corps determined that a lion could have killed him. Chris Raymaker, Mark's younger brother, believes otherwise:

> I have long resigned myself to his disappearance. But after recalling and rereading the press and official Peace Corps accounts of the search and the final conclusions regarding his fate, much remains unanswered, some 40 years later. Why was his compass left in the land rover? Why no cigarettes taken with a chain smoker, why no gunshots, why no physical equipment... found, no clothing, human remains, vultures, bloodstains, carrion, etc.[?]
>
> I cannot help but intuitively conclude that either information was omitted from the official action accounts, or the search was very poorly managed and initiated long after it should have been. My brother Mark Raymaker was no hero. But it would be a blessing to better understand the incident which took him from us all. It was a mystery which haunted his mother to her last breath.[10]

However, another brother, Mike Raymaker, does not believe that Mark could have staged his disappearance for whatever reason. Mike believes that the Peace Corps story about the circumstances under which his brother went missing is not very convincing. He told the author that the family had just returned from a Parkers game when they got a call from the Peace Corps informing them that Mark had gone missing after going shooting for the pot (i.e., hunt for meat) with two other colleagues. Thirty days after his disappearance, the Peace Corps informed the family that Mark was presumed dead, although the cause of death could not be determined.

Subsequently, the Peace Corps decided to put a marker up for Mark in the Allouez Catholic Cemetery in Wisconsin, next to where his mother and father Catherine and Leonard Raymaker are buried. According to Mike, when this came to Chris's knowledge, he clandestinely arranged to have the marker removed. Later, Mike had the marker replaced.

Over the years there have been many turns and twists to the story of Mark's disappearance. According to Eugene Mihaly, who was assistant country director at the time, after the futile search for Mark, the Peace Corps presumed that either a lion or some poachers had killed him. It thus came as a surprise, Mihaly said, when "about ten years ago [circa 2009] Peace Corps had a major shock":

> A newspaper report in Nairobi stated that Mark and his family had just been killed in a car accident in Kenya. Our conclusion: To avoid the US draft, Mark had arranged for a friend to pick him up near the camp site and then he had gone to ground, i.e., officially disappeared. Where he went remains part of the mystery. But clearly he had staged his own fake demise—one that cost PC Tanzania and the US Government much angst, time and money. We have no idea what country he lived in for all those years, nor how he managed to escape notice. This is a fascinating episode.[11]

Another bizarre twist to Mark's disappearance was that many years later it was reported that he had been killed in automobile accident in Kenya. His reported automobile death was accompanied by a fake death certificate. On the one hand, this author was unable to get any evidence of such an automobile accident in which the victims included Mark Raymaker. On the other hand, we know that the death certificate is fake because the details on the document are false. For instance, there is no such place as the "State of Nairobi" and the name "BRENDA J. MCCAN" is likely fake, as is the signature. The title "Clerk of Nairobi commission, Kenya" is also fake.

Death Certificate

State of Nairobi — **Republic of Kenya**

I, BRENDA J. MCCAN, clerk of the commission in the country and state aforsaid, it being an office of record, and having a seal, do hereby certfy that the records in my office show that Mark A. Raymaker died at 14:22 GMT in Nairobi, the Republic of Kenya on the 14th day of January 2000. Sex Male, Age 67, Race White, Cause of Death Auto crash, Nationality United States of America, Duration of residence in the city of Nairobi 17 Years, Occupation Contractor / Consultant, Married Yes, Widowed NIL, Single NIL, Divorced NIL, as shown by the death records returned by Federal Medical center, Nairobi Kenya, and recorded in death record No. 054 at page 36, certificate filed March, 2000, in testimony whereof, I have hereunto affixed my signature and official seal in Nairobi, Kenya, this 26th day of March 2000. Clerk of Nairobi commission, Kenya. Cert No. 26241

Fake death certificate of Mark Raymaker. The origin/source is unknown.

When looking at the document, notice that the word *commission* is in lowercase. Nor is there such a thing as the "Nairobi Commission."

To date, Mark Raymaker's family has not had a sense of closure about his fate. Did he "disappear" on his own accord? Is it plausible that he decided to disappear just before he was to return to the United States because there was a pending felony case that he had to face? Or did he "disappear" in order to avoid the draft? According to George Brose, a T-10 volunteer stationed in Moshi from December 1965 to December 1967, Chris, Mark's younger brother, informed him that Mark had a pending felony charge, which he would have to answer were he to return to the United States.

Over the years, those who were involved in his strange "disappearance" continue to grapple and deal with this bizarre story. Former assistant Peace Corps country director, Eugene Mihaly, is one of them. In a recent email correspondence with Peace Corps volunteer George Cummins, Mihaly had this to say about Raymaker's "disappearance": "That was an unforgivable stunt. The only mystery that remains is how Mark went undetected or perhaps unreported all those years. I gather he lived in Kenya where the expat[triate] community isn't all that large. And the newspaper report of his death in a car accident suggests that he did not change his name."[12]

According to Mihaly, Paul Sack, country director at the time, sent him a newspaper clipping about the automobile accident in which Mark had supposedly died. However, my efforts to trace down and get hold of this newspaper clipping was to no avail. Almost in anguish, Mihaly has concluded: "We ran a massive air/ground search for two weeks in August. I was in charge, and I had to make the awful decision to call it off. We are divided in our thinking about his fate. I think he was bitten [by] a snake or attacked by a rhino or elephant and then eaten. Barry [Bloom] is convinced that a poacher murdered him and then buried him. All gruesome. And, as someone so wisely said, the worst thing is that a family has no corpse to grieve over—no entity on which to focus grief and thereby release it. How terrible."[13]

John M. Peterson's Fatal Hit-and-Run Case

An investigative report by *USA Today*, published on December 21, 2021, alleged that on August 24, 2019, a Dar es Salaam–based American Peace Corps staff member hit and killed a street vendor with his car in the predawn hours while driving under the influence. The *USA Today* investigative report identified the American as John M. Peterson, who, it is alleged, had hit and killed a street vendor, identified as Rabia Issa, a mother of three. *USA Today* alleged that Peterson was intoxicated at the time of the accident.

In its semiannual report to Congress (October 2020 to March 2021), the Office of the Inspector General (OIG) for the Peace Corps in Washington submitted the following brief report about the incident:

> OIG and the Department of State's Diplomatic Security Service, Office of Special Investigations, investigated a Peace Corps employee's involvement in the traffic death of a host country national. The investigation disclosed that after drinking an undetermined amount of alcohol at a bar, the employee picked up a sex worker on a street in his diplomatic-plated vehicle and brought her back to his U.S. government-leased residence, where he exchanged money for sexual activity with her. While driving her back to the area where he picked her up, the employee's car struck three host country nationals in separate but successive incidents, causing injury to the employee and severe injury to

bystanders, including one fatality. After the initial accident, a group of onlookers pelted the employees' vehicle with rocks. The employee then sped off in the vehicle and was chased down by a group of motorcycles. During the chase the employees' vehicle struck and killed a street vendor. The employee was eventually transported to a police station where he refused a breathalyzer and was released so that he could receive medical attention. The Peace Corps and [the] U.S. Embassy arranged a medevac to the United States for the employee. The host country was unable to pursue prosecution before the medevac took place, and the U.S. Department of Justice declined prosecution, citing a lack of jurisdiction. OIG referred the matter to the agency for administrative action and security clearance review. The employee's clearance was revoked, and he resigned from his position.[14]

The case of John Peterson presents us with some issues and questions. One issue has to do with Peace Corps staff and volunteers' sexual behavior. While the matter of sexual behavior is a highly personal one, volunteers are required to follow certain legal and policy requirements. It is important that volunteers understand the host country's sexual mores, including those in relation to dating, premarital sexual activity, adultery, and the consequences of transgressing them. What remains unclear is why, after he returned to the United States, Peterson was not dismissed but remained on the Peace Corps's payroll for more than a year before he resigned.

Peterson immediately left Tanzania for medical care in the United States even though he could have received adequate care in Dar es Salaam. How the medevac was conducted and why Tanzania police allowed it raises the suspicion of collusion to prevent Paterson from being held accountable for the fatal hit-and-run case, as had been the case with Bill Kinsey in 1966. Since *USA Today* published its investigative report, former Peace Corps volunteers have called for change at the agency. The author is unaware of what steps the Peace Corps has taken. It also remains unclear how this case has affected the Peace Corps's aspirational mission of promoting "world peace and friendship," especially if those in charge of fulfilling that promise have done so at the expense of the communities they and the agency's volunteers are meant to serve.

CHAPTER 9

Anecdotes of Peace Corps Volunteer Experiences

Introduction

The Peace Corps has no age limit for volunteers. Since its inception in 1961, most volunteers have been young men and women, most unmarried at the time of recruitment, and fresh out of college. The Peace Corps believed that young volunteers were better suited to venture off the beaten path and to the opportunity to develop "one's own resourcefulness toward a larger good in settings where resourcefulness and the sincere application of it [could] be useful to recipients."[1]

It is fair to say that the Peace Corps placed too much emphasis on physical hardship as a problem that new volunteers could expect to face in their host countries. As it turned out, it was not physical deprivation but rather not having someone to talk to on a social and intellectual level that was harder to endure. In other words, the lack of companionship in which volunteers could feel they were in a warm personal relationship with another was also a difficulty the Peace Corps needed to address. Early volunteers in Tanzania endeavored to alleviate loneliness by visiting one another, dating, and partying whenever an opportunity arose.

Dating and Marriage Between Volunteers

In the early days (1961–64), volunteers saw each other only occasionally in Tanganyika. However, when they did, the gatherings were festive and sometimes wild, as they partied and shared stories from their experiences in their host country. Schreiber remembers the gatherings and partying of T-1 and T-2 volunteers as resembling the television show *M*A*S*H*. Some volunteers went to great lengths not to miss such gatherings. According to Katus, when faced with the possibility of missing a party with the newly arrived nurses of T-2, he lied his way out of his predicament:

> I was on safari deep in the Eastern Region "pori" [the bush] the week before the Nurses [T-1I] arrived. I was translating for a UN official from the Netherlands, mostly translating his English for the Africans and Asians who had difficulty with his accent.... He was a real dawdler and he wanted to stay in Mikumi Saturday night. I said, "No way, I had to get the PWD [Public Works Department] Land Rover back to the compound." Not true, but it worked. However, I arrived at about 8:00 pm, well after dark, and the party was well underway at Tom and Jerry's bachelor quarters [in Morogoro].[2]

Furthermore, Katus remembers occasional weekends in Dar es Salaam, especially after the nurses arrived, and meetings on Saturday afternoons in the courtyard of the New Africa Hotel. Katus also recalls that he and two other T-1 volunteers, Burt Segall and Jerry Parson, had a dhow[3] excursion with eight T-2 nurses from Bagamoyo to Pangani (near Tanga) on the Indian Ocean coast. Subsequently, Segall married one of the nurses, Mary Briggs. Katus, Young, and Parson would later be Segall's best men at his wedding. Mary's folks flew in from the United States. The couple wedded at the Dar es Salaam Anglican Church. After the ceremony, the wedding party returned to the nurses' quarters at the Princess Margaret Hospital (Muhimbili) for the reception. There was much drinking and dancing, and Katus recalls passing out: "I woke up around midnight, sprawled out on the lawn, still in the white dinner jacket, with considerable grass stains. With an enormous head (ache), I struggled to the nurses' common area to sleep it off. The next morning, I saw Lee Overstreet [a T-2 nurse] and remembered that she had been dancing on a tabletop. I congratulated her for her style, and she said, 'Don't you remember? You were on the tabletop dancing with me!'"[4]

In Morogoro, Katus and Parson had plenty of fun when they were not in the field. To begin with, they patronized local pubs and clubs. Katus remembers that the Morogoro European Club attempted to recruit Parson as their first Black member. Parson told the club's management that they had best find a Tanganyika African member before he would ever consider becoming a member. Instead, Katus and Parson patronized the Goan Club, which was only a block from their bachelor quarters.

Other volunteers who married while in Tanganyika were Annie and Peter DeSimone, Pat and John King, Art and Ann Young, Jim and Maria Ohara (a British nurse he had met in Dodoma), and Will and Tereza Julian. Tereza was a young Goan woman who had been born in Tanzania. While these volunteers met and fell in love in Tanganyika, as we have noted, Earl Brown invited his fiancée Mary Ann from the United States and they married at Nyegina, Musoma.

There were also flirtatious and dating relationships that did not lead to marriage between a few other T-1 and T-2s. Carole Siriani was already engaged when she arrived in Tanganyika. Nevertheless, Katus pursued her for months before she finally took off her engagement ring. Although they became very close and planned to marry, they did not. According to Katus, Parson and Proctor were also very close and flirtatious, as were Alex Veech and Donna Annetta. Jim Belisle and Art Young pursued Ann Quink, but Art Young won out in the end.

Socializing with Nationals

Socializing between volunteers and nationals in Tanzania depended upon several variables, especially a volunteer's gender, type of job, personality, and willingness to socialize with nationals. Regarding gender, male volunteers, more than their female counterparts, were more likely to socialize with nationals, both male and female. Some types of jobs, more than others, were amenable to developing close relations between volunteers and nationals. Forms of socialization included visiting nationals at their homes, visiting local bars and music dance halls, and giving and receiving invitations to parties.

To begin, there was, of course, unwanted attention on the part of female volunteers, which Peace Corps training had never prepared them to deal with. Proctor recalls that she and another nurse, Ann (née Quink) Young, were invited to the Mwanza Club that was just down the road from where they lived. The Mwanza Club was a members-only club, meaning for whites only. She recalls going there two or three times in the year they lived in

Mwanza but was unaware of any restrictions on membership. As she puts it, "I must plead being young and dumb on that issue. I think I just did not pay much attention. On the occasions I was at the Mwanza Club, Ann and I had typically been invited by someone. The last time I vividly remember while there, someone told me/us about the assassination of John Kennedy. I was physically ill after that."[5]

On the question of unwanted male attention, Proctor recalls that Asian men often accosted her: "I had two interactions with Asian men, one nonviolent, the other, potentially violent. In the first episode, two young men came to our house in Mwanza and asked us how much we 'charged.' They were not at all aggressive—more like teenagers daring each other with boyish dares. Ann handled them kindly but directly. She will recall this event perhaps better than me. I would not categorize this as sexual harassment."[6]

However, Proctor did have one episode later in Dar es Salaam where she was accosted from behind while walking home from a movie in the evening. A young Asian man came up to her from behind, grabbed her by the neck, and attempted to pull her into some nearby bushes. She fought back and hit him, and he ran away. An overhead streetlight lit up his face and that is how she recognized him as Asian. She never reported this incident. As she puts it, "Things like that happened to women regularly and it never occurred to me to ever call the police or to report it to the Peace Corps. It never crossed my mind to tell anyone other than my roommate. It was 1965!!! There was no awareness of the importance of reporting such events! There were no laws against sexual harassment! There were no definitions of sexual harassment! No one even discussed it in the public sector. It was a man's world. One just dealt with it as a female."[7]

In terms of normal socializing, perhaps not many early volunteers socialized with Tanzania nationals more than Donna (née Abner) Chalmers, a T-2 volunteer nurse, did. She developed close friendly relations with several nationals, some of whom she kept in touch with years after returning to the United States. When she worked at the Princess Margaret Hospital (Muhimbili) at Dar es Salaam, she became close friends with Shose Mawalla, with whom she kept in touch for years after she had returned to the United States. Chalmers recalls that Shose's sister, Vicki, married Nsilo Swai, who was one of the ministers in Tanganyika's first cabinet under President Nyerere. According to Chalmers, President Nyerere attended the wedding.

While at Dar es Salaam, Chalmers became friends with Mark Bomani, who was at the time a lawyer in the Ministry of Justice. According to Chalmers, she was a frequent visitor at Bomani's house in Oyster Bay, where she listened to American and African music and went to the beach. Bomani's chauffeur would get her from the nurses' quarters and take her back. During her stay in Dar es Salaam, Chalmers also attended Dar es Salaam's "high society" parties. She recalls that in August 1963 the mayor of Dar es Salaam invited the volunteer nurses to a dance, which officials and ministers attended. One of the guests was the exiled king of Burundi, with whom Chalmers remembers dancing.

Besides attending parties, Chalmers attended sundowners, one of which she remembers was also attended by Jeremiah Kasambala, minister of community development, and the minister of health. Donna recalls joining a Conga line, singing, "TANU Yajenga Nchi" (TANU builds the nation). She felt so privileged to be there because attendance was by invitation only and there were just three other white (European) people there.

In 1964, a member of a United Nations' mission who was visiting Dar es Salaam invited Chalmers (as his "wife") to a state ball where the guest of honor was Emperor Haile Selassie of Ethiopia. Chalmers remembers sitting only twenty feet from the emperor. In addition, in 1964 Chalmers attended parties with Nigerian officers who at the time were in Tanzania at the invitation of President Nyerere following the mutiny of the armed forces. The Nigerians had just replaced the British Commandos that President Nyerere had called to quell the 1964 mutiny.

Donna Abner's invitation card to a sundowner graced by Rashidi Kawawa, Tanzania's vice president (Donna Abner)

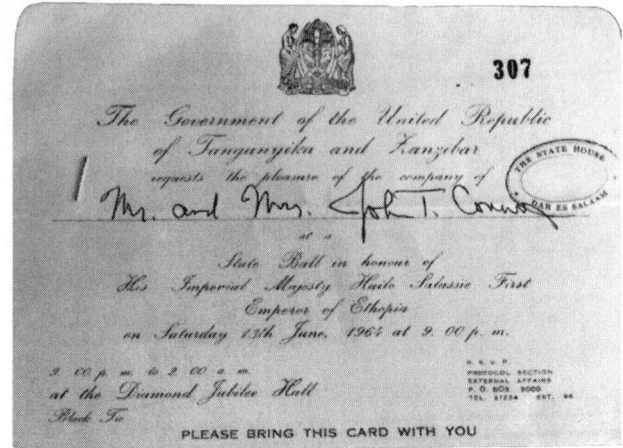

Donna Abner's invitation (as "Mrs. Conway") to state ball in honor of Emperor Haile Selassie of Ethiopia (Donna Abner)

When Chalmers was transferred to Tabora she developed a close relationship with Mirisho S. H. Sarakikya, who was at the time an army captain. She recalls that there were fewer parties to attend but with Sarakikya they went to movies or went out to eat. During the mutiny, Sarakikya remained loyal to President Nyerere and managed to keep the soldiers in Tabora under control.[8] As a result, President Nyerere promoted him to brigadier and subsequently to major general. He was also the first chief of the Tanzania People's Defense Force from 1964 to 1974.

T-1 Geological Team Suspected of Being *Mumiani* (Vampires)

In parts of East and Central Africa, beginning in the 1910s and early 1920s, there emerged a popular belief about certain categories of colonial government employees whom people came to associate with abducting people for purposes of draining their blood. In an article titled "Cars Out of Place: Vampires, Technology, and Labor in East and Central Africa," Luise White outlines the origins and contours of this belief.[9] In Tanganyika, people believed to engage in the practice of collecting human blood were known as *mumiani*. As White notes, besides the belief being a figment of people's imaginations, stories about certain colonial employees going about abducting people and then draining their blood also disclose the concerns and anxieties of people at a specific time and place.[10] The concerns and anxieties were related to specific occupations such as firefighters, health inspectors, and surveyors, whose performances were alien to people. Hence, the stories describe not only the way in which blood was extracted but also how it occurred, who performed it, and under what conditions and inducements.[11]

While conducting mapping work among the countless coastal villages, T-1 geologist Tamura notes that he made it a point to visit with the headman or elders of the villages and wards to notify them of the presence of the survey team and to explain the kind of work that they were doing. Not everyone understood the nature of survey work and the interest in rocks. When Tamura and his team reached Pangani, he visited with the first Tanganyikan Provincial Commissioner of Pangani, soon after Tanganyika became independent. He remembers it was a cordial, but friendly, meeting and he took Tamura and his crew around and introduced them to all his constituents around the town and up the Pangani River to visit some of the Arab coconut plantations. Tamura thinks that, in those days, everyone thought he was another "European," since the country of "America," (much less the concept of being a Japanese American) was less known to the villagers. Nevertheless, he says that, for the first time, he appreciated drinking cinnamon-flavored coffee.

Working along the coast, Tamura and his crew became aware of *mumiani*, a superstitious belief that strangers went around collecting human blood. The villagers suspected Tamura and his men were there to waylay and capture unsuspecting women and children, tie them up, withdraw blood, and sell it to the hospitals. According to Tamura, the locals had answers for all the equipment the team had carried with them. The Land Rover was used to transport the victims, the rope they used to pull the truck out of the mud was used to tie down the victims, the forty-five-gallon gasoline drum (which was painted red) used to fuel the Land Rover was used to store blood, the geologic pick he carried to break open rocks was supposedly used to knock the victims unconscious, the notebook he carried to record his findings was used to record the number of victims, and the hand lens he carried to examine rock minerals was used to examine blood samples.

The manner of conducting surveys was to examine rock outcrops and collect samples wherever they cropped out. In his work along the coast, the only rock exposures were along the banks of streams and rivers, often in remote areas. During the team's traverses, they often encountered and surprised women collecting water along the streams and rivers. Just the nature of the team's appearance and their rock examinations and random collections probably looked suspicious to those not understanding what survey work was all about. It only added to the superstitious rumors and beliefs of *mumiani*.

As they worked their way further north to the Kenya border, the suspicions grew graver to the point that Tamura's crew felt threated and feared for their lives if they set foot in some of the villages. At the last village in Tanganyika before the Kenya border, Tamura was awakened at 2 A.M. by members of his field party to attend a meeting requested by the elders of the village. They were aware of the heightened fears by the villagers about *mumiani* and wanted to talk to Tamura about it. As he and his men sat around the campfire, each elder spoke of his concern and wanted them to be aware of it. When it came time to try to find a way to mitigate the problem, they asked for counsel from the old man of the village. Tamura and his men were all surprised when they discovered he was fast asleep and had not listened to the discussion. The tension of the meeting then dissipated. Tamura suggested to the elders that in the morning he would set up the survey equipment in the village center and demonstrate the use of each piece of equipment for all the villagers to see how it worked. When they watched the demonstration like using the rope to hook up to the winch to pull the Land Rover, opening the gasoline drum so they could smell the gasoline, using the geology pick to break rocks, then it became obvious to the villagers. Their response was, essentially, "Oh, those were obvious uses." When his crew asked about *mumiani*, their excuse was that it was not them who held such a belief but the Makonde who had emigrated from Mozambique that believed in such things.

Anyone for a Scrambled Ostrich Egg for Breakfast?

Lee Hedges was twenty-two years old when he volunteered for the Peace Corps and was part of T-1 that arrived in Tanzania before independence in 1961. After the Independence celebrations, he and another T-1 volunteer, Denis Galvin, were posted to the provincial Public Works Department (PWD), with headquarters at Arusha. Like other T-1 volunteers, Lee Hedges had an assortment of skills that enabled him to carry on his work as a surveyor: typing, drafting, vehicle mechanics, surveying, crew leadership, organization, and field preparation, as well as learning to make do with little.

While at Arusha, Hedges made topographical maps of several areas, including hospital grounds, police installations, two bridge sites, and a reservoir. He conducted general surveys for several hundred miles of feeder roads for the Community Development Program, involving drainage problems, horizontal and vertical alignment, and economic feasibility. Hedges supervised the survey and construction of five miles of drainage improvements for the main Arusha-Dodoma part of the renowned Great North Road (from Cape Town to Cairo).

One day, the engineer in charge, Bill Rowe, called Hedges into his office and assigned him the task of locating a four-by-four-mile site for a proposed airport about thirty miles east of Arusha on the Sanya Chini plains, east of Mount Meru and south of Mount Kilimanjaro. A topographical survey was to be made of the four-mile square area. This provided the layout of the future four-hundred-acre Kilimanjaro International Airport.

In early 1962, Hedges and Galvin took off from Arusha in a loaded Land Rover, followed by a PWD flatbed, gear-laden truck pulling a three-hundred-fifty-gallon water bowser trailer. Arriving near a previously built weather station, they established their camp. This camp would serve as a home for the next nine months. Fortunately, the town of Arusha was only thirty miles away, allowing weekly returns and thus giving the crew fresh food and welcomed mail.

With Galvin's help, solar ephemeris sun readings were made to locate true north for the airport's true bearings. Once this was completed, then the four-mile layout could begin. A typical survey workday commenced at 8 A.M. with the workday lasting for eight hours without a lunch break. This was the policy of the new African government and the choice of the African crew. The men preferred not having to work any longer than necessary in the midday sun and not having to put in the effort of preparing lunch. As Hedges put it: "We would start by going to the last completed survey point [to] obtain our bearings and [then] continue to project the line with the Swiss made Wild T-2 theodolite [which was the best available equipment at that time]."

Then, the milled wooden survey markers began to go missing and Hedges suspected that the local herds boys liked to get their hands on "finished" wood. This activity caused the survey team to have to resurvey the missing line, resulting in wasted work. A fellow Peace Corps surveyor in another providence told Hedges that he had the same problem: "PCV

Lee Hedges at the Sanya Chini survey campsite (Lee Hedges)

Roger Hagler [from Jonesboro, Louisiana] recalled from our training red was a taboo color. He had his survey markers painted red—problem solved. The next time we were in Arusha at PWD headquarters I obtained red paint and brushes. Our painted markers then stayed put. Then we started having trouble with the concrete markers being dug up."[12] At this point, Hedges and his crew visited all the nearby settlements. The local people told them that whoever dug them up believed there must be something of value beneath to warrant such a marker. Hedges assured them there were no valuables hidden. The headmen agreed to inform their people to cease removal of any more markers in the future.

After nine months, Hedges and Galvin completed the topographical survey of the future Kilimanjaro International Airport. Ten years later, in December 1971, construction of the airport began, financed by a $13 million loan. An Italian construction company built the airport. The main runway is over two miles long and is oriented at 090/270 degrees, just like Hedges and Galvin had originally laid out in their east–west orientation! The largest commercial passenger aircraft at the time (e.g., Boeing's 747-400 and Antonov planes) could take off and land here. Just as all airports have identifying codes such as Seattle/SEA or Chicago/ORD, Kilimanjaro International Airport also had its own code: JRO.

As already noted, the survey site for the future Kilimanjaro International Airport was located in the Sanya Chini plains, in an area straddling the Arusha and Moshi districts. There were various kinds of wild game to be found on the Sanya Chini plains. The game ranged from antelope, including Impala, Thompson's, and Grant's gazelles. Ostriches, giraffes, Cape buffalo, and lions also made their presence known. Sometimes the survey crew would come across ostrich nests. Hedges told the author, "To collect an egg was a treat for us all. We would cook it up like a scrambled chicken egg. One ostrich egg could feed all six of us plus the weatherman."[13]

Perhaps the most foolish and dangerous thing Hedges did during this survey job was catching a very young giraffe. This occurred over fifteen years before Robin Williams starred in the movie *Dead Poets Society,* where Williams admonished his students to *"carpe diem,"* which is Latin for "seize the day or time." As Hedges was returning to camp from the southeast corner to the northwest of the survey area—constituted of over eight miles of bumpy plains—he noticed a small group of giraffes. There were five or six adults and a few newborns. He seized the moment by driving the Land Rover slowly toward these giraffes and singled out one of the young ones. He then hazed it away from the herd, meaning that he isolated it and then chased it with his vehicle. As the Land Rover's speed steadily increased over time, and given the duration of the chase, the young giraffe soon tired. Sliding the window down, Hedges was able to grasp the animal's tail. Then he slowed the vehicle down, causing the giraffe to exert more energy and be unable to run away. This very soon exhausted the animal. As it stopped running, his crew hopped out of the Land Rover and put a rope on one of the giraffe's hind legs. Hedges also quickly got out and grasped its neck and held its mouth closed in case it would attempt to bite. He did all this while standing smartly to the side should it try to kick. Soon they had the animal on the ground and secure. Hedges used a soil sample bag to cover the giraffe's eyes.

This technique worked as well on the giraffe as it had when using eye coverings on Texas horses to calm them down. Realizing he did not have his camera with him that day, he asked Abdula to drive to camp and collect it. As he continued to hold the animal down, much to his surprise, the entire crew abandoned him, hopping into the Land Rover with Abdula. At this point, he realized that he was very alone, with the nearby adult giraffes looking on. To them, he most likely appeared to be some kind of beast eating one of their young. If they had attacked, then he would have been defenseless and soon dead! Good fortune was with him, however, as the adult giraffes just continued to watch and Abdula soon arrived with the camera. After taking some pictures, Hedges released the young giraffe, which returned to the herd.

CHAPTER 10

Peace Corps Volunteer Early Departures

Introduction

The early termination of volunteers and trainees has been a concern for the Peace Corps since it sent its first volunteers overseas in 1961. Over the decades the Peace Corps has used a variety of methods to study, measure, predict, and combat volunteer and trainee attrition. Based on current available records, precise early termination (ET) rates are difficult to determine for the first several years of the Peace Corps. The Peace Corps Act of 1961 stipulated that the president of the United States could terminate the service of a volunteer at any time. However, the act did not call attention to any reasons that could make the president terminate a volunteer's service. It appears that until 1969 the Peace Corps did not have any manual with policies and procedures governing the circumstances under which a volunteer or trainee's service could end prior to completion of service date. Instead, volunteers received letters from the Peace Corps with information deemed necessary to prepare them before departure such as what type of clothing, personal care products, and appliances they would need.

The Peace Corps appears to have first issued a rule of conduct manual in 1984. The 2020 Peace Corps manual indicates that it partially supersedes several manuals that date back to 1984. The manual outlines comprehensive policies and procedures regarding the circumstances under which a Peace Corps volunteer's service may end early. Specifically, the Peace

Corps Manual stipulates that an early termination should occur when a volunteer cannot or should not remain in service until his or her projected completion of service (COS) date.

Service in the Peace Corps is voluntary, but once a volunteer commits to serve, the Peace Corps and the host country expect that he or she will complete the term of service. By accepting an invitation to serve, volunteers commit themselves to serve the people of the host country to the best of their abilities for a specified period, usually about two years, within the framework and support systems established by the Peace Corps. The manual identifies four types of early termination:[1]

- Medical Separation: If a volunteer has or develops a medical condition that the Peace Corps cannot medically accommodate or resolve within forty-five days, then the volunteer will be medically separated. This decision is made by the Office of Health Services in consultation with the Peace Corps medical officer at the post and as needed, alongside the appropriate medical consultants.
- Administrative Separation: Pursuant to the Peace Corps Act, 22 U.S.C. 2504 (j) and Peace Corps policy, the service of a volunteer may be terminated at the discretion of designated Peace Corps staff. This option may be invoked on several grounds—for example, when a volunteer commits a major violation of Peace Corps policy, including certain policies designed to ensure health and safety.
- Resignation: A resignation is a decision made by a volunteer who no longer wishes to continue his or her Peace Corps service. With certain exceptions, such as the use, possession, or distribution of drugs, volunteers who are informed by their country director that they will be administratively separated from the Peace Corps can be given a twenty-four-hour window to resign voluntarily from service.
- Interrupted Service: A volunteer may be separated with "interrupted service" status if the country director determines that circumstances beyond the control of the volunteer make it necessary for the volunteer to leave his or her present assignment.[2] Because the nature of the circumstances is beyond the volunteer's control, interrupted service is not used in lieu of administrative separation. Examples of cases in which this type of early termination is used include civil unrest, conflict,

and outbreaks of major diseases in the country of service that put the volunteer's health or safety at risk.³

In the case of medical separation, a country director will arrange transportation for a volunteer or trainee to his or her home of record—with personal effects delivered as unaccompanied airfreight.

As noted above, a volunteer may be administratively separated for unsatisfactory conduct or performance; violation of any Peace Corps policy, whether agency-wide or post-specific; or any other grounds that diminish the effectiveness of the volunteer or the Peace Corps program. The Peace Corps will pay return transportation costs for early terminating volunteers and trainees who, upon termination from the Peace Corps, return directly and immediately to their home-of-record from their country of assignment. Volunteers and trainees traveling at Peace Corps's expense must be given (1) an international travel authorization, (2) an economy class air ticket from post to home-of-record, and (3) travel allowances in accordance with MS 221 Volunteer Allowances or MS 222 Trainees Allowances.

The following allegations regarding Peace Corps policy violations could result in termination of a volunteer's service:

a. Sexual misconduct,
b. Commercial sex,
c. Fraud, theft, embezzlement, or misuse of Peace Corps funds,
d. Fraternizing with students or subordinates contrary to Peace Corps policy,
e. Involvement with drugs,
f. Failure to disclose legal or medical record, and
g. Serious violations of US or local law.

Over the decades Peace Corps has used a variety of methods to study, measure, predict, and combat volunteer and trainee attrition. However, precise Early Termination (ET) rates are difficult to determine for the first several years of the Peace Corps. It appears that in the early 1960s, the ET rate fluctuated between 30 and 35 percent of all volunteers and trainees. The ET rate of the late 1960s rose to all-time agency highs, ranging between 45 percent in 1966 to 65 percent in 1968. It is uncertain why such high rates existed, but one contributory factor could have been high trainee attrition when the "de-select" practice was common. Nevertheless, there was a common fear that the rates were rising due to the feeling that the Peace Corps had lost some of its mystique. Therefore, the Peace Corps decided that it could best lower attrition by increasing volunteer satisfaction and improving recruitment and selection.

During the early 1970s, the overall ET rate was approximately 50 percent in 1970, then it fell to 43 percent in 1972, rose again to nearly 50 percent in 1974, and finally decreased to about 37 percent by 1976. During the late 1970s, overall ET rates declined from the previous high attrition of the late 1960s and early 1970s. Although the rate rose to nearly 45 percent in 1978, it fell back to under 40 percent by 1980 and continued to decrease from that point onward. In the early 1980s, the overall ET rates hovered at, or slightly above, the 30 percent mark.

In 1979, the Peace Corps conducted a study involving all the ETs to date. The study indicated that no information in the letters of recommendation, for instance, predicted the length of service. However, the more references applicants provided, the more likely they were to ET. Overall, the 1979 study showed that age and sex are the best indicators for ET (ET for males is less common than female ET, and older volunteers terminate early more often than younger volunteers). The study also showed that one-half of married volunteer terminate early, and it was suggested that the rate is so high because married couples joined the Peace Corps in order "to resurrect" a failing marriage. In turn, volunteers that are more educated serve longer.

On December 22, 1983, Director Loret Ruppe sent a memorandum to country directors, and it outlined the creation of an Attrition Task Force whose purpose was to identify areas of manageable attrition and take action to improve COS chances for PCVs. A limited exercise (only nine posts returned complete exercises) designed for "quick response" by the Task Force showed that programming and volunteer support were major factors of ET. Consequently, the Attrition Task Force recommended:

1. Strengthening training for overseas staff in programming and Peace Corps volunteer support by enhancing training of new hires in addition to in-service skill development.
2. Every country should address current ET rates and develop plans to reduce its ET rate as part of its annual Country Management Plan exercise.

3. Staff in high ET countries should be given consideration by senior managers in determining agency resource allocations: Reduction of ET rates should be both a budgetary and planning priority.
4. An agency focus on attrition should continue beyond fiscal year 1985. A volunteer tracking system should be built into the computer system and the Country Program review monitoring system.
5. Countries should be encouraged to conduct ET management exercises.
6. High ET countries should be encouraged to conduct management exercises every two to three years.

There is no evidence to indicate whether the Peace Corps implemented these recommendations. Nevertheless, this was the first time that it had been suggested to reduce the ET rate, especially by improving Peace Corps policies and management skills as opposed to "weeding out" applicants.

In the late 1980s, the Peace Corps continued to monitor the ET rate closely. Attrition remained at, or slightly above, 30 percent. The agency began to analyze the ET rate based on various demographics in an effort to pinpoint the causes for ET among different groups. Among minorities, American Indian and Alaskan Natives had the highest ET rate (38 percent), followed by Hispanic Americans (31 percent), and Black Americans (30 percent). Besides high attrition rates for minorities, age was also a factor because high ET rates were also common among older volunteers, including those over the age of 30 and not just 50-year-old and above.

The Attrition Task Force reached a consensus that a variety of isolated disappointments and frustrating experiences (i.e., dissatisfaction with assignment, culture shock, or unmet expectations) conspired to result in volunteer attrition. The task force also cited problems related to Peace Corps operations, which had contributed to volunteers' decisions to shorten their service. The Attrition Task Force cited three main factors concerning volunteer attrition that had not been "adequately considered" previously:

1. Attrition must be viewed as being the collective result of actions taken by volunteers and the agency. The Peace Corps has the responsibility to support and train volunteers adequately, just as applicants have a responsibility to be free of stateside obligations and relationships and must carefully consider the depth of their commitment before taking the Peace Corps oath.

2. There are numerous places throughout the Peace Corps system that, together, can cause attrition: At any stage of the volunteer's service, an old disappointment, such as errors in processing or a negative encounter with a staff member can have a residual effect.
3. Strategies to reduce and end attrition need to be institutionalized into one policy or effort, in contrast to the various uncoordinated efforts that had taken place in the past.

Moreover, the Attrition Task Force cautioned that although there could be no quick fixes to the problem of volunteer and trainee early termination, a willingness to give of oneself and modify old habits and ideas is essential to succeeding as a Peace Corps volunteer. This is because volunteers can be vulnerable to very stressful experiences of varying types (medical, psychological, cultural, professional), which can often result in a hasty decision to terminate their service. It was therefore suggested that each post should have someone trained in a variety of counseling techniques and that there should be assistance for senior volunteers, couples, and ethnic minorities. Peer counseling should also be made available. The task force also recommended that special services should redesign the ET procedure and incorporate a "reflection period" of several days to prevent hasty ET decisions.

Furthermore, the Attrition Task Force recommended that a standing committee be established, which would make periodic reports to the director and chief of staff about agency attrition rates. This committee would have the sole authority to design activities that would increase retention rates for volunteers. The task force also recommended that the committee be made up of the three chiefs of operations from IO (Impact and Outcomes) as well as other staffers from similar offices.

During the 1990s, the overall ET rate remained at about 30 percent but the debate about how to reduce ET continued, focusing especially on "older" volunteers. The possibility of developing a database to monitor rates was at the forefront of discussions. This was in recognition that the expensive staging models of the past, CAST (Community Analysis and Strategy Tool) and PRIST (Project Review and Implementation Strategy Tool), proved to be ineffective at predicting an applicant's length of service. Most interestingly, a question was raised whether the Peace Corps should shift its emphasis from retaining senior volunteers to minority volunteers. Seniors, it was noted, tended to ET at a higher rate partly because they had a difficult time mastering foreign languages. The concern was also raised about the cost of early terminations to the Peace Corps. By the 1990s, the Peace Corps was spending approximately $6,230 per volunteer for medical services, training, and other costs. Because 30 percent of each class terminated early each year, the Peace Corps lost approximately $5.8 million of its initial investment.

Furthermore, to obtain data about volunteer attrition and the reasons why volunteers terminated early, Director of Peace Corps Mark Gearan sent a memorandum to country directors containing a questionnaire for volunteers, trainees, and staff to complete once a volunteer had chosen to terminate early. The questionnaire followed the favorable results of a 1994 pilot study, in which reasons for ET were obtained from 62 percent of those who had terminated early—up from 47 percent the previous year. The 1994 pilot study had shown that early terminations were the result of several factors, including "family-related," the most common reason given by 41 percent of volunteers and trainees and 43 percent of overseas staff. Other reasons were "qualifications" (12 percent of volunteers and trainees, 22 percent of staff), "job-related dissatisfaction" (18 percent of volunteers and trainees, 10 percent of staff), and "health-related problems" (10 percent of volunteers and trainees, 7 percent of staff).

During the 2000s, the ET rate fluctuated between 24 percent and 34 percent. In fiscal year 2015, of the 3,444 volunteers who began their Peace Corps service, 1,188 terminated early. Resignations accounted for most of these early terminations, coming from 21 percent of the volunteers in the fiscal year 2015 cohort, or 734 people. The latest data on ET rates by sex show a parity between male and female volunteers. In fiscal year 2018, 788 of 6,834 female volunteers (12 percent) and 472 of 3,984 male volunteers (12 percent) left service early. Early termination by marital status during fiscal year 2018 shows that of the volunteers who terminated their service early, 12 percent were single or engaged, 15 percent were divorced or separated, and 16 percent were married. None of the six volunteers who were widowed terminated early.

The percentage of global ETs in fiscal year 2020 by type shows that resignations accounted for 52 percent of ETs, followed by medical separation (39 percent), and interrupted service (8 percent). In fiscal year 2020, five hundred twenty volunteers who served during the fiscal year, and prior to the global evacuation of volunteers because of the COVID-19 pandemic, did not complete their full service. Of these five hundred twenty volunteers, 272 (52 percent of all ETs) resigned. Thirty of the 272 people who resigned in fiscal year 2020 (11 percent of resignations) chose to do so in lieu of an administrative separation. The second-largest number of fiscal year 2020 ETs came from medical separations (204 volunteers, or 39 percent of all ETs).

Given the central role of volunteers in advancing the Peace Corps mission, there can be a significant impact on agency operations when volunteers leave before completing their two years of service. When a volunteer terminates his or her service early, it disrupts the performance and delivery of services anticipated by host-country communities. This may have an adverse effect on local community morale and future support of other volunteer-driven endeavors.

As already noted, in the early years of the Peace Corps, attrition was attributed to "bad" applicants, who hopefully could be weeded out before they were sworn in as volunteers. As time passed, the Peace Corps's focus shifted toward correcting and modifying its approach to early terminations. In the 1980s and 1990s, attrition was seen as both a problem resulting from uncontrollable factors and from volunteer and Peace Corps inadequacies. The new data collected during the 2000s, and the adoption of more precise and regular ET monitoring and analysis, offer some hope of ET reduction in the future.

Early Departures and Terminations from Tanzania

For the early 1960s, precise early termination and early departure rates are difficult to determine, except for T-2 volunteers. Proctor, one of the T-2 nurses, provided the data in Table 6 on the following page. The T-2 term of service was September 1962 to June 1964.

The major reason for the early departure of T-2 volunteers was marriage. All the marriages occurred in 1963 and, as noted in chapter 3, the volunteers were nurses in their early twenties. According to Proctor, for them, marriage was their first priority, not a career:

> This was 1963. Most American women expected—in fact wished to be married—and there was a reciprocal cultural expectation that they do so. During this era, the US was barely out of the 50s, the decade of the ideal housewife

Table 6: T-2 Early Departures and Terminations

Peace Corps Volunteer Name	Station	Reason for Departure	Approx. Date of Departure	Remarks
1. Gail Croy, RN	Tanga	Dissatisfaction	Late 1962 (exact date unknown)	Resigned because she felt the assignment was not for her.
2. Mary Briggs Segall, RN	DSM	Marriage	June 1963	Mary married T-1 civil engineer Burt Segall. She notes in a memoir that the Peace Corps had a policy against married couples and, furthermore, had no mechanism in place for extending service at that time.
3. Pat Hogan King, RN	DSM	Marriage	June 1963	Pat married Tanganyika Peace Corps physician Dr. John King. They continued in Peace Corps service with an immediate subsequent assignment to Somalia.
4. Mary Stafford Merselis, RN	DSM	Marriage	June 1963	Mary departed to marry her physician fiancé in her home country. They immediately returned to East Africa and served in a small rural hospital in Uganda.
5. Patricia "Annie" Hohlstein DeSimone, RN	Tanga	Marriage	June 1963	Annie married T-1 civil engineer Peter DeSimone. Because there was no option for extending and there were policies against married couples, the couple continued service in Uganda through USAID.
6. Sally Lazar, RN	DSM	Adoption	June 1963	Sally adopted a Tanganyikan child. This was apparently against Peace Corps policy, and she was asked to leave.
7. Marlys Bralic Hector, RN	Tanga	Marriage	June 1963	Marlys married Teachers for East Africa (TEA) teacher Henry Hector. They continued in the Tanga area with TEA. Because she married, she could not continue as a Peace Corps volunteer.
8. Rebecca Davis Henderson, MT	DSM	Illness	May 1964	Becky departed the country slightly early due to illness.

Source: Susan Proctor, *Tanganyika Two: Bio Sketches and Life Stories*, mimeograph. (In author's possession.)

and mother who was expected to spun [sic] a career in favor of marriage and family only. It was not uncommon for college to be seen as something "to fall back on" should marriage not come one's way. Indeed, this was very much my experience despite an intense, rigorous, five year baccalaureate program in nursing. Careers were something to be engaged in until marriage came along.[4]

Volunteer Resignations

According to the Peace Corps manual, a resignation is a decision made by a volunteer who no longer wishes to continue his or her Peace Corps service. The first volunteer to have resigned from service in Tanzania was Gail Croy, RN, who resigned from her post in Tanga in late 1962. According to Susan Proctor, Croy left because she felt that the assignment was not for her. What made Croy feel the assignment was not for her? It could be that she was unable to cope under conditions that were very challenging in terms of working in a British-style nursing context, dealing with ailments she had little knowledge of, or having to do work with very few resources in terms of medical supplies.

Medical Separations

The first medical separation of a volunteer in Tanzania was that of Rebecca "Becky" Davis Henderson, a T-2 medical technologist. Henderson was one of two medical technologists who, together with twenty-five registered nurses, arrived in Tanzania on September 5, 1962. Due to an illness, Henderson departed the country in May 1964 before having completed her service. Obviously, her departure deprived the Princess Margaret Hospital (Muhimbili) in Dar es Salaam of her specialized expertise as a medical technologist.

Another early volunteer who was subject to a medical separation was Richard Scrivner. Scrivner was born on June 21, 1944. He joined the Peace Corps in 1965. According to George Cummins, who was in the same cohort (T-5) as Scrivner, he was involved in a bicycle accident. Scrivner was seriously injured (it may have been a neck injury) and evacuated. Because of his injuries, he became a quadriplegic and spent the rest of his life in a wheelchair. Scrivner died on May 22, 2005, and was buried in Phoenix, Arizona, on May 27.

Stephen "Steve" McNown was a T-6 teacher. According to Sanna Poorman Thomas, a T-6 teacher who taught in Korogwe, "He got involved with a bunch of ex-pats in Dodoma and started playing rugby. In one game, he had a terrible hit and suffered a concussion. Steve blacked out in 1967 during one of Dr. Jim Morrisey's medical projects up near Loliondo so Jim sent him back to the US for tests, etc. Steve died in Washington DC in the winter of 1967/1968."[5]

Administrative Separations

Administrative separation is the termination of a volunteer's service according to policy regulations that a volunteer may have contravened. The first administrative separation of volunteer service in Tanzania may have been that of Peace Corps volunteer John White. Peace Corps terminated his service in the spring of 1963 for engaging in an extramarital relationship with a young wife of a British expatriate.

In this category of administrative separation, Peace Corps female volunteers were likely more affected than their male counterparts. We have noted that some T-2 early departures were due to marriage. This is because the Peace Corps had a policy that did not allow female volunteers to continue serving if they married while in service. Due to marriage, the twenty-seven-strong cohort of T-2 registered nurses and medical technologists lost five of its members. It is paradoxical that the Peace Corps had a policy that required women who married while in service to quit serving, despite their husbands not having to quit.

Another Peace Corps policy that contributed to early terminations and departures by female volunteers was that female volunteers could not give birth in their assigned host countries, although initially the Peace Corps had allowed them to. The initial policy adopted by Robert Sargent Shriver that women could give birth in their assigned country was later changed to require a termination of service if a woman became pregnant. In 2013, the policy was changed again to allow women to continue serving while pregnant.

Thus, the Peace Corps did not give female volunteers enough leeway or any option to choose to serve during pregnancy. Regarding pregnancy, the Peace Corps based its policy on medical grounds. Pregnancy was treated in the same manner as other volunteer health conditions that require medical attention. Given the circumstances under which volunteers live and work in their host countries, it is possible that the Peace Corps's medical standards for continued service during pregnancy may not be met except in large cities like Dar es Salaam.

Other cases of early administrative separation had to do with volunteer misconduct deemed as compromising the image of the Peace Corps and its good relations with the host country. Most of these cases arose out of cultural misunderstandings or insensitivities on the part of Peace Corps volunteers. The termination and transfer of Francis "Fran" Koster, Gayle "Gay" Singer, and Patricia "Trish" Berry out of Tanzania constituted one such case. In 1965, Peace Corps whisked the three volunteers out of the country after what happened at a hospital at Tabora. At a T-5 reunion in 2011, Koster asked if he could have a few minutes to tell his story.

According to Koster, who worked for the provincial Public Works Department (PWD) in Tabora, one weekend he happened to visit Gay Singer and Trish Berry, Peace Corps nurses who worked at a hospital in Tabora that was thinly staffed. That weekend, Singer was on call. After dinner, Singer was called to the hospital to attend to a pregnant woman in labor. She asked Koster to walk her to the hospital because there were no streetlights, and she did not want to go on foot alone. He did and waited outside on the hospital steps. A trainee nurse assisted Singer. A second woman had also gone into labor in an adjoining bed. When Singer performed an episiotomy on the first patient, the trainee fainted at the sight of blood and dropped the lantern, setting the spilled fuel on fire across the delivery room. Singer screamed for Koster to come and help. He dragged the trainee out and put out the fire. While Singer was assisting the first woman, the second started to deliver. Singer asked Koster to assist and instructed him on what to do. He noticed that the umbilical cord was wrapped around the baby's neck. She verbally walked him through the procedures and the baby was safely born. The next day, Koster visited the hospital and received thanks from the patient, who asked that a picture be taken of her and the baby. He took a photo of the mother and her baby and returned to the field. Midweek, the police came and arrested him. A short time later, the Peace Corps evacuated Koster, Singer, and Trish Berry. Apparently, the woman that Koster had helped deliver was Muslim; she had a jealous husband who was incensed that another man (especially a white man) had seen his wife naked. More damaging was the fact that, in the picture, the baby's eyes were red from the camera's flash. As a result, the couple thought their child had been bewitched. In response, the Peace Corps transferred the three volunteers to other countries.

CHAPTER 11

Peace Corps Volunteers and the Reentry Problem

Introduction

By 1965, there were some 3,500 returned volunteers of the Peace Corps in the United States. The Peace Corps expected the number to rise over the years. As more and more volunteers returned, the Peace Corps headquarters became aware that some of them were facing "challenges" like the "culture shock" they may have experienced upon arrival in their host countries. In its March 19, 1965, edition, *Life* magazine carried a long article by Richard B. Stolley titled "Peace Corps' Re-Entry Crisis," in which Stolley asserted that the Peace Corps was facing a serious problem with its returned volunteers. Two weeks before Stolley published his article there was a conference in Washington, DC, attended by more than one thousand returned volunteers. According to Stolley, the volunteers expressed concern about their inability to readjust to life in the United States.[1] Furthermore, Stolley wrote that the Peace Corps headquarters was aware of the problem because of the number of letters it had received from returned volunteers, letters with expressions of anguish such as "The first month [back home] was hell," "I was depressed for six months," and "I don't feel at home anymore."[2]

Moreover, Stolley reiterated that the cause of the returned volunteers' inability to readjust was because, upon returning to the United States, they found the country had changed "mysteriously" while they had been away. According to Stolley, typically, the difficulties began as the homecoming welcome congealed rapidly into disillusionment: "Returning joyfully to old friends they discover that they have nothing much to talk about. 'I came back more serious, I suppose, much more concerned about things like peace and civil rights,' said Joseph Mullins of Griffin, G[eorgi]a. 'But my friends seem to think mostly about their own pleasures.'"[3]

Peace Corps officials at headquarters were quick to claim that what Stolley said did not represent the average returning volunteer. Peace Corps staffer David Gelman, a former reporter for the *New Yok Post,* ridiculed Stolley's article in a staff newsletter: "Was it a documentary about ex-junkies?" he quipped. Although top officials at Peace Corps headquarters said that news media had overemphasized difficulties experienced by volunteers in rejoining American society, they admitted that returning volunteers did require a readjustment period that could last from four months to a year.

According to Dr. Joseph English of the Peace Corps medical division, the reentry process was a "challenge." The main problem for the returning volunteer, English said, was to find a meaningful employment position that came with responsibilities. His colleague, Deputy Associate Director Dr. Joseph Colmen concurred, saying that volunteers working overseas held responsible jobs and it made sense that upon returning to the United States, they needed stimulating jobs, which provided independence and a sense of commitment. Failure to get a good job could easily lead to disillusionment and depression.[4]

From its inception, the Peace Corps anticipated that returning Peace Corps volunteers would likely face reentry difficulties and would require a readjustment period. It was due to such an anticipation that the original Peace Corps legislation in 1961 included a clause that stipulated the establishment of the Peace Corps Career Planning Board to aid returning volunteers with issues of reentry and readjustment. However, the proposal was premature because Congress had not yet even approved the program. Therefore, the Peace Corps deleted the clause from the proposed legislation.

In 1963, following the return of the first group of volunteers, the Carnegie Corporation provided funds to establish the Peace Corps Career Information Service. Career Information Service (CIS) staff were responsible for facilitating volunteer reentry and aiding volunteers to readjust to American society psychologically as well as finding appropriate career opportunities. In this regard, the Peace Corps recognized that the returning volunteer would likely face unique problems by virtue of having been away for two or more years from the United States.⁵

The CIS was responsible for helping volunteers with reentry by publishing monthly career bulletins that listed scholarship, employment, and service opportunities.⁶ After returning to the United States, volunteers could contact consultants in various academic and vocational fields. The CIS also published rosters of volunteers interested in continued education, government service, and business and industry. Besides assistance from the CIS, returning volunteers were eligible to use placement offices at their former college or university.⁷

Besides anticipating volunteer career needs upon reentry, the Peace Corps also anticipated that some would likely have psychological issues to deal with. This was in fact a concern that necessitated the vetting of applicants to determine whether they were psychologically fit for service in foreign lands. In June 1962, Dr. Joseph English was hired by the Peace Corps as a full-time psychiatrist. In July 1963, a second full-time psychiatrist joined the Peace Corps staff at headquarters.⁸

Peace Corps psychiatrists had two functions. They were involved in the recruitment and vetting of Peace Corps applicants to determine if they were psychologically healthy and well suited to Peace Corps work (i.e., able to withstand emotional stress while working abroad).⁹ Upon termination, they also assisted volunteers in dealing with the attendant problems of reentry into American culture. However, one returning volunteer has questioned the Peace Corps's ability to play that second role: "No one should expect PC to be able to keep track of every individual as they re-enter and readjust. There are resources and communities there if you reach out for them and ask. But everyone's re-entry struggle is as unique as everyone's PC service. We're all returning to something different, and that can have different impacts on us. I do think some of the Peace Corps friendships will be my strongest friendships in all of life. Those are what save you when you re-enter."¹⁰

Indeed, reentry poses several challenges that some returning Peace Corps volunteers may have to cope with for a long time after their return to the United States. As we shall see, returning Peace Corps volunteers do not receive adequate preparation for reentry, whereas when they leave the United States, many have some expectation that adjustment in their host country might be challenging. In other words, many Peace Corps volunteers anticipate the foreignness of their host culture, but they do not realize that their own American culture, friends, and family may feel foreign to them after two years or more of service overseas.

As Eleanor Q. Burton indicates, people returning home may experience many of the same symptoms of cultural adjustment to a new country when readjusting to their home country: "It is frequently difficult for people to accept or give much attention to the idea that returning home might pose unforeseen challenges. After all, home is home—what is there to 'adjust' to?"[11] As we shall see, Peace Corps volunteers who expect reentry to be easy and a return home where everything is "normal" have had some rude awakenings.

Peace Corps volunteers who adjust most easily to their host country's culture may have the most difficulty readjusting to American life when they return. As one of the letters cited by Stolley above indicates, they come back home but do not feel they are home! Some volunteers have lived in less comfortable circumstances overseas; when they return, they feel guilty, disturbed, or upset at American materialism or the waste of resources that Americans seem oblivious to.

Moreover, Peace Corps volunteers' experiences overseas may cause personal changes in attitude to life and one's values. American values, ideas, and customs that a volunteer had considered important before going overseas may no longer hold the same significance or garner the same interest upon reentry into the United States. Topics and issues that concern friends, family, and others may seem irrelevant or unimportant to a returning volunteer. Conversation becomes difficult because friends and relatives have little experience or knowledge about the country the returned volunteer was living in and may have little interest in sharing the returned volunteer's reminiscences.

In the United States, attitudes and lifestyles changed rather dramatically in the mid-1960s. More specifically, a shift occurred from 1965 onward. As returned volunteer John Ratigan observes:

> That is when what is often called the "Eisenhower era" of sort of blandness, general acceptance of life in the US among white people at least, conformist clothes of chino pants and button-down shirts came to a close. And what took its place was a greater consciousness of the unfairness or failings of American life began to take hold, perhaps initiated by the Martin Luther King march in Washington in 1963, along with increased drug use, beginning with marijuana and then moving on to other things, and also more anti-establishment

clothes. Consciousness of and doubts about the war in Vietnam caused these sentiments to grow, student protests began to occur and then grew. The latter reached a crescendo at the Democratic convention in 1968.[12]

The point Ratigan makes is that after 1965 changing conditions worsened the reentry of returning volunteers. However, there were also continuities in America's underlying social, economic, and political dynamics. The United States, both before and after 1965, remained a market-driven economy and culture in which materialism and self-centeredness were the core of American culture. As we shall see, some returning volunteers found both "disturbing." Of course, racism and racial discrimination against Blacks was a specter that returning African American volunteers both before and after 1965 had to contend with upon reentry.

Reentry Experiences and Varied Career Paths

According to Peace Corps psychiatrist Dr. Joseph English, the main problem and cause of concern for returning volunteers is to find a job that provides independence, responsibility, and a sense of commitment. His perception is due to an understanding that while abroad many volunteers work in positions that not only give them great responsibility but also a degree of independence, especially in terms of decision-making. However, concern about securing a job is not the only reentry issue that returned volunteers face. Returning volunteers from Tanzania have faced reentry issues that are racial, social, political, and economic in nature.

Politically, the escalation of the Vietnam War was accompanied by an increase in young American men being drafted. During the 1960s, the majority of volunteers were young men and women aged between twenty-two and twenty-five, most fresh out of college. Most were, therefore, eligible to be drafted. Many young men who enrolled in the Peace Corps did so to avoid the draft. However, even while serving overseas the possibility of being drafted upon reentry remained in the back of many volunteers' minds. Those who returned and were still eligible were drafted. Some sought deferment by enrolling in graduate school.

Socially, given the age of most volunteers, romance and dating have been a part of the Peace Corps experience. Most Peace Corps volunteers were (or remain) single, and a few were engaged before they left the United States for Tanzania. In Tanzania, some dated and married there; others got engaged and married after they returned to the United States. Many returned to the United States expecting to find prospective significant others whom they would marry. According to George Cummins (T-5), many volunteers tried to contact friends still on college campuses looking for people to date. They also inquired about the social scene back in the United States from volunteers who had happened to visit the United States for a special occasion and then had returned to Tanzania to finish their service.

Ed Connerley was a member of T-5 who took leave and went home for several months to deal with some urgent family matters. When he returned to Tanzania, other volunteers asked about his social life back in the States. He indicated that he had trouble communicating with and relating to college female students. He found them shallow, self-centered, and not interested in the world off-campus. He says, "I found several [of them] attractive and wanted to get better acquainted [with them] until they opened their mouths and their heads fell off. Time to break out the tinker toys."[13] When George Cummins went back to graduate school three years after having served in the Peace Corps and then three years in the army, he found college female students much as Connerley had: "I found women who were out of college, employed and aware of the wider world more attractive and good company."[14]

Politically, serving overseas took the edge off President Kennedy's idealism that had motivated many volunteers to join the Peace Corps. This was especially the case for those who had served during the turbulent times of racial riots in the United States and the Vietnam War. In this regard, it is important to note how some volunteers began to view the United States differently while serving overseas. According to Susan Proctor, a T-2 nurse, her experience of living in Tanzania created strong emotional challenges:

> The emotional challenges largely involved politics and my slowly growing awareness that the US was not all "pure" as I had been taught. I saw my country from the outside with all her triumphs but also her foibles. This awakening is perhaps not unusual for any early twenty-something, and is in fact, a normal developmental phenomenon. However, to have it occur while living in a different culture was particularly unsettling. I began questioning my faith and my country. And the war in Vietnam didn't help. When

President Johnson escalated the bombing of Hanoi in January 1965, I told new people I met that I was an Mcanada—a Canadian—because the Canadians always come off so squeaky clean.

Another volunteer, Tom Katus (T-1 surveyor) struggled to explain to local people in Tanzania what was happening in the United States regarding the riots and violent police encounters with Black rioters, who looked like themselves:

> As civil rights were very hot in the US, including [Theophilus Eugene] Bull Connor's use of dogs on demonstrators, we had many discussions with our educated Tanzanian-African, European and Asian and young expatriate friends. Many were appalled and sympathetic to the demonstrators. Because I am from "South" Dakota and the confrontations were mostly in the US "South", I posted a large map of the US on our wall to demonstrate to our friends that South Dakota was hundreds of miles north of the deep South. But I admitted that the plight of the American Indians with whom I grew up, while not currently as violent as the rednecks beating up African-Americans, historically the Native American suppression was comparable to African slaves suppression. I remember one rather heated discussion when some of our young expatriate friends were promoting equality; Jerry [Parson], in his own quiet way, simply said, "You folks have all the right answers but you have never lived it."

Indeed, Parson, who was Black, was right that white volunteers could not claim to understand American racism because they belonged to the privileged mainstream cultural milieu. According to Cummins, who spent his formative years in rural, white, Protestant America (Iowa), he knew few people of color and felt safe with his surroundings. The Peace Corps introduced him to and provided him with the opportunity to live and work with a diverse group of Americans. However, he said that "Before Peace Corps, I was unaware of / not involved with the civil rights movement that was growing in the US. When I returned to the US in 1967, it was having an impact. While I was in the Army (1967–70) and in Korea (1968–69), the antiwar movement was also gaining strength. Those movements created some of the 'culture shock' I experienced when I returned to the US permanently."[15]

Moreover, before Cummins deployed to Korea, he had a personal experience with race and racism that left him shaken up. Cummins notes that while serving in Tanzania he realized he was a member of the white minority. However, he never felt threatened in any way. He got a rude awakening when he returned to the United States:

> In early January 1968 I arrived in Washington, D. C. on a Friday morning before I was scheduled to report for Army Combat Engineer Officer Candidate School (OCS) early the next week at nearby Ft. Belvoir, Virginia. I checked into the downtown YMCA and headed over to Peace Corps headquarters. I had a brief reunion with several PC/Tanzania staff that I had worked with (Paul Sack, Jack McPhee, Norm [Leon] Parker and Brenda Brown) who had now assumed fairly influential positions in PC Headquarters. Brenda and I had worked closely together supervising the Tanzania XII PCVs who were initiating a pilot agriculture training program in elementary grades. We had lunch together.
>
> She indicated she had a couple of hours of afternoon work to finish and then was headed to her apartment to pack for an evening bus to her home in Baltimore. She invited me to join her for supper so we could continue our discussion of the progress and surprising success of the TXII volunteers we had worked with. She needed to get to Baltimore to start making arrangements for her wedding to Dick Schoonover, a Foreign Service officer we had served with in Tanzania. After supper she asked if I would walk her to the nearby bus station in downtown D. C. which I readily agreed to do. She got her ticket, I carried her travel case to the bus, gave her a peck on the cheek and wished her well in her upcoming marriage. As I turned to leave I realized I was the center of attention—a white GI in uniform kissing a black girl with a traveling case getting on a bus. There had been considerable racial unrest in Washington, D. C. and I was the only white [person] in the bus station and one of the few in the neighborhood where the YMCA was located. The bystanders assumed Brenda and I had a business relationship, and their glances were hostile. I hurried out of the bus station, jogged to the YMCA and locked my room door behind me. It is one of the few times in my life that I have been scared and feared for my safety.[16]

Both before and after 1965, African American volunteers returned to a country that was still embroiled in racism and overt racial discrimination.

James "Jim" Crawford was an African American T-6 volunteer teacher stationed at a school just west of the capital, Dar es Salaam, together with another volunteer, Stephen McNown (a white man). One being Black and the other being white, their close relationship disregarded the color line that would have been an obstacle to their closeness in the United States. They hosted several dignitaries as poster boys for the Peace Corps. Cummins was one of those invited to their termination celebration. At the party, Cummins observed that Crawford's demeanor showed that his thoughts were elsewhere: "Jim seemed a bit melancholy and withdrawn. I later found out he was from the deep South, his father was a Baptist minister and in college he was attracted to the Black Panthers. Feeling he wasn't accepted in the USA and not wanting to embarrass his father, he joined the Peace Corps. After 2 years in Tanzania, he didn't feel he fit in there either. The nagging question was where did he belong and where would he be accepted?"[17]

The experience of another African American volunteer, serving not in Tanzania but in the Philippines, illustrates the shocking experience of racial discrimination upon reentry. Brenda (née Brown) Schoonover was an African American volunteer teacher in the first group that went to the Philippines in 1961. Schoonover came home in the fall of 1963. She notes:

> Back home, not long after my return from my volunteer assignment, there would be one comeuppance on the racial front. Another African American returned volunteer and I went to our alma mater, Morgan State College, on a Peace Corps recruiting trip. Afterwards, he and I stopped at a very casual restaurant for a meal, and we were refused service. Bluntly reminded that segregation in my country was alive and flourishing, I was hurt, disgusted. I had left our country to represent our great democracy. Yet less than 35 miles from our nation's capital and only one mile away from my old campus, I could still be refused service because of the color of my skin.[18]

Unlike Black volunteers, in Tanzania white volunteers like Charles Fels became accustomed to being the only white face in a sea of Black faces. However, his Tanzanian students were deeply respectful of him as a person and as a teacher. When he returned to the United States, he became a seventh-grade English teacher in an inner-city school in Syracuse, New York. There he experienced the opposite of what he had experienced in

Tanzania: "The students were almost entirely black and hated white teachers. They were rude and disrespectful to most teachers. My last day on the job the principal called the state police to come put down a riot in the school refectory. The police used tear gas to put down the students and the school made the national news that night. I was glad to get out alive."[19]

According to Fels, unlike at the schools he had taught at in Tanzania (Dodoma and Lyamungu), he never established order in the classes in Syracuse: "Every class was a struggle. Most students did not want to be in school and did not value the experience. Many acted out. I was white. Most of them were black. They were super charged with hormones and racial animosity. As a white person, I was the recipient of 100 years of understandable hatred."[20] Consequently, Fels says,

> I never felt I re-entered American society. For three years, I was adrift in the sea of protest, racial tension and controversy that characterized America from 1968 to 1971. Things began to settle only after I knew I could not be sent to fight in Vietnam. Three years in law school were not easy but that is when the transition back to America began for me.
>
> I cannot blame the Peace Corps for not helping with that re-entry. It was a turbulent time and while no doubt I received occasional letters from the Peace Corps, they were generic, more suited to people who were at a different stage of life than I.

Fels went on to law school, in Nashville, Tennessee, and experienced what he says were an odd set of circumstances. His first roommate was from Tanzania, his second roommate was from Tanzania, and his third roommate was from Tanzania! Later, he chose to become a priest and went to seminary in Alexandria, Virginia. Each of his three years there, he had a new friend from Tanzania, all Anglican clergy. Also, remarkable.

Although Fels explains his experience at Syracuse as the result of being white in a predominantly Black school, some returning African American volunteer teachers had similar experiences. At the end of her volunteer stint in the fall of 1963, Brenda Schoonover joined the Cardozo Project in Urban Teaching, a yearlong pilot program in curriculum development utilizing returned Peace Corps volunteers in an urban setting, at Cardozo High School in Washington, DC. She had grown up in a small town, so while the project was an invaluable experience, she admits to a degree of culture shock. For her, working in the rough-and-tumble of an inner-city American high school was quite an adjustment. She found the students a stark contrast to the well-behaved youngsters she had taught in the Philippines.[21]

Being able to earn a living after returning to the United States concerned many returning volunteers. The Peace Corps addressed volunteer reentry financial concerns by providing an escrow readjustment allowance. Each volunteer had $75 per month remitted to an account while overseas. Thus, at the end of a two-year service, a returning volunteer was given $1,800. A married couple would get $3,600. Some used this money to pay for graduate school expenses. Others used the money to cover down payments for rental apartments and other living expenses.

The Peace Corps was also a springboard for a variety of career opportunities. African American returning volunteers took advantage of such career opportunities. The post–Peace Corps career of Tanzania returned volunteer Earl Brown is a case in point. Brown joined the Peace Corps in 1964. The Peace Corps posted him at Nyegina Upper Primary School, Musoma. In November 1966, Brown and his wife Mary Ann, as newlyweds, left Tanzania to return to the United States. Upon his return, Peace Corps Washington employed Brown as a staff recruiter in their talent search section in 1967. The Browns lived in Washington, DC.

As a staff recruiter, Brown recruited personnel for overseas positions such as country directors, deputy directors, and administrative officers, which meant constant travel. He established many contacts while at the agency and he was instrumental in getting some of his Tanzania Peace Corps members employed. Brown remained in that position for a year and then moved to New York City to pursue his master's degree in city and regional planning at Hunter College in Manhattan.

Although returning white volunteers did not face racial discrimination, some volunteers experienced a frosty reentry. One white volunteer thought he was coming back to a friendly country but the reception he got was not friendly: "I got in the airport in Seattle and I got taken aside by DEA agents who thought maybe I had drugs on me or something, and got everything gone through, including me. And you know, that's a disappointment...And I didn't have a reentry problem especially, I just felt like things were a little frostier, that you know, the great Camelot experiment was over somehow."[22]

Similarly, Susan Proctor found her reentry troubling because she did not expect to experience reverse culture shock: "The cultural shock I experienced was upon reentry to the US. After two years, I returned overnight to the US to assume a staff training position with the next group of nurses, again at Syracuse University. The Peace Corps did not prepare us for reentry to the US. I served my five months as a staff trainer and immediately returned to Tanzania for another two years. Even with several weeks in transit back to the States the second time, it took me years to readjust to American culture."[23]

Like Proctor, Chris Biles struggled to readjust to American life after serving in Tanzania. Biles told the author,

> It was difficult. It still is difficult sometimes—it takes a long time to adjust, and I still feel I am at times not at home back here in the States, even after about 2 years. You need to totally rebuild your life when you come back. Sure you may have your friends and your family, and the places you love, but you don't fit into these spaces and these relationships as you did before you left for the PCs. Rather than returning and fitting back into the mold of yourself that you left behind, you have to discard that and create a new existence as your new self in these places and with these people. It takes time, patience, and self-kindness.[24]

Readjusting to American culture was for some volunteers difficult considering the kind of social life they had had in their host communities. Bonnie Jo Dopp Hurley found it difficult to adjust to American social life: "I was shocked by how lonely I felt. I had had a rich social life in Njombe, mainly among other PCVs, British expats, and other kinds of volunteers of the American Society of Friends, Russian cryptographers. I came 'home' to nothing like that, for I had gone to Tanzania straight out of college, which had not been near 'home'—so I had zero old contacts, socially."[25]

Because of her difficulty adjusting, Hurley volunteered for another round of Peace Corps service, this time in South Korea. She spent two years teaching English in South Korea. Her living in South Korea further expanded Hurley's worldview, which she considers an asset. She recalls that after she came back from South Korea, she had trouble "respecting people or groups that thought only of the U.S."[26] Her second reentry from South Korea also proved emotionally difficult:

> After Korea, I needed psychological counseling and got it from the US government via Peace Corps. After essentially five years away from the US,

adjusting to a country at war, where JFK had been assassinated when I first went to Tanganyika, his brother also assassinated 3 days after I returned from Korea, [the] public figures Malcolm X and Martin Luther King, Jr. being murdered in between those [assassinations], and a big family problem that had developed while I was gone made me wonder where I was and where I belonged. The counseling helped.

After South Korea, Hurley easily got a job at the local public library because of her BA. That led to her pursuing a master's degree in librarianship and a career in that field. She had applied for graduate school in the field of international education and had been accepted, but the school wanted her to go straight back to South Korea to do research. After nearly five years overseas, she decided she needed to stay put for a while, so she asked for a yearlong extension of her acceptance. Librarianship "called" to her instead and she never lived overseas again.[27]

Likewise, Biles had difficulty adjusting to the American "survival mode" of life:

Relearning all the expectations of American culture, especially the difference in concepts of time—rushing to do this or that, always doing something. This still throws me. Also, the expectation that everyone is totally tuned into everything—with the internet, fast communication, the expectations are high.

The wealth and lack of appreciation for it can also simply disgust me at times—seen through the love of, and therefore assigned need for, THINGS. This of course leads to so much WASTE. So many Americans are quite privileged and cannot recognize that fact. There is a lack of appreciation as so many people live their lives too fast without really seeing the world around them and their fellow humans as much as they should—not everyone! But there is a lot of ignorance in the States.[28]

Katie Songer's experience upon reentry is particularly poignant. Songer describes her reentry experience in a more nuanced way than either Hurley or Biles. She told the author that:

Despite having traveled back and forth between Africa (Ghana) and the United States three times previously and largely overcome my culture shock on those trips, my return from two years in Tanzania still came with more culture shock. For me, it wasn't the inability to find meaningful work that was hardest, and it wasn't a lack of "serious" friends or people with whom to talk... about my experience. It was just a genuine culture shock. Americans in my hometown moved and talked faster than the rural Tanzanians I'd been surrounded by. I had come to value slowness and lack of busyness. I longed for the long, quiet moments sitting with people in my village, not always talking, just sipping tea, shucking corn, knitting, or weaving baskets together. Americans always have to be talking; there is constant pressure to keep conversations interesting, and everyone is busy. Conversations seemed to move at a dizzying pace at first. And I longed for the softness of time—the common understanding, in the village, that meetings don't have to start on the dot, that it's okay to linger and talk to someone in the street if you happen to encounter them. I have always felt that the rushed pace of American life, and the way our capitalist society pulls us from our families, is unnatural. Returning from rural Tanzania and back into this life, I felt a deep sadness realizing that I could never have what I wanted: the slow village lifestyle, but with my family nearby. I could only have one or the other, because my family is American. I eventually readjusted to the American pace, but even now, fifteen years after reentry, I feel sad about this and miss that slowness.

Furthermore, as was the case with many others, upon returning to the United States, Singer had to deal with a lifestyle she had become oblivious to for two years. She had to adjust to America's fast-paced life, the "anonymity" of being white, and some of the things she had taken for granted before she went to Tanzania:

> Although being home was difficult, it was also wonderful in other ways. I missed the slowness of village life, but other things were a relief. It was a relief to relax into anonymity: as the only white person in my village, I had not been able to leave my house without attracting attention. I had always felt to some extent like an outsider, even though I'd had many good friends in the village. I also desperately needed modern health care by the time I came home. In [the] Peace Corps, I hadn't really understood nutrition and had become malnourished, and had developed various minor ailments that, all added together, made me feel pretty sick. It took several months to feel like I was really healthy again. So while culturally I was missing [the] Peace Corps, physically it was a relief to be home, without the stress of a language barrier and outsider status,

and with access to excellent medical care. It was also a great relief to be closer to my family, who[m] I had missed very much when I was gone.

For a volunteer who had been away for two years or more, it helped one's reentry if one had connections on the ground. For some volunteers, family was the first support they depended upon when they returned to the United States. Songer was one of those for whom family support was crucial in their reentry. She says, "Since I initially had no place to live, I moved in with my parents, which was an adjustment after living independently for so long."[29]

For others, it was old connections or friends. When Tom Katus, T-1, returned to the United States, he went to Washington, DC, and reconnected with Padric Kennedy at Peace Corps headquarters. Kennedy is the person who telephoned and informed Katus of his selection for T-1. They stayed in touch while Katus was in Tanzania. According to Katus, Kennedy was very helpful in getting him enrolled at the University of Wisconsin, Milwaukee, as a major in political science and in getting him a job at the Peace Corps training center there. Subsequently, Katus, together with others from T-1— Jerry Parson, Rodgers Stewart, and Gil Griffiths—formed their own Peace Corps training company, Volunteer Training Specialists Inc. (VTSI).

Likewise, before they returned to the United States, John and Barbara Ratigan, T-7, decided that they would not return to their hometowns in Minnesota and Massachusetts, respectively. Instead, they chose to settle in Denver, Colorado. Several factors facilitated their move to Denver. John's college roommate and closest friend had already resettled with his wife in Boulder, about thirty minutes away, several years before. They had stayed in touch while they were in Tanzania. A high school friend and college fraternity brother and his wife, whom John also knew, were settling in Denver at the same time. Thus, John and Barbara had known while they were still serving in Tanzania that they would have some very good friends in Denver when they got there.

Moreover, with his law degree, John Ratigan was able to get a job with a Denver law firm within a month of their arrival there. Barbara landed a job in about the same time as a baby photographer at a shop in a local shopping mall. They rented an apartment largely with the funds from their combined Peace Corps resettlement allowances, totaling $3,600, and so they got themselves settled quickly.

Many volunteers changed careers or career plans while still serving in the Peace Corps. Engineers and surveyors became political scientists, business majors became history teachers. These options invariably entailed getting into graduate school. It appears that returning to campus lessened reentry anxiety. A university campus was a good place to readjust. As Stolley notes, "In addition to its relative tranquility, there are other reasons favoring the campus. Liberal scholarships, grants and fellowships earmarked specifically for the Volunteers make it financially easy for many to re-engage in academic life."[30]

Few volunteers upon returning to the United States went into private business. According to Stolley, by 1965 only 8 percent had. The numbers may have increased over the years but not in the same magnitude as those who went into healthcare, social work, teaching, and government service. The small number of Tanzania returned volunteers who went into business include Alex Quattlebaum Jr. and James (Jim) Belisle, both T-1 volunteers (1961–63).

When Alex Quattlebaum Jr. joined the Peace Corps in 1961, he held a bachelor's degree in civil engineering from Clemson University, where his father had previously been a professor of engineering. During his service in Tanzania, Quattlebaum was responsible for surveying, as well as for the design and construction of roadways, bridges, and infrastructure in the Southern Province. When Quattlebaum returned from Tanzania, he enrolled in graduate school at Clemson University and graduated in 1965. After graduating Quattlebaum began working for his family's construction company in a variety of roles, rising from assistant superintendent to president.[31] He left the Harllee-Quattlebaum Company in 1986 to pursue development work on his own, but in 1996 he took over the company after the death of his uncle, renaming it Quattlebaum Development Company.

Quattlebaum Development Company (QDC) clients have included governments; the World Bank; the CIA; the Free Zone division of the Services Group in Washington, DC (of which he was a founding board member); the US Agency for International Development (USAID); United Nations Educational, Scientific and Cultural Organization (UNESCO); and more. During the early 1970s, Quattlebaum was instrumental in creating the first Foreign Trade Zone in South Carolina and has owned and operated Foreign Trade Zones since 1974. Subsequently, he handed the reins over to his sons, Alex Quattlebaum III and Scott Quattlebaum.

James R. Belisle was twenty-three years old when he joined the Peace Corps in 1961. He was a graduate of the University of California with a degree in electrical engineering. After he graduated, the Naval Ordnance Test Station (NOTS) employed Belisle in their junior professional training program. He was stationed at China Lake, San Bernardino, California, when he joined the Peace Corps.[32]

Other returned volunteers sought employment with philanthropic organizations and in various US government agencies, including the Peace Corps. Besides starting a company to train volunteers for the Peace Corps, Tom Katus was recruited by the Phelps Stokes Fund (hereafter: the Fund), which was headed by Ambassador Franklin Williams and Vice President Dr. Marie Gadsden. At the Fund, Katus codirected the Fund's Southern African workforce development program, which provided education to 245 Africans from throughout the African continent. The Fund placed most of them at historically Black colleges and universities in the United States. Under Jimmy Carter, the Fund's operating budgets jumped from $2.5 million to $13 million in four years. However, the Fund lost virtually all its federal contracts with USAID when Reagan came to power.

After working for the Fund, the African Development Foundation employed Katus as regional manager for Eastern Africa. Although it was a very enjoyable experience, Katus wanted to get back to South Dakota and be engaged in the politics of his home state. He worked on Democratic national campaigns for the McGovern-Shriver presidential campaign in 1972, the Carter-Mondale campaign in 1976, the Mondale-Ferraro campaign in 1984, and the Dukakis-Benson campaign in 1988. Following the 1988 election, Katus returned home to South Dakota. He served in South Dakota's state senate from 2007 to 2008.

CHAPTER 12

The Friends of Tanzania (FOT) Make a Difference

Introduction

In the spring of 1991, a small group in the Washington, DC, area, mainly returned Peace Corps volunteers (RPCVs) met to explore the formation of an organization they named Friends of Tanzania/Marafiki wa Tanzania. On August 3, 1991, during the Peace Corps thirtieth anniversary conference, Friends of Tanzania (FOT) became a reality when about fifty people participated in the first business meeting. They reviewed and discussed the initial purpose statement and contributed $800 for dues, start-up funding, and project money. Each offered his or her time and skills and approved $500 for FOT's first project.

Since 1991, FOT has contributed monetary funding to various projects in Tanzania for the purpose of making a difference in people's lives. Projects have been funded through the FOT budget and through FOT's Giving Back program. The former are projects chosen by FOT's Projects Committee from grant inquiries and applications from Tanzania. The latter projects are chosen and funded by individual RPCVs and are normally operating in the areas in Tanzania where these volunteers have worked. Projects chosen by FOT are funded from membership dues and donations. According to the fall 2011 FOT newsletter, by 2011 (the twentieth anniversary of FOT) FOT had spent $350,000 to finance community development projects in Tanzania. Among the projects funded were simple water or sanitation systems for schools, community reforestation efforts, micro-loans, beehive projects, and many more.

Money, as they say, not only tempts but is also the cause of crime. So it was that FOT's donations were likely to be stolen. In the fall 2017 FOT newsletter, FOT President Candy Warner reported that the women and children of Jitegemee Women had had their FOT funds stolen. In 2016, Jitegemee Women in Njombe applied for funding for a water tank for the school and village. Their request for $5,000 was approved by FOT and the money was wired in May 2017 directly to them through a local Tanzania bank. However, FOT's communications with Jitegemee were hacked and the funds were stolen. The funds were diverted to an unauthorized bank account for a woman in Dar es Salaam!

By 2017, the FOT had disbursed thousands of dollars to various projects in Tanzania, as Tables 7 and 8 show. However, because of the fraudulent diversion of FOT funds intended for Jitegemee, FOT stopped inviting project proposals for the remainder of 2017. In February 2018 at their board retreat, board members received recommendations on "the way forward." That being said, the manner in which FOT acquires funds for projects has not changed. Yearly budgeted grants are donations given to FOT by members or others who do not designate a specific project for fund allocation, but rather allow their contributions to finance projects that FOT deems worthy.

In 2008, the FOT General Fund received $25,000, the biggest donation to date given by a volunteer, who had worked in Tanzania from 1965 to 1967. The FOT used about $5,000 of this money to finance the Shashui water project in Lushoto District. The donor allowed the FOT to use the money for any other projects deemed worthy of cause.

Table 7: FOT Grant Activity, 1991-2017

ALL FOT Grants Yearly Budgeted + Member Sponsored, 1991-2017: 340 Projects Totaling $688,715

AREA	AMOUNT	AREA	AMOUNT
Education & Textbooks (includes scholarships)	$245,814	Agriculture, Beekeeping & Fishing	$41,643
Water	$85,465	Health, Sanitation, Housing & Basic Needs	$40,685
Equipment, Bldg. Supplies, Tools, & Electrification	$81,214	Reforestation & Nurseries	$31,905
School Renovation	$71,512	Sewing	$24,175
Animal Husbandry	$44,402	Microfinance	$21,900

Table 8: FOT Yearly Budgeted Grants, 1991-2017
YEARLY BUDGETED GRANTS, 1991-2017: 297 PROJECTS TOTALING: $412,815

AREA	AMOUNT	AREA	AMOUNT
Equipment, Bldg. Supplies, Tools, & Electrification	$75,250	Reforestation and Nurseries	$31,905
Water	$74,890	Health, Sanitation, Housing and Basic Needs	$30,985
School Renovation	$55,005	Sewing	$24,175
Animal Husbandry	$44,402	Education & Textbooks	$17,660
Agriculture, Beekeeping & Fishing	$41,643	Microfinance	$16,900

Table 9: FOT Member Sponsored Funds, 1991-2017
MEMBER SPONSORED FUNDS, 1991-2017: 43 PROJECTS TOTALING: $274,900

AREA	AMOUNT	AREA	AMOUNT
Education & Textbooks (including scholarships)	$228,154	Water	$9,575
School Renovation	$16,507	Equipment, bldg. supplies, tools & electrification	$5,964
Health, Sanitation, Housing & Basic Needs	$9,700	Microfinance	$5,000

In 2021, the FOT Board approved the following projects for funding from the General Fund. Nangwanda Girls Secondary School, Newala, was a recipient of $4,198 for the construction of two dormitories that will house forty girls each, eighty more boarding students who need accommodations. The Southern Highlands Participatory Organization (SHIPO) received $5,162 to finance its public health project, also known as WASH (Water, Sanitation, and Hygiene), at Mbuga Primary School in Mbozi. The project included improvements to a water well, installation of an electric pump and water storage tank, construction of a handwashing station, and the building of a water point for domestic use. Other General Fund outlays included $8,500 for the construction of a computer lab for instruction at Makongoro Secondary School at Nyamuswa, Musoma; $8,475 for milling equipment and micronutrients to fortify maize flour at Kakonko, Kigoma; and the Lorna Dadi Foundation applied and received $4,200 to purchase and distribute *Nisitiri* reusable menstrual pads for adolescent pupils in Lindi Region.

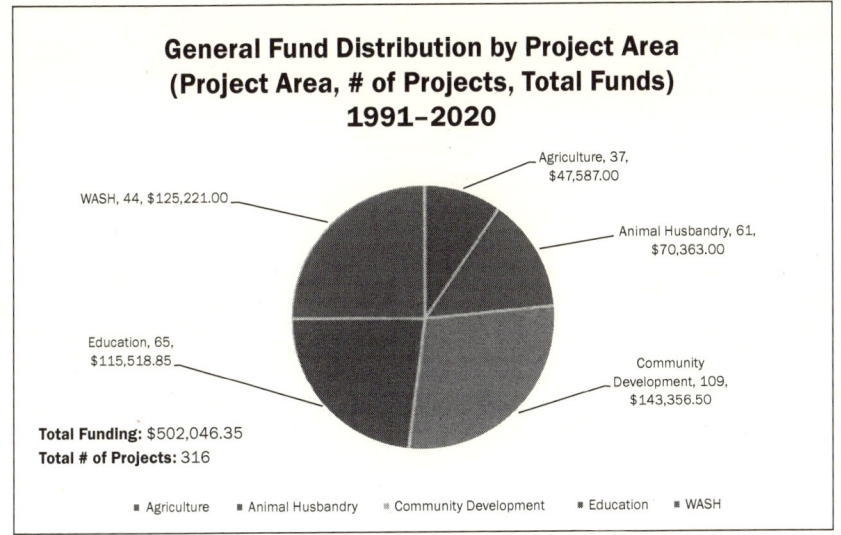

Summary of grant distribution from the general fund

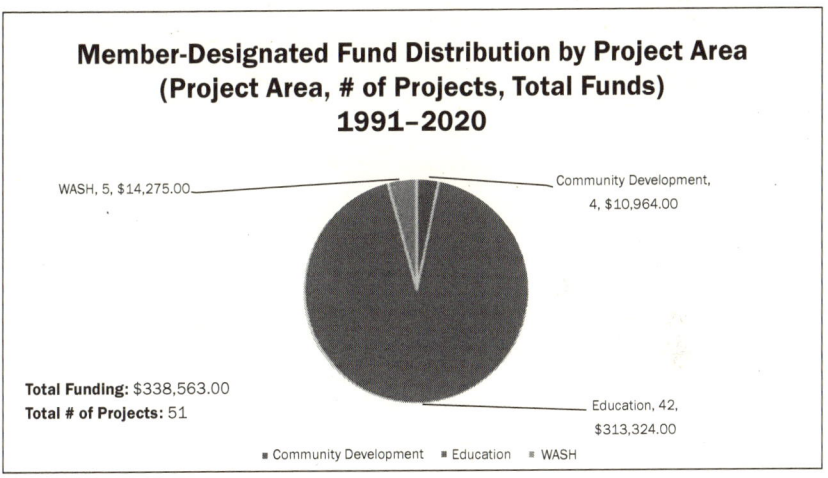

Summary of grant distribution from the member-designated fund

Over the years since FOT's inception, members have initiated and sponsored projects of their own choice, usually for people and places in Tanzania where these volunteers worked. Others have chosen to support projects that they simply determined were worthy, regardless of where these volunteers had worked in Tanzania. Among the notable member-sponsored projects are the Lutengano Scholarship and the Ilboru School for children with disabilities, highlighted on the following page.

Scholarships for Lutengano Secondary School
(Sponsored by Anita Johnson, PCV 1963–65)

Lutengano Secondary School is a private school located in the village of Makeje, about ten miles south of Tukuyu, about twenty miles south of Rungwe, and some fifty miles south of Mbeya. The Moravian Church, Tanzania, owns it, and the school has a long-lasting tradition. The Moravian Church founded Lutengano in 1950 as a girls' middle school. In 1972, it became an inclusive primary school especially focused on supporting children with disabilities. However, in 1982 it became a coeducational secondary school (O-

Lutengano Secondary School (Friends of Tanzania newsletter)

Left: Students at Lutengano Secondary School (Friends of Tanzania newsletter). *Right:* Judge Neema Ephraim, former student at Lutengano Secondary School (Friends of Tanzania newsletter).

Level and A-Level) and remains as such today. Most of the buildings are old, but renovation efforts started in July 2019 (see photos on the previous page).

When Anita Johnson, a T-3 volunteer (1963–65), was teaching at Lutengano Middle School, she never dreamed her actions many decades later would make such a difference. After returning to the United States, she established the Lutengano Scholarship Fund, which to date (2022) has funded one hundred fifty scholarships supporting secondary education for eligible girls for tuition, room, and board. One of the girls who received a scholarship, Neema Ephraim, completed her secondary schooling and went on to the University of Dar es Salaam, where she studied law. In September 2021, President Samia Suluhu Hassan appointed her to a judgeship in the High Court of Tanzania.

**Scholarships for High School Students, Geita
(Sponsored by Barbara Torrey, PCV)**

Barbara Boyle Torrey was a T-3 volunteer teacher at Geita (1963–65). In 2004, Barbara and her husband started a scholarship fund specifically to support girls in Geita whose families could not afford to pay their school fees from their scarce resources. In the beginning, 90 percent became secondary students, but retention rates were low. By 2015, 75 percent of the students were borders and retention was over 90 percent. In addition, by 2015, sixty-two girls had finished Form IV (O-Level) and 11 Form VI (A-Level), with six girls who were in college.

To safeguard against fraud, FOT transmits the funds to the Microfinance Bank in Geita, which controls their distribution to recipients. Periodically, Barbara and her husband update the Memorandum of Understanding to make sure the bank, the directors (a former student and an ex-secondary school teacher), and the FOT, are all on the same page. Funds disbursed are tax deductible in the United States.

Ilboru School for Children with Special Needs

In 2001, Loy Yamat, a teacher at the Government of Tanzania (GOT) Ilboru Primary School, convinced his principal to let him use an abandoned storeroom to begin a class of six special needs students who were deaf or mentally disabled. Loy is a charismatic teacher who graduated O-Level (high school) and received a variety of teacher training certificates, including fluency in sign language.

In 2006, Donna Chalmers, a RPCV nurse in T-2 (1962–64) was introduced to the children of the Special Needs School by Julu Metili, a local board member. Yamat asked Chalmers if she could help provide the students with a cup of *Uji* (porridge). Chalmers returned to her home in Alexandria, Minnesota, and appealed to her local church's congregation, as well as to fellow RPCVs from T-1 and T-2 (1961–63). She was successful with her fundraising, and the students began to receive their cup of *Uji* daily. A clean supply of water was also required for the Special Needs School and the government primary school nearby. With Chalmers's support a borehole was completed. The Lutheran Church provided a water tank and paid the pumping bills. In 2012, one of Chalmers's RPCV friends, Tom Katus, a T-1 volunteer, brought three engineering students from South Dakota School of Mines and Technology's Rotary Club to visit the school. With the guidance of Yamat, the team surveyed the compound of the two schools and church and designed a water system and site for a new kitchen. A proposal was prepared and submitted to FOT, which donated $3,000 to the project.

CHAPTER 13

Peace Corps Volunteers Who Died While Serving in Tanzania

Introduction

When the Peace Corps began in 1961 it started with a small number of volunteers that went to serve in Colombia, Ghana, and Tanganyika (later Tanzania). By 2019, the Peace Corps had grown to an enormous organization with volunteers totaling more than 235,000 and serving in 141 countries. Although volunteer deaths have been a common occurrence, they have rarely been a central focus of published works about the Peace Corps, even though the agency has endeavored to recognize those who have died in service. Of the 235,000 dedicated men and women who have served in the Peace Corps, 309 have to date lost their lives while pursuing the Peace Corps mission overseas. Figure 1 shows the causes of death among volunteers by category. Accidents (motor vehicle and other unintentional) accounted for the highest number of deaths (65 percent), followed by natural causes, homicide, suicide, and indeterminate causes.

Health for Peace Corps volunteers has been an ongoing concern since the inception of the Peace Corps in 1961. Because the Peace Corps was very much concerned about the health of volunteers while serving overseas, each volunteer was equipped with a medical kit. Yet, some volunteers lost their lives due to sickness while others died from accidents, including motor vehicle and plane crashes. Between 1966 and 2015, six volunteers lost their lives while in service in Tanzania. One disappeared and was presumed dead shortly before the end of his service; another died shortly after returning to the United States for medical reasons. The following volunteer fatalities in Tanzania included death due to an alleged homicide, an elephant attack, motor vehicle and other accidents, and a drug overdose.

Peverley Dennett Kinsey (d. 1966)

Peverley "Peppy" Dennett Kinsey joined the Peace Corps in the fall of 1964. She and her husband, Bill Kinsey, were posted to Tanzania, where they taught at a school in up-country Maswa. In March 1966, Peverley died under mysterious circumstances. Her demise has been examined by Peter H. Reid in *Every Hill a Burial Ground: The Peace Corps Murder Trial in Tanzania*, which was published in 2020.

Robert Spencer Lehman (d. 2015)

Robert "Robbie" Spencer Lehman, the son of Dr. Gregory T. Lehman and Dr. Dawn L. Martin, was born in Minneapolis, Minnesota, on April 23, 1992. Lehman attended St. Olaf College, Minnesota, where he graduated with a bachelor of science degree. After graduating from St. Olaf, Lehman joined the Peace Corps and was thrilled to become a community health volunteer in Tanzania. At 23, Lehman passed away unexpectedly in a tragic bus accident near the town of Mbeya in southwestern Tanzania on May 24, 2015.

Joseph Chow (d. 2009)

Joseph Lawrence Chow, 23, a native of Scarsdale, New York, graduated from Amherst College in 2007. He joined the Peace Corps in September 2007. In his Peace Corps aspiration statement, Chow wrote that one of the reasons he decided to serve with the Peace Corps was because he had never spent a long period of time in a different culture. He hoped to meet the challenges of teaching in a classroom in Africa and understood that the work he faced would be much more difficult than any work he had previously accomplished.

Initially, Chow volunteered in Kenya, where he taught chemistry and physics at Saint Clement Secondary School at Ndalat. When the Kenya program closed in 2008, he went to Tanzania, where he volunteered as a math, physics, and chemistry teacher at Ndanda Secondary School, in southern Tanzania. Chow died in a rock-climbing accident near the village of Mbuji in the Ruvuma region in the southern part of Tanzania. He was scheduled to complete his Peace Corps service in November 2009.

David Schaeffer (d. 1990)

David Schaeffer, 27, was from Springfield, Missouri. Schaeffer was one of the Peace Corps volunteers whose expertise was aquaculture, with a specialty in fisheries. On September 7, 1990, Schaeffer was riding a motorcycle when he collided with a truck near the town of Korogwe in northeastern Tanzania. Schaeffer sustained multiple injuries including a cranial fracture that resulted in his death. A host-country national who was riding with Schaeffer died several hours later at a local hospital.

Natalie Waldinger (d. 2001)

Natalie Waldinger, 24, was born in Bolivia in November 1976. An American family adopted her in 1977 when she was only four months old. She grew up in Brooklyn and Oceanside, Long Island, New York. She graduated from Oceanside High School in 1994 and enrolled at the University of Michigan, Ann Arbor, to study aerospace engineering. As a college undergraduate, Waldinger helped design and test a wind tunnel on the X-31 escape module for the National Aeronautics and Space Administration's (NASA) space station.

In 2000, Waldinger volunteered for the Peace Corps as a science teacher at Bihawana Secondary School, a few miles southwest of Dodoma, Tanzania. In early January 2011, Waldinger and fellow Peace Corps volunteers were on vacation touring Ruaha National Park. While Waldinger, together with some friends, was taking pictures of some elephants, she was charged by one of them and trampled to death.

Wyatt Pillsbury (d. 2001)

Wyatt Simeon Pillsbury, 23, son of Richard and Rosemary (née Constable) Pillsbury was born in Waterville, Maine, on September 12, 1977. After graduating from Mount View High School, he was awarded a Presidential Scholarship and attended Brandeis University, where he majored in sociology and minored in environmental studies. He graduated from Brandeis University in 1999. He joined the Peace Corps in September 2000 and was posted to Imilinya, Tanzania. He died unexpectedly on July 11, 2001, while on vacation in Zanzibar, Tanzania.

CHAPTER 14

Conclusion

On December 9, 1961, Tanganyika (later mainland Tanzania) was granted independence by Britain, which had administered the territory as a mandate after World War I and under the Trusteeship Council of the United Nations after World War II. Before independence, Prime Minister Julius K. Nyerere had requested technical assistance from the United States to begin major improvements of the country's infrastructure under what was dubbed "the roads-to-markets" project. Just before independence in November 1961, the first group of Peace Corps volunteers arrived in Dar es Salaam. They consisted of surveyors, civil engineers, and geologists, known as Tanganyika One, or T-1.

The year 2021 marked the sixtieth anniversary of the Peace Corps. After reaching this milestone, it is pertinent to ask: Is the Peace Corps mission still relevant after sixty years? What lessons can the Peace Corps draw from the past sixty years of administering programs in developing countries like Tanzania? To what extent have volunteers succeeded or failed to promote American goodwill in host countries and promote a better understanding of foreign cultures among American citizens?

To start with, the Peace Corps has never conducted an overall evaluation of its programs worldwide, from which it could draw country-specific and general lessons for the purposes of making the institution better. Over the years, the Peace Corps has endeavored to interview and conduct surveys of returning volunteers about their individual opinions, feelings, and experiences. These interviews and surveys have not influenced the Peace Corps to change its policies or to make fundamental administrative changes.

The relevance of the Peace Corps after sixty years of service hinges on the first of its major objectives in its mission, namely, to provide technical and other expertise needed in the host countries. Is the Peace Corps sending volunteers where they are needed the most? I believe it is. When the US Congress established the Peace Corps in 1961, three countries were the first recipients of those who had first volunteered to serve abroad. These were Colombia, Ghana, and Tanganyika (Tanzania).

By the 1980s, half of all volunteers in the Peace Corps served in sub-Saharan Africa, whose numbers equaled the combined numbers for the Americas (the Caribbean and Central and South America) and the NANEAP (North Africa, the Middle East, Asia, and the Pacific). Regarding the Americas, volunteer numbers declined from a large presence in the 1960s and 1970s, so that by the mid-1980s only Ecuador and Paraguay had volunteers serving there. Nevertheless, some data show that in 2019, 45 percent of all Peace Corps volunteers served in Africa compared to 19 percent in Central and South America, and 12 percent in Asia. These percentages suggest that Peace Corps is sending more volunteers to Africa because there continues to be greater need for volunteer services there than in Asia and Central and South America.

However, why are Tanzania and other African countries continuing to require Peace Corps volunteer services when other regions' numbers have declined? Does this reflect African countries' growing need for expertise, which the Peace Corps volunteers can provide? Are the education systems of African countries perpetuating this continued dependence? Are there shortcomings in Peace Corps programs that are creating continued dependence on Peace Corps volunteers? We can answer these questions by drawing lessons from Tanzania, which may be applicable to other sub-Saharan African countries. In Tanzania, during the Three-Year Development Plan (1961–64), Peace Corps volunteers provided vital technical expertise to the newly independent nation. However, during the launching of the following Second Five-Year Development Plan (1965–70), President Julius Nyerere reiterated the goal of the country to achieve full self-sufficiency in technical manpower requirements by 1980, including science teachers. Yet, to date, Tanzania continues to receive Peace Corps volunteer teachers for science subjects as well as volunteers working in various other areas.

For Tanzania to achieve self-sufficiency in technical manpower, it is required that the number of secondary, technical college, and university graduates rise in both quantitative and qualitative terms. However, for nearly two and a half decades after independence, students were unmotivated to study science subjects despite the government's emphasis on the sciences. Consequently, the performance of students in science subjects until now remains abysmal.[1] Limited motivation and poor performance are also due to the shortage of science teachers because, to date, there continues to be a preponderance of graduates in the humanities and social sciences from Tanzania's tertiary institutions.

The continued need for Peace Corps volunteer teachers is also due to the expansion of Tanzania's education system. Tanzania's secondary and teacher education systems have changed dramatically over the past decade. The number of secondary schools has exploded from 927 in the year 2000 to 1,745 in 2005, and to over 4,200 in 2010, and most of them are in rural locations. The increase in number of secondary schools is vastly outpacing the availability of qualified teachers. Peace Corps volunteers are increasingly one of the few—or in some cases the only—math or science teachers at Tanzanian schools. Peace Corps volunteer teachers are placed in O-level and A-level schools, with a limited number of positions in teacher training colleges and other institutions of tertiary education.

Between 1961 and 1969, Tanzania requested, and the Peace Corps provided, volunteers in areas where the country felt their expertise would greatly make a difference and enable the newly independent country to embark on its journey as a sovereign developing nation. The program of the first Peace Corps volunteers who arrived in November 1961, a month before independence, was named the "roads-to-markets" program. It was constituted of engineers and surveyors who put their skills and expertise to work to create a new network of trunk and secondary roads that connected hitherto isolated rural areas from local and global markets. The geologists in the group were instrumental in mapping out the country's geological resources. It is important to note that President Nyerere specifically asked President Kennedy for volunteers in these areas because he had identified a pressing need that the Peace Corps could alleviate, and it did. Likewise, the Peace Corps volunteers who went to Ghana had expertise in the areas requested by President Kwame Nkrumah, who specifically told President Kennedy that he did not need volunteer teachers!

The second Peace Corps volunteer group to Tanganyika was constituted of nurses and laboratory technicians, who were thirty-six in number. They served in referral hospitals in five of the major towns at the time, namely, Dar es Salaam, Moshi, Mwanza, Tabora, and Tanga. Derek Bryceson, the minister of health at the time, specifically requested this group because the newly independent nation was facing an acute shortage of nurses. Many British nurses left soon after independence at the same time when Tanganyika needed to send some African nurses abroad for training. The American nurses' contribution, as highlighted in chapter 2, was very much needed. The third and largest group of Peace Corps volunteers were middle and secondary school teachers. Again, Tanganyika very much needed their expertise due to shortage of teachers and the need for the new nation to provide more education opportunities in its endeavor to build its human capital.

In 1969, the government of Tanzania terminated the Peace Corps program. It remained closed until 1980 when, at the request of the government of Tanzania, it reopened. In the 1960s, several other African countries also terminated their countries' Peace Corps programs. These included Malawi and Somalia. The reasons for these closures ought to provide the Peace Corps with lessons that should enable the agency to navigate the political landscapes of host countries more effectively. In Tanzania, as in other African countries, the country's politics turned out to be antithetical to US politics at the time. In Tanzania, volunteers came under suspicion as CIA agents, while the Vietnam War and racial discrimination against African Americans added further suspicions about American intent, especially because Tanzania had declared to become a socialist country.

Nevertheless, since its inception in 1961, the Peace Corps has tried to present an image of being apolitical in its endeavors in host countries. However, this has been difficult because given its legislative mandate and funding, the Peace Corps has continued to be seen as a US government agency. In Tanzania, as elsewhere, the country director sits in all embassy meetings even though he or she does not vote on any decisions made. Moreover, the Peace Corps staff reside and relate with other embassy staff in ways that suggest to local people there is no difference between them.

In 1980, the government of Tanzania invited the Peace Corps to reopen its program. However, negotiations preceding the signing of the agreement between the governments of Tanzania and America pivoted on issues of concern that Tanzania raised if the Peace Corps were to return. Tanzania's needs no longer required "generalist" volunteers fresh out of college who wanted to test their ability to do whatever a situation required them to do. Instead, Tanzania in the 1980s wanted experienced professionals, especially in agriculture (food storage), range management, maternal/childcare, nutritionists, and those with skills in water supply systems. Moreover, the Tanzanian government wanted to be involved in the recruitment process as well as vetting the credentials of volunteers before they arrived in Tanzania. Another new requirement was that volunteers needed to apply for work permits. These requests put Tanzania at loggerheads with the Peace Corps.

The Peace Corps, while adept at recruiting generalists and training them sufficiently to carry out useful assignments, has historically not prioritized attracting highly skilled professionals. This approach has long been a source of debate. Some have argued that the Peace Corps should recruit experienced specialists to meet the growing demands for experts in an increasingly complex world. Others have argued that demonstration of US values through personal interaction is as important as technical assistance, and recent college graduates may be less resource-intensive to recruit and manage.[2]

Moreover, when Tanzania and other host countries receive Peace Corps volunteers, they expect them not only to perform their duties but also to complete their tours of service. However, over the years the Peace Corps has had to deal with early termination of service for a considerable number of volunteers, not only in Africa but also in other regions of the world.[3] In Tanzania and elsewhere in sub-Saharan Africa, these early terminations have not only interrupted completion of grassroots projects but also have dampened host communities' hopes of and possible support for future proposed projects.

In Tanzania, reasons for early departures and termination of volunteers' services have varied. Marriage and illness have been the most prevalent. However, there have also been cases of administrative separation pursuant to the Peace Corps Act. 22 US C. 2504 (j). A few have left because they did not feel up to whatever job they had volunteered to do. Data on early departures and terminations from the 1960s are sketchy. However, between 2003 and 2016, about 1,107 volunteers served in Tanzania, out of which the Peace Corps terminated 318.

Furthermore, in Tanzania, as in other host countries, the Peace Corps's safety protocols call for reevaluation. According to the Fallen Peace Corps

Volunteer Memorial Project, as of 2011, around 279 volunteers have died or been murdered during their service since 1961. Many others have been victims of assault, theft, burglary, robbery, and rape. At a hearing before the House Foreign Affairs Committee in March 2011, its chairperson, Rep. Ileana Ros-Lehtinen (R-FL), said, "Despite critical reports by its own Inspector General, the General Accountability Office, and prior Congressional hearings, Peace Corps' safety and security failures have been a recurrent problem with tragic consequences for thousands of volunteers."[4] Although the risk of crime is not unique to serving in the Peace Corps, for the agency, the challenge has been how to help volunteers adapt their US-based understanding of crime risks to the situational and cultural realities of the host communities where they live and work. For instance, although volunteers live modestly by US norms, local people may view them as well-off by host-country standards. This may make them attractive targets for property crimes.

However, on rare occasions Peace Corps volunteers and staff have committed crimes in host countries. How the Peace Corps has handled these cases has raised questions about the lack of transparency and fairness. In Tanzania, the Peace Corps's handling of the case of William "Bill" Kinsey, the volunteer accused of killing his wife, Peverley Dennett Kinsey, antagonized the then attorney general Mark Bomani, who believed the Peace Corps was interfering with the investigation.

Nevertheless, in response to the Kinsey case, Congress passed legislation to provide for defense counsel and coverage of other legal costs for Kinsey. This remains Peace Corps policy to date. If a volunteer is a party to a foreign judicial or administrative proceeding during the volunteer's service, the Peace Corps may:

(a) Retain counsel for the volunteer and pay the related legal fees.
(b) Pay court costs, bail, and other expenses incidental to the volunteer's defense, including costs relating to investigations, counsel's travel, witness fees, and so on.
(c) Continue to pay such expenses after the volunteer leaves his or her Peace Corps service.

However, the Peace Corps retains sole discretion to determine whether to retain counsel, or to continue the services of counsel. Further, the Peace

Corps will not pay for fines or damages. The Peace Corps will retain counsel for a volunteer who is the victim of a sexual assault if requested by the volunteer. The Peace Corps may retain counsel in support of a volunteer who is a party to, complaining witness of, or participant in the prosecution of a crime against the volunteer.[5]

In the case of John Peterson, a *USA Today* investigative report published on December 21, 2021, alleged that in 2019, this Dar es Salaam–based American Peace Corps staff member hit and killed Rabia Issa, a street vendor, with his car in the predawn hours while driving under the influence. Peace Corps and embassy staff hurriedly evacuated Peterson to the United States before local police could file charges against him. To what extent this decision has affected the reputation of the Peace Corps in Tanzania remains unknown.

Another facet of this study, from which lessons maybe applicable to other programs, is reverse culture shock, about which returning volunteers from Tanzania have expressed to the author, indicating that coming back and readjusting to life in the United States was hard. A 2010 *Special to CNN* program highlighted five common grievances or complaints of returning Peace Corps staff and volunteers, commentary similar to those expressed by volunteers returning from Tanzania. These include:

Waste: "The ridiculous amount of trash we produce in the U.S. was hard for me to look at every day," said returning Peace Corps volunteer Erin Curtis from Kazakhstan.
Choice: Many volunteers feel overwhelmed by the wide variety of choices in the United States.
Pace of life: "You feel so rushed in this culture and bombarded with things."
Relationships: After spending two years overseas: Volunteers find they have grown apart from their friends and loved ones at home.
Language/Communication: Sometimes it is hard to find the right words after speaking another language for a long time.[6]

Moreover, returning volunteers have found it difficult to share their experiences from the communities and cultures in which they have lived and worked. One volunteer from Tanzania said that people are not interested in listening to them. No one really wants to hear about a Tanzanian village at which they had taught English or mathematics. Paradoxically, this disinterest on the part of the American public undermines the Peace Corps's third objective, that is, upon returning, the Peace Corps expects volunteers to share their knowledge of other peoples and cultures with the American people.

Although each Peace Corps country office is supposed to organize what is called a "close of service conference" at the end of a program to prepare volunteers for some of the hurdles of reentry, such conferences may not be adequate. A much longer period of transition may be necessary to address the many scenarios they encounter when restarting life in the United States. However, it is to be noted that the Peace Corps Reauthorization Act of 2021 addresses other issues, besides those cited above, that returning volunteers face when they return to the United States. These include employment and healthcare. The Reauthorization Act provides statutory authority for an executive order that grants returned volunteers noncompetitive eligibility for federal civil-service positions. Additionally, the Reauthorization Act entitles returned volunteers to three months of healthcare benefits (and a three-month extension at the volunteer's expense). The Peace Corps must also provide volunteers with (1) information about enrolling in US health plans no more than thirty days prior to service termination, (2) adequate access to menstrual products, and (3) mental healthcare during and after service.

Nevertheless, after sixty years, an overall view of the Peace Corps shows that since 1961 the agency has evolved and gone through many other significant changes. In the 1980s under the direction of Loret Miller Ruppe, the Peace Corps embarked on a series of initiatives in Africa, the Caribbean, and Central America. The objective was to make the agency even more relevant in the fight against hunger, poverty, and lack of opportunity. To maximize impact, the Peace Corps's programming emphasis was readjusted. More volunteers than ever before worked in agriculture and food production (25 percent), and in fisheries, forestry, and water supply (24 percent). Twelve percent worked in health and nutrition. Education continued to be the largest Peace Corps program (29 percent). In the 1980s, the average age had risen nearer to thirty, with 8 percent of all volunteers being over fifty. Recruitment focused on applicants with a relevant degree, skill, or experience. The number of generalists fell to an average of 40 percent.

More women joined in the 1980s, bringing the male-to-female ratio to about one to one, whereas in the 1960s it had been three to two. Minority participation also went up slightly from about 5 percent in the 1960s and 1970s to an average nearer 7 percent for the early 1980s. By 2020, 34 percent of volunteers serving overseas were minorities. Of course, unlike in the 1960s when many volunteers joined the Peace Corps as an adventure and an opportunity to travel to foreign countries, by the 1980s most volunteers and employers viewed Peace Corps service as a bridge to future careers.

Since the 1980s, the Peace Corps has gone through further changes aimed at enabling it to meet its mandate. One of these changes has been in training, shifting from predeparture training in the United States to training volunteers in the host country for eight to thirteen weeks. The endeavor has been to adapt training to the locale and to the projects in which volunteers work. Instead of US predeparture training, in the 1980s Peace Corps applicants went through one of four forms of "staging," or predeparture modules, during which motivation and commitment to the Peace Corps were rigorously examined. Still in use today, the four forms of staging are as follows:

(a) Center for Assessment and Training, or CAST, lasting eight days (for the most difficult volunteer assignments)
(b) Center for Reassessment and Training, CREST, lasting five days (70 percent of trainees went through this module)
(c) Traditional comprehensive training, or COMP, lasting three and one-half days (for about 20 percent of trainees)
(d) Medical/administrative staging, lasting two days

Yet, despite adapting training to host-country conditions, culture continues to be one cause of problems often overlooked by volunteers. When volunteers do not know enough about the culture in which they will be or are working, this can lead to misunderstandings that may jeopardize a volunteer's job performance. Eight to thirteen weeks of in-country training may still not be enough to sensitize volunteers to the host country's cultural sensitivities, something that is necessary to create and maintain effective interpersonal working relations. A Peace Corps handbook for volunteers, *A Few Minor Adjustments*, notes that wherever volunteers serve, there will be numerous cultural differences between the United States and the host country in work-related behaviors and values. While these will not be the same for every country, four differences are widespread throughout the

Peace Corps and are particularly difficult to adjust to for many Peace Corps volunteers. These are the concept of power/authority, cultural dichotomies, direct and indirect communication styles, and the pace of events.

While people join the Peace Corps for different reasons, most volunteers hope for the "Peace Corps experience," which is having a profound encounter with a foreign culture that changes forever the way one thinks about the world, one's own country, and oneself. Many returned volunteers from Tanzania have indicated that living and working in Tanzania, indeed, has changed their view of the world, of the United States, and of themselves. However, others have come back only slightly changed, not because the "Peace Corps experience" was not available to them but because of some other competing experiences. By choice or other circumstances, some volunteers found themselves working in proximity with other volunteers or expatriates from other Western countries. Therefore, the tendency was to spend most of their time, both on and off the job, with other volunteers rather than socializing with nationals.

Other "Peace Corps experiences" have much to do with the nature of the program or job. The T-2 group of nurses is a case in point. Although they worked with host-country nurses and other medical staff, they lived together in a hostel in Dar es Salaam or shared housing when posted to up-country stations. They also spent weekends with the T-1 volunteers, with whom close relationships formed, even resulting in a few marriages.

Yet, many returned volunteers developed friendships, and have remained in contact, with nationals. Even more important, many volunteers have continued to make a difference in their host communities by supporting grassroots endeavors, such as funding classroom construction, funding small-scale economic projects, and paying scholarship fees, especially for girls from marginalized rural communities. The Friends of Tanzania (FOT) has been exemplary in this regard.

Finally, in March 2020 the Peace Corps evacuated approximately one hundred fifty to one hundred sixty Volunteers from Tanzania due to the COVID-19 pandemic. Before they were evacuated, these volunteers worked in three sectors, secondary education, community health, and sustainable agriculture, in different parts of the country. Beginning in late 2021, preparations were under way to reopen the program. However, as Stephanie Joseph de Goes notes, Peace Corps Tanzania has also had to look at how to fortify its relationship with the government of Tanzania, especially by liaising with government representatives from each of the ministries in the program sectors in which volunteers work.[7] The objective of these liaisons is to identify priorities and strategic country partnerships and to talk about the criteria and qualifications that Tanzania would like to see in the volunteers that arrive.

Peace Corps Tanzania has also endeavored to look at how it can do things better, to update the program's approaches, travel policy, and action plans in preparation for reentry. According to de Goes, reentry will be on a small scale: "And so as we look to the future, we look to start small. We look to maintain our program areas and [sic] education, stem, science, technology, and math. We look to continue with community health. We will stay close to Dar es Salaam in terms of our site locations. We're also looking to implement a few innovations looking at site-specific goals so that we can monitor and capture our impact with a bit more precision."[8]

NOTES

Introduction

1. Hilary Parkinson, "The Peace Corps' Not-So-Peaceful Roots," National Archives and Records Administration (NARA), *Pieces of History*, accessed Nov. 28, 2018, https://prologue.blogs.archives.gov.
2. Parkinson, "The Peace Corps' Not-So-Peaceful Roots."
3. Parkinson, "The Peace Corps' Not-So-Peaceful Roots."
4. Parkinson, "The Peace Corps' Not-So-Peaceful Roots."
5. Timothy Nicholson, "Empire of Individuals: American Expansion, British Angst and Tanzanian Anger," *US Abroad: Journal of American History and Politics* 1 (2018): 3.
6. Ron Hert, "No Room for PC in Tanzania's Policy of Self-Reliance," *Peace Corps Volunteer* (Sept. 1969): 5.
7. National Archives, "Statement of Robert Sargent Shriver, Jr., Director of the Peace Corps, in Chicago, Illinois, May 17, 1961," in "Sargent Shriver and His Peace Corps Guerrillas," accessed Dec. 6, 2018, https://prologue.blogs.archives.gov/2011/01/19/mr-shriver-and-his-peace-corps-guerrillas/.
8. National Archives, "Statement of Robert Sargent Shriver."
9. Peace Corps, *2nd Annual Peace Corps Report* (Washington, DC: Peace Corps, 1964), 12–13.
10. Charles Cobb Jr., "Harry Belafonte & A Committed Life," in *No Easy Victories: African Liberation and American Activists Over a Half-Century, 1950–2000,* ed. William Minter, Gail Hovey, and Charles Cobb (Trenton, NJ: Africa World Press, 2008), 98.
11. Peace Corps, *2nd Annual Peace Corps Report,* 64.
12. John Lunstrum, "The Mystique of the Peace Corps: A Dilemma," *The Phi Delta Kappan* 48, no. 3 (Nov. 1966): 98.
13. Peace Corps, *2nd Annual Peace Corps Report,* 54.
14. Peace Corps, *2nd Annual Peace Corps Report,* 56.
15. Peace Corps, *2nd Annual Peace Corps Report,* 56.
16. Peace Corps, *2nd Annual Peace Corps Report,* 56.
17. Peace Corps, *2nd Annual Peace Corps Report,* 57.

1. Tanganyika One (T-1)

1. Scott Stossel, *Sarge: The Life and Times of Sargent Shriver* (Washington, DC: Smithsonian Books, 2004), 226–27.
2. Stossel, *Sarge,* 227.

3. "Special to the New York Times," July 18, 1961, 7.
4. "Special to the New York Times," July 18, 1961, 7.
5. Susan Proctor and Mary Segall, eds., *Peace Corps Tales from the Tanganyika I and II Peace Corps Groups*, 2nd ed., Sept. 21–25, 2016 (Washington, DC: n.p., 2016), 8.
6. Proctor and Segall, *Peace Corps Tales from Tanganyika*, 8.
7. Tom Katus, email message to author, Mar. 10, 2020.
8. Katus, email, June 5, 2024.
9. Katus, email, June 5, 2024.
10. Proctor and Segall, *Peace Corps Tales from Tanganyika*, 29.
11. Proctor and Segall, *Peace Corps Tales from Tanganyika*, 9.
12. Peace Corps, *1st Annual Peace Corps Report* (Washington, DC: Peace Corps, 1962), 48.
13. Peace Corps, *Tanganyika Public Works: Peace Corps Program Description* (Washington, DC: Peace Corps, 1964), 3.
14. Peace Corps, *Tanganyika Public Works*, 3.
15. International Bank for Reconstruction and Development, International Development Association, *Highway Project, Tanganyika* (Washington, DC: Department of Technical Operations, 1964), 1.
16. International Bank for Reconstruction and Development, *Highway Project, Tanganyika*, 7.
17. United Republic of Tanganyika and Zanzibar, *Parliamentary Debates (Hansard), National Assembly Official Report*, tenth meeting, June 16–July 3, 1964 (Dar es Salaam: Government Printer, 1964), col. 381.
18. United Republic of Tanganyika and Zanzibar, *Parliamentary Debates (Hansard)*, col. 386.
19. United Republic of Tanganyika and Zanzibar, *Parliamentary Debates (Hansard)*, col. 388.
20. There were 60 village settlement schemes planned in the Five-Year Development Plan.
21. Aaron Segal, "Kitete: Birth of a Community," *Africa Today* 12, no. 2 (Feb. 1965), 5.
22. Segal, "Kitete," 5.
23. Government of Tanganyika, Public Works Department, Morogoro, Tanganyika, 1963.
24. Susan Proctor, "In Memoriam: Peter De Simone, 06.1937–08.2018," *Mbegu za Urafiki/Seeds of Friendship Newsletter*, Spring 2019, 5.
25. Robert Milhous, email message to author, Nov. 29, 2020.
26. It is unclear why the chief geologist said this. It could have been out of prejudice or concern for Robbins's safety. Out in the field, Robbins was once chased by a Cape buffalo and ran away from a rhino. Robbins notes that the surveys intended to identify potential deposits for copper, lead, and zinc.
27. Eric Ries, email message to author, July 20, 2021.
28. He was nicknamed Bwana Mnegro in Kiswahili.

29. He was trained as a civil engineer in Bulgaria.

30. Joseph G. Colmen, Peace Corps, Office of the Director, "Report of Meeting of Peace Corps Volunteers in Tanganyika I Project at Dar-es-Salaam, November 20–22, 1962," Dec. 17, 1962, 1.

31. Colmen, "Report of Meeting," 1.

32. Colmen, "Report of Meeting," 1.

33. *Sun* (Baltimore, MD), May 18, 1962.

34. Colmen, "Report of Meeting," 9.

35. Colmen, "Report of Meeting," 10.

36. Colmen, "Report of Meeting," 1.

37. Colmen, "Report of Meeting," 3.

38. Colmen, "Report of Meeting," 8.

39. William McTeer, "Peace Corps Draws Praise in Tanganyika Newspaper," *Tanganyika Standard*, Feb. 25, 1962, 20–21.

2. Race and Peace Corps Recruitment and Training

1. Julius A. Amin, "The Peace Corps and the Struggle for African-American Equality," *Journal of Black Studies* 29, no. 6 (July 1999): 813.

2. Amin, "The Peace Corps," 813.

3. Amin, "The Peace Corps," 812.

4. "Remarks of the President at Peace Corps Meeting in Chamber of Commerce Auditorium, Washington, D.C.," typescript, 7, Peace Corps Folder, Box 86, President Office Files (Kennedy Library). Quoted by Jonathan Zimmerman, "Beyond Double Consciousness: Black Peace Corps in Africa, 1961–1971," *The Journal of American History* 82, no. 3 (Dec. 1995): 1006.

5. Amin, "The Peace Corps," 817.

6. Office of Volunteer Support, Peace Corps, "Black Graduates See the Peace Corps as a Costly Interlude," *Peace Corps Volunteer*, Aug. 1968, 4.

7. Office of Volunteer Support, "Black Graduates See the Peace Corps as a Costly Interlude," 4.

8. Office of Volunteer Support, "Black Graduates See the Peace Corps as a Costly Interlude," 6.

9. Quoted by Jonathan Zimmerman, "Crossing Oceans, Crossing Colors: Black Peace Corps Volunteers and Interracial Love in Africa, 1961–1971," in *Sex, Love, Race: Crossing Boundaries in North American History*, ed. Martha E. Hodes (New York: New York Univ. Press, 1999), 517.

10. Ernest Dunbar, *The Black Expatriates: A Study of American Negroes in Exile* (New York: E. P. Dutton & Co., 1968), 67.

11. "Peace Corps' Former Director Carolyn Payton Dies at Age 75," *Washington Post*, Apr. 12, 2001.

12. Carol Word, email message to author, May 5, 2020.

13. Word, email, May 5, 2020.
14. Gaddi Vasquez, accessed July 10, 2022, Wikipedia-en.wikipedia.org/Gaddi_Vasquez.
15. "Peace Corps Looks for More Negroes," *New York Times,* Jan. 14, 1962, 62.
16. "Peace Corps Looks for More Negroes," 62.
17. Office of Volunteer Support, "Needed: Abroad or at Home?," *Peace Corps Volunteer* 6, no. 9 (July–Aug. 1968): 7.
18. Office of Volunteer Support, "Needed: Abroad or at Home?," 7.
19. Office of Volunteer Support, "Needed: Abroad or at Home?," 7.
20. Office of Volunteer Support, "Needed: Abroad or at Home?," 8.
21. Paul Conkin, "A Question of Black or White," *New Republic* 145, no. 19 (Nov. 6, 1961): 8.
22. Zimmerman, "Beyond Double Consciousness," 1010.
23. Zimmerman, "Crossing Oceans, Crossing Colors," 517.
24. Tom Katus, correspondence with author, Aug. 8, 2022.
25. What follows is gleaned from various email exchanges between Tom Katus, member of T-1, and the author.
26. Tom Katus, email message to author, June 10, 2024.
27. Allen Tamura, email message to author, July 20, 2022.
28. Tamura, email, July 20, 2022.
29. Loretta Ann Helms, "The Special Concerns of African-American Peace Corps Volunteers" (EdD diss., Columbia Univ. Teachers College, 1990), 2.
30. Carter G. Woodson, *The Mis-Education of the Negro* (Washington, DC: Associated Publishers, 1933), 4.
31. Woodson, *The Mis-Education of the Negro,* 12.
32. Woodson, *The Mis-Education of the Negro,* 10.
33. Quoted by Martin Staniland, *American Intellectuals and African Nationalists, 1955–1970* (New Haven: Yale Univ. Press, 1991), 179.
34. The author witnessed this firsthand when he took a group of William Paterson African American students to Ghana in 2000. All they were interested in was taking photographs of signs of "backwardness," such as barefoot children, ramshackle dwellings, and rickety automobiles. No one took pictures of the airport or the motel where we had breakfast after we landed.
35. David Peterson del Mar, "At the Heart of Things: Peace Corps Volunteers in Sub-Saharan Africa, 1961–1971," *African Identities* 9, no. 4 (Nov. 2011): 358.
36. Zimmerman, "Beyond Double Consciousness," 1022.
37. When Smith met Malcolm X and introduced himself as a Peace Corps volunteer, Malcolm X scoffed at Smith's service as a volunteer in Ghana. That was the proverbial last nail in the coffin for Ed Smith's affinity with Africa.
38. Malcolm X, "We're One with You," *Tanganyika Standard,* Oct. 13, 1964.
39. Wesley Lynch, "Peace Corps Leader Replies to Malcom," *Tanganyika Standard,* Nov. 2, 1964.
40. Lynch, "Peace Corps Leader Replies to Malcom."
41. Zimmerman, "Crossing Oceans, Crossing Colors," 355.

42. Zimmerman, "Beyond Double Consciousness," 1015.
43. Word, email, May 17, 2020.
44. Word, letter to her mother, Jan. 7, 1965. In author's possession.
45. Word, letter to her mother, Jan. 7, 1965.
46. Word, letter to her mother, Jan. 7, 1965.
47. Norrie Robbins, email message to author, July 11, 2021.
48. Tamura, email, July 20, 2022.
49. Mary Ann Brown, interview the author, May 19, 2020.
50. Brown, interview, May 19, 2020.
51. Best known for its 161 theatrical short films by MGM, the series centered on a friendly rivalry between the title characters Tom, a cat, and Jerry, a mouse.
52. Zimmerman, "Crossing Oceans, Crossing Colors," 517.
53. *Congressional Record,* 62d. Congress, 3d. Sess., Dec. 11, 1912, 502–3.
54. Zimmerman, "Crossing Oceans, Crossing Colors," 516.
55. Interracial marriages were banned in Maryland until 1967, when that law was repealed. Therefore, Brenda and Dick Schoonover's marriage would have been illegal had they married before 1967.
56. Ambassador Brenda Schoonover, email message to author, June 26, 2020.
57. Lineberger, "Crossroads Africa," *Negro History Bulletin* 24, no. 3 (Dec. 1960), 64. The volunteers were carefully selected from some seven hundred applicants.
58. Johanna Lesley Lineberger, "Crossroads Africa: An Experiment in International Communication," *World Affairs* 126, no. 4 (Winter 1963–64): 256.
59. John David Cato, "James Herman Robinson: Crossroads Africa and American Idealism, 1958–1972," *American Presbyterians* 68, no. 2 (Summer 1990): 104.
60. Operation Crossroads Africa, *A Decade of Achievement* (New York: n.p., 1968).
61. Amy Lee, *Throbbing Drums: The Story of James H. Robinson* (New York: Friendship Press, 1968), 78.
62. Lineberger, "Crossroads Africa," 259.
63. Charles J. Wetzel, "The Peace Corps in Our Past," *The Annals of the American Academy of Political and Social Science* 365 (May 1966): 7.
64. Operation Crossroads Africa, *Decade of Achievement.*
65. James Forman, "Manifesto to the White Christian Churches and the Jewish Synagogues in the United States of America and All Other Racist Institutions," Riverside Church Archives, Papers of the Benevolence Committee (1930–80), catalog 9.2.1.
66. Forman, "Manifesto."
67. Forman, "Manifesto."
68. "Nation Building Jobs in Africa," Riverside Church Archives, Papers of the Benevolence Committee (1930–1980), catalog 9.2.1.
69. Brenda Gayle Plummer, *In Search of Power: African Americans in the Era of Decolonization, 1956–1974* (Cambridge, UK: Cambridge Univ. Press, 2013), 276.
70. Plummer, *In Search of Power,* 276.
71. James P. Garrett, interview by author, Nov. 18, 2023.
72. Garrett, interview, Nov. 18, 2023.

73. Benjamin F. Scott, "The Technology of Liberation: Proposal for a Pan African Academy of Science," *Black World* (July 1972): 34.

74. Scott, "Technology of Liberation," 31.

75. Sylvia I. B. Hill, "Sixth Pan African Congress: Planning, Preparation and Implementation, 1969–1974," Black Power Chronicles, https://www.blackpowerchronicles.org/cool_timeline/sixth-pan-african-congress-planning-preparation-and-implementation-1969-1974/.

76. Hill, "Sixth Pan African Congress."

77. Alma Robinson, "A Meeting with Nyerere," *New Directions* 1, no. 4 (1974), https://dh.howard.edu/newdirections/vol1/iss4/4.

78. Neville Parker, "The Pan African Imperative for Increased Emphasis on Science and Technology," *Resolutions and Selected Speeches from the Sixth Pan African Congress* (Dar es Salaam: Tanzania Publishing House, 1976), 203.

79. Parker, "The Pan African Imperative," 205.

80. Parker, "The Pan African Imperative," 205.

81. Parker, "The Pan African Imperative," 206.

82. Parker, "The Pan African Imperative," 206.

83. Andrew Ivaska, "Learning from Dar es Salaam: Harvard's 'Project Tanganyika' and the Nodal Perspective on Decolonization Itineraries," *Humanity: An International Journal of Human Rights, Humanitarianism, and Development* 14, no. 1 (Spring 2023): 105.

84. Eliza M. Nguyen, "Project Tanganyika Fosters International Service," *Crimson*, accessed Sept. 10, 2022, https://www.thecrimson.com/article/2012/5/21/project-tanganyika-international-service/?page=single.

85. Ivaska, "Learning from Dar es Salaam," 103.

86. Neil Sheehan, "Foundations Linked to CIA Are Found to Subsidize 4 Other Youth Organizations," *New York Times*, Feb. 16, 1967, 26; Neil Sheehan, "5 New Groups Tied to CIA Conduits," *New York Times*, Feb. 17, 1967, 1; James Reston, "Washington: The CIA and the Universities," *New York Times*, ProQuest Historical Newspapers: New York Times, 184; Richard M. Hunt, "The CIA Exposures: The End of an Affair," *Virginia Quarterly Review: A National Journal of Literature and Discussion* (Spring 1969): 211–29.

3. Tanganyika Two (T-2)

1. In addition, there were sixty-eight hospitals and four hundred fifty dispensaries, most owned and run by voluntary agencies.

2. Anna K. Tibaijuka, "Trends and Issues in Health Service Delivery Under Economic Adjustment," in *The Social Services Crisis of the 1990s: Strategies for Sustainable Systems in Tanzania*, ed. Anna K. Tibaijuka (Aldershot, UK: Ashgate, 1998), 132.

3. Tibaijuka, "Trends and Issues in Health Service Delivery," 132. These goals were part of the government's objective to eliminate disease that it identified as one of the major "enemies" to fight. The other two were poverty and ignorance.

4. Tibaijuka, "Trends and Issues in Health Service Delivery," 146.

5. Tibaijuka, "Trends and Issues in Health Service Delivery," 136.

6. The two technologists, Virginia Lee Overstreet and Becky Davis, had college degrees and both had completed a yearlong internship following graduation. Of the twenty-five nurses, twelve RN diplomas from hospital schools of nursing (thirty-six-month programs), and thirteen held baccalaureate degrees, twelve BSNs (bachelor of science in nursing), and one BSW (bachelor of social work)—this person became a nurse after changing profession from social work to nursing. Of those holding a BS in nursing, one nurse also held an MS in nursing. I thank Dr. Susan (née Tonskemper) Proctor for this information.

7. William H. Friedland, "Nurses in Tanganyika," in *Cultural Frontiers of the Peace Corps*, ed. Robert B. Textor and Comitas Lambros (Cambridge, MA: MIT Press, 1966): 142.

8. The principal secretary at the time was Dr. Charles Mtawali, who received the group at the airport when they arrived.

9. Friedland, "Nurses in Tanganyika," 153–54.

10. Syracuse University, syllabus for Syracuse University training program, Tanganyika Peace Corps Project, July 2–Aug. 25, 1962 (Syracuse, NY: Syracuse Univ., 1962), 2.

11. Susan Proctor, email message to author, Nov. 13, 2019.

12. Syracuse University, syllabus, 3.

13. Syracuse University, syllabus, 14.

14. Syracuse University, syllabus, 3–4.

15. Proctor, email, Nov. 13, 2019.

16. Syracuse University, syllabus, 4.

17. Syracuse University, syllabus, 4.

18. Syracuse University, syllabus, 5.

19. Three members of T-2 missed the flight: Donna Abner had just lost her father, and Patsy Mason and Jeannie Read missed the plane for unknown reasons. However, the three nurses arrived in Dar es Salaam later, in time for the in-country training and orientation.

20. Richard M. Titmus, "The Health Services of Tanganyika: A Report to the Government," *Medical Care* 2, no. 1 (Jan.–Mar. 1964): 27.

21. Titmus, "Health Services of Tanganyika," 28.

22. Susan Proctor's response to a questionnaire administered by the author to volunteers about their Peace Corps experiences in Tanzania.

23. Proctor, email, Sept. 22, 2020.

24. Ruth Elizabeth Dygert (Shiers), response to a questionnaire administered by the author on Peace Corps experiences in Tanzania.

25. William R. Duggan, "A Study of Ujamaa and Nationhood," in *Tanzania and Nyerere: A Study of Ujamaa and Nationhood*, ed. William R. Duggan and John R. Caville (Maryknoll, NY: Orbis Books, 1976), 75.

26. Proctor, questionnaire response.

27. Proctor, email, Sept. 22, 2020.

28. In late 1963 some of the nurses in Dar es Salaam were reassigned to two other towns, Mwanza and Tabora.

29. Friedland, "Nurses in Tanganyika," 141.
30. Friedland, "Nurses in Tanganyika," 142.
31. Friedland, "Nurses in Tanganyika," 141.
32. Friedland, "Nurses in Tanganyika," 150.
33. Friedland, "Nurses in Tanganyika," 151.
34. Friedland, "Nurses in Tanganyika," 152. Friedland suggests that even though such interactions were routine, it did not establish a friendship of any depth between the volunteers and African nurses.
35. Friedland, "Nurses in Tanganyika," 151.
36. Proctor, email, Nov. 13, 2019.
37. Friedland, "Nurses in Tanganyika," 141.
38. Proctor, email, Nov. 13, 2019.
39. Proctor, email, Nov. 13, 2019.
40. Friedland, "Nurses in Tanganyika," 152.

4. Tanganyika Five (T-5)

1. Joseph Nye Jr., "Tanganyika's Self-Help," *Transition* 11 (Nov. 1963): 35.
2. Nye, "Tanganyika's Self-Help," 37.
3. Nye, "Tanganyika's Self-Help," 36.
4. Dennis Herlocker, "Transits and Culverts: Peace Corps Engineers in Tanzania, 1964–66," accessed June 29, 2022, http://storiesofeastafrica.com/page2/.
5. Herlocker, "Transits and Culverts."
6. Herlocker, "Transits and Culverts."

5. Tanzania Six (T-6)

1. United Republic of Tanganyika and Zanzibar, *Parliamentary Debates (Hansard): National Assembly Official Report* (Dar es Salaam: Government Printer, 1962), col. 29.
2. United Republic of Tanganyika and Zanzibar, *Parliamentary Debates (Hansard)*, col. 29.
3. P. C. C. Evans, "American Teachers for East Africa," *Comparative Education Review* 6, no. 1 (June 1962): 70.
4. These were teachers sent to East Africa to teach in lower- and upper-primary schools.
5. Syracuse University, syllabus for Syracuse University training program, Tanganyika III Peace Corps Project, Aug. 31–Oct., 1963 (Syracuse, NY: Syracuse Univ., 1963); letter from the university, Aug. 26, 1963.
6. Syracuse University, syllabus, 6.
7. Syracuse University, syllabus, 6.
8. Syracuse University, syllabus, 7.
9. Students were untrained in analytical thinking. They had instead been encour-

aged to memorize and reproduce information during examinations.

10. Justin A. Amin, *The Peace Corps in Cameroon* (Kent, OH: Kent State Univ. Press, 1992), 101.

11. From September 1966 to 1967, Cummins was acting PC advisor to the T-12 volunteers who would introduce agricultural training in primary schools.

12. Author unknown.

6. Termination of the Peace Corps Program in Tanzania

1. Lawrence Fellows, "Peace Corps Quietly Folding up in Tanzania: Once-Ambitious Plan is Victim of Harsh Political Climate," *New York Times*, Feb. 3, 1969, 14.

2. Ron Hert, "No Room for Peace Corps in Tanzania's Policy of Self-Reliance," *Peace Corps Volunteer* 7, no. 10 (Sept. 1969), 2.

3. Ikaweba Bunting, interview by author, Dec. 1, 2023.

4. Bunting, interview, Dec. 1, 2023.

5. Cranford Pratt, "Foreign-Policy Issues and the Emergence of Socialism in Tanzania, 1961–8," *International Journal* 30, no. 3 (Summer 1975): 461.

6. In diplomacy, a *persona non grata* (Latin: "Person not appreciated," pl. *personae non gratae*) is a foreign person whose entering or remaining in a particular country is prohibited by that country's government. Such designation is the most serious form of censure that a country can apply to foreign diplomats, who otherwise are protected by diplomatic immunity from arrest and other normal kinds of prosecution.

7. Staff reporter, "Washington Envoy Recalled," *Standard, Tanzania*, Feb. 15, 1965, 3.

8. Staff reporter, "Washington Envoy Recalled," 1.

9. Paul Bjerk, "Postcolonial Realism: Tanganyika's Foreign Policy under Nyerere, 1960–1963," *International Journal of African Historical Studies* 44, no. 2 (2011): 240.

10. Gilbert P. Verbit, "Negotiating with China: A Minor Episode," in *China's Practice of International Law: Some Case Studies*, ed. J. A. Cohen (Cambridge, MA: Harvard Univ. Press, 1972), 155.

11. Verbit, "Negotiating with China," 155.

12. Tom Katus, email message to author, June 16, 2020.

13. Katus, email, June 16, 2020.

14. Allen Tamura, email message to author, June 16, 2020.

15. Verbit, "Negotiating with China," 165.

16. New China News Agency, "Shanghai Cheers Mwalimu," *Standard, Tanzania*, Feb. 17, 1965, 1.

17. "Nyerere Has Talks with Chinese Leaders," *Standard, Tanzania*, Feb. 19, 1965, 1.

18. "Nyerere Has Talks with Chinese Leaders," 7.

19. The conference was canceled in the wake of the overthrow of Algerian President Ahmed Ben Bella.

20. Azaria Mbughuni, "Why Did Che Guevara Come to Tanzania Secretly: Part I & II," *Africa United* (Oct. 9, 2017).

21. Martin Bailey, "Tanzania and China," *African Affairs* 74, no. 294 (Jan. 1975): 44.
22. Hert, "Peace Corps in Tanzania," 3.
23. Sean Jacobs, "When Malcolm X Went to Africa," accessed June 22, 2020, https://africasacountry.com/2011/06/malcolm-x-in-africa1.
24. FEATURE, "Malcom X and Tanzania," Business Times, accessed June 22, 2020, https://businesstimes.co.tz/malcolm-x-and-tanzania/#:~:text=Malcolm%20came%20to%20Tanzania%20first,known%20as%20Tanganyika%20and%20Zanzibar.&text=More%20importantly%20Malcolm%20had%20made,human%20rights%20of%20African%20Americans.
25. Malcolm X's visit to Tanzania happened just a few months after "Che" Guevara visited the country.
26. Godfrey Mwakikagile, *Relations Between Africans and African Americans: Misconceptions, Myths and Realities* (Dar es Salaam: New Africa Press, 2007), 255.
27. James Garrett, interview by author, Dec. 1, 2023.
28. United Republic of Tanzania, Extradition Act, Cap. 368, 1965, Section 5 (2).
29. James C. McKinley, "A Black Panther's Mellow Exile: Farming in Africa," *New York Times,* Nov. 23, 1997.
30. Andy Alcock, "New Pardon Push for Kansas City Black Panther Founder Pete O'Neal Living in Exile in Africa," *KSHB,* Apr. 5, 2018.
31. George Cummins, email message to author, May 28, 2020.
32. Hert, "Peace Corps in Tanzania," 4.
33. Acronym for Tanganyika African National Association, the party that led the country to independence.
34. Karim Hirji, *Cheche: Reminiscences of a Radical Magazine* (Dar es Salaam: Mkuki na Nyota, 2010), viii.
35. Peace Corps, "Tanzania: Peace Corps Memorandum," 7.
36. Peace Corps, "Tanzania: Peace Corps Memorandum," 7.
37. Stossel, *Sarge,* 228–29.
38. Julius K. Nyerere, "The Costs of Nonalignment," *Africa Report* 11, no. 7 (Oct. 1966): 62.
39. Nyerere, "The Costs of Nonalignment," 62.
40. Stossel, *Sarge,* 270.
41. Stossel opines that it would certainly have made some strategic sense for the Peace Corps to have been a tool of the Pentagon or that of American espionage operations. However, "Shriver had been at great pains to establish an impenetrable firewall between the Peace Corps and the CIA." Stossel, *Sarge,* 270.
42. Stossel, *Sarge,* 270–71.
43. Stossel, *Sarge,* 271.
44. Stossel, *Sarge,* 272.
45. Stossel, *Sarge,* 272.
46. Ambassador John Howard Burns, interview by Charles Stewart Kennedy, May 1, 1995, accessed Nov. 10, 2020, https://www.adst.org/OH%20TOCs/Burns,%20John%20Howard.toc.pdf. The personnel of the American embassy at the time were

constituted of one political officer, one economic, one administrative, one consular (who also worked for the CIA, as did the code clerk).

47. Burns, interview, May 1, 1995.
48. Burns, interview, May 1, 1995.
49. Hirji, *Cheche*, 180.
50. Stanley Meisler, "Peace Corps Teaching in Africa," *Africa Report* 11, no. 9 (1966): 16.
51. C. Mwalongo, "Teachers Hit at Peace Corps' Lowering Standards of Profession," *Tanganyika Standard*, Nov. 12, 1963, 3.
52. Meisler, "Peace Corps Teaching in Africa," 16.
53. Meisler, "Peace Corps Teaching in Africa," 18.
54. Solomon Eliufoo, "You're Needed Here, Peace Corps Told," *Tanganyika Standard*, Nov. 13, 1963, 2.
55. Special to the *New York Times*, "Tanzania Critical of U.S. Peace Corps," *New York Times*, Mar. 5, 1967.
56. Jim Hoagland, "Tanzania's Ban on Soul," *Washington Post, Times Herald*, Jan. 8, 1970, C 1.
57. Hert, "Peace Corps in Tanzania," 4.
58. Hert, "Peace Corps in Tanzania," 6.

7. Return of the Peace Corps Program to Tanzania

1. Ron Hert, "No Room for Peace Corps in Tanzania's Policy of Self-Reliance," *Peace Corps Volunteer* 7, no. 10 (Sept. 1969): 2.
2. Roger Mann, "Nyerere Visit Seen as Symbol of Shift in U.S. Policy on Africa," *Washington Post*, Aug. 4, 1977.
3. Mann, "Nyerere Visit Seen as Symbol."
4. "Nyerere Says Carter Is Firm over Africa," *New York Times*, Aug. 8, 1977, 3; Jacqueline Trescott, "Nyerere May Invite U.S. Peace Corps to Return to Tanzania," *Washington Post*, Aug. 11, 1977.
5. Ambassador James Spain to US State Department, telegram, Oct. 4, 1977, Canonical ID: 1977DARES03994_c.
6. Spain to State Department, telegram, Oct. 4, 1977.
7. Ambassador James Spain to secretary of state, telegram, Aug. 15, 1978, Canonical ID: 1978DARES03483_d.
8. Ambassador James Spain to secretary of state, telegram, Sept. 1, 1978, Canonical ID: 1978DARES03752_d.
9. Ambassador James Spain to secretary of state, telegram, Nov. 21, 1978, Canonical ID: 1978DARES05075_d.
10. Spain to secretary of state, telegram, Nov. 21, 1978.
11. Spain to secretary of state, telegram, Nov. 21, 1978.
12. Spain to secretary of state, telegram, Nov. 21, 1978.
13. United States, *Report by the U.S. General Accounting Office: Changes Needed for a Better Peace Corps*, Washington, DC, Feb. 6, 1979, ii.

14. American ambassador, letter to the Tanzanian minister of manpower development, *Agreement Effected by Exchange of Letters Signed at Dar-es-Salaam January 9, 1979; Entered into Force January 9, 1979,* accessed July 13, 2020, HeinOnline.

15. Staff reporter, "Peace Corps to Work Here," *Daily News,* Jan. 10, 1979, 3.

16. "Comment," *Daily News,* Jan. 11, 1979, 1.

17. Ambassador James Spain, telegram to US State Department, Jan. 11, 1979, Canonical ID: 1979DARES00157_c.

18. B. Omu-Mura, "Suspicious of Peace Corps," *Daily News,* Jan. 15, 1979, 5.

19. Lawrence F. Lihosit, *Peace Corps Chronology, 1961–2010,* 2nd ed. (New York: iUniverse, 2011), 16.

20. Lihosit, *Peace Corps Chronology,* 16.

21. Lihosit, *Peace Corps Chronology,* 27.

22. Lihosit, *Peace Corps Chronology,* 27.

23. Lihosit, *Peace Corps Chronology,* 28.

24. Marilyn S. Chakroff and Random DuBois, *Marine Fisheries Case Studies* (Washington, DC: Peace Corps, 1982), 11.

8. Peace Corps Volunteer Mishaps in Tanzania

1. The reported disappearance and presumed death of Peace Corps volunteer Mark Raymaker remains contentious, whether or not a lion killed him.

2. Susan Proctor, *Tanganyika Two: Bio Sketches and Life Stories,* mimeograph (in author's possession).

3. Proctor, *Tanganyika Two.*

4. Proctor, *Tanganyika Two.*

5. Amirali A. Jetha, "Document Denouncing Ownership of Child," Nov. 22, 1961. In author's possession and received from Cathy Lee Lazar, formerly named Katrina.

6. Barthazar A. Rwezaura, and Ulrike Wanitzek, "The Law and Practice Relating to the Adoption of Children in Tanzania," *Journal of African Law* 32, no. 2 (Autumn 1988): 124.

7. American embassy, Dar es Salaam, telegram to US secretary of state, Nov. 6, 1963.

8. Everett Jordan, letter to Hugh D. Mills, May 23, 1966.

9. Peace Corps, *The Peace Corps' Contributions to the Global Smallpox Eradication Program* 19, accessed Nov. 20, 2019, https://s3.amazonaws.com/files.peacecorps.gov/documents/open-government/Peace_Corps_Global_Smallpox.pdf.

10. Chris Raymaker, online post, Peace Corps Online News Bulletin, Apr. 1, 2009, accessed Nov. 11, 2019, peacecorpsonline.org/messages/messages/2629/3214347.html.

11. Eugene Mihaly, email message to author, Dec. 6, 2019.

12. George Cummins, email message to author, Oct. 20, 2021.

13. Cummins, email, Sept. 12, 2020.

14. Peace Corps Office of Inspector General, "Report of Staff Involvement in a Traffic Death in the Africa Region (UPDATE)," Oct. 1, 2020–Mar. 21, 2021, accessed June

13, 2024, https://s3.documentcloud.org/documents/21165462/semiannual-report-to-congress-october-2020-to-march-2021_traffic_death.pdf.

9. Anecdotes of Peace Corps Volunteer Experiences

1. Stanley Meisler, *When the World Calls: The Inside Story of the Peace Corps and Its First Fifty Years* (Boston: Beacon, 2011), 145.
2. Tom Katus, email message to author, Feb. 18, 2020.
3. A dhow is a local single-mast sailboat.
4. Katus, email, Feb.18, 2020.
5. Susan Proctor, email message to author, Nov. 13, 2019.
6. Proctor, email, Sept. 23, 2021.
7. Proctor, email, Nov. 13, 2019.
8. "Cool Captain of Tabora Took Command," *Tanganyika Standard*, Jan. 30, 1964, 5.
9. Louise White, "Cars Out of Place: Vampires, Technology, and Labor in East and Central Africa," *Representations* 43 (Summer 1993): 27–50.
10. White, "Cars Out of Place," 27.
11. White, "Cars Out of Place," 29.
12. Jan LeMoyne Hedges, email message to author, Jan. 25, 2022.
13. Hedges, email, Jan. 25, 2022.

10. Peace Corps Volunteer Early Departures

1. Peace Corps, "FY 2018 Peace Corps Early Termination Report: Global, March 2019," 2.
2. In March and April 2020, the Peace Corps evacuated all its volunteers around the world in response to the global COVID-19 pandemic. With a small number of exceptions, the evacuated volunteers were considered to have completed their service regardless of the stage of their service. Exceptions are predominantly medical separations with a very small number of interrupted services.
3. Michael Sheppard, "Early Termination in the Peace Corps," Department of Statistics and Probability, Michigan State Univ., mimeograph, Apr. 2008, 6.
4. Sheppard, "Early Termination in the Peace Corps," 6.
5. George Cummins, email message to author, Oct. 21, 2021.

11. Peace Corps Volunteers and the Reentry Problem

1. Richard B. Stolley, "Back from Overseas, Peace Corps Volunteers Suffer Reverse Homesickness: The Re-Entry Crisis," *Life*, Mar. 19, 1965.
2. Stolley, "The Re-Entry Crisis," 98.
3. Stolley, "The Re-Entry Crisis," 102.
4. Walter Grant, "Re-Entry Crisis: Officials Claim Overemphasis," *Peace Corps News* (Autumn 1965): 3.

5. Calvert, Robert, "The Returning Volunteer," *The Annals of the American Academy of Political and Social Sciences* 365 (May 1966): 106.
6. These were sent to volunteers in the field during the last year of their service.
7. Calvert, "The Returning Volunteer," 105.
8. Leonard J. Duhl, Robert L. Leopold, and Joseph T. English, "A Mental Health Program for the Peace Corps," *Human Organization* 23, no. 2 (Summer 1964): 135.
9. The rigors of the selection process and training tended to eliminate the most seriously disturbed applicants. Many dropped out during training as a result.
10. Chris Biles, email message to author, May 25, 2020.
11. Eleanor Q. Burton, "Re-entry: Part I," *Insight Turkey* 10 (Nov. 1997): 167.
12. John Ratigan, email message to author, May 31, 2020.
13. Cummins, email, May 28, 2020.
14. Cummins, email, May 28, 2020.
15. Cummins, email, May 28, 2020.
16. Cummins, email, May 30, 2020.
17. Cummins, email, May 28, 2020.
18. Brenda B. Schoonover, "On Being an American," *American Diplomacy* (Mar. 2011). Originally published in Parker W. Borg, Maureen J. Carroll, Patricia MacDermot Kasdan, and Stephen W. Wells, eds., *Answering Kennedy's Call: Pioneering the Peace Corps in the Philippines* (Oakland, CA: Peace Corps Writers Book, 2011).
19. Charles Fels, email message to author, May 10, 2021.
20. Fels, email, May 10, 2021.
21. Schoonover, "On Being an American."
22. Meghan Elizabeth Kallman, "Home Again: Political, Civic, and Occupational Consequences of Volunteering," in Kallman, *The Death of Idealism: Development and Anti-Politics in the Peace Corps* (New York: Columbia Univ. Press, 2020), 193.
23. Susan Proctor, email message to author, Aug. 5, 2021.
24. Biles, email, May 25, 2020.
25. Bonnie Jo Dopp Hurley, email message to author, Sept. 7, 2021.
26. Hurley, email, Sept. 7, 2021.
27. In the meantime, Bonnie Hurley's Peace Corps experience made her multilingual. Bonnie recalls that after she returned from Korea, she attended a Peace Corps training event where all the people were either East Africans, Koreans, or Americans, and she could converse with all of them in English, Swahili, or Korean, whichever they chose. That made her wonder if she should work on a Korean-Swahili dictionary one day!
28. Biles, email, May 25, 2020.
29. Katie Songer, email message to author, June 4, 2021.
30. Stolley, "The Re-Entry Crisis," 103.
31. His father, a well-known philanthropist, was a professor of engineering at Clemson University and eventually opened Harllee Construction Company in 1927 in Florence with his brother.
32. "James Belisle Starts Peace Corps Duty," *San Bernardino Sun*, Sept. 6, 1961, 13.

Conclusion

1. Frank Florah Edward, "Circulation and Appropriation of Urban Technologies: Drainage and Traffic Infrastructures in Dar-es-Salaam, 1913–1999," (DPhil diss., Technische Universitat Darmstadt, 2022), 225.

2. Congressional Research Service, "The Peace Corps: Overview and Issues," updated Dec. 17, 2021, accessed May 20, 2020, https://sgp.fas.org/crs/misc/RS21168.pdf.

3. Peace Corps, "Reports and Documents," accessed May 20, 2020, https://www.peacecorps.gov/about/open-government/reports/?search_text=early%20termination.

4. Joshua Norman, "Peace Corps Regrets Response to Rapes, Deaths," *CBS News*, May 11, 2011, accessed May 21, 2022, https://www.cbsnews.com/news/peace-corps-regrets-response-to-rapes-deaths/.

5. Sec. 10. (a) Memorandum of Agreement with Bureau of Diplomatic Security of the Department of State.

6. Tas Agarwalla, "Dealing with Reverse Culture Shock," *CNN*, Aug. 24, 2010, accessed May 25, 2020, http://www.cnn.com/2010/TRAVEL/08/24/cultural.reentry/index.html.

7. Stephanie Joseph de Goes, "FOT's 30th-PCTZ Country Director's Remarks," accessed June 13, 2024, https://vimeo.com/649552009?utm_campaign=5250933&utm_source=affiliate&utm_channel=affiliate&cjevent=5be9c71d29c211ef819d00d10a82b82a&clickid=5be9c71d29c211ef819d00d10a82b82a.

8. de Goes, "FOT's 30th-PCTZ Country Director's Remarks."

Index

Page numbers in *italics* refer to illustrations. The letter *t* following a page number denotes a table.

ABC, 42
Abdula, 153–54
Abner, Donna: invitation to state ball, *148;* in T-2, 69t
Abraham Baldwin Agricultural College (ABAC), 119
ACTION, 38, 119, 127
Adoption of Infants Ordinance, No. 5 of 1942, Cap. 14, 132
Adoption Ordinance, No. 42 of 1953, Cap. 335, 132
Africa: African American Peace Corps volunteers and, 48; African Americans' psychological rupture with, 46; colonial, 47–48; independence movement, 47–48, 57; racism and, 46–47
African American Institute, 63
African Development Foundation, 183
African Medical and Research Foundation, 70
African National Congress (ANC), 99
Agency for International Development of the State Department, 86
Air Force, Morogoro headquarters, 21
All God's Children Need Traveling Shoes (Angelou), 48
Allouez Catholic Cemetery, 139

Almasi, John, 27
Alpha Phi Alpha, 106
American Colonization Society, 47
American Council of Education, 85
American Liaison Committee, 87
American Society of Friends, 178
Anderson, Ed, 63
Andrews, Julie, 14
Angelou, Maya, 40, 48
Angola, 60, 117
Annetta, Donna, 145
Army Combat Engineer Officer Candidate School (OCS), 174
Arusha Declaration, 102
Asian-African Conference, 102
Attrition Task Force, 158–60
Augusto, Geri Stark, 60

Babu, Abdulrahman, 104–5
Bagnall, P. Stanley "Stan," 24
Bakari, Gabriel, 29
Baldwin, Abraham, 119
Baldwin, James, 47
Barbera, Joseph, 53
Barcas, John, 95
Barclays Bank, 82
Basch, Samuel, 57
Bates, Margaret, 67
Bayley, Edwin R., 2
Belafonte, Harry, 2, 4–5, 34

Belgium, 103
Belisle, James "Jim": in T-1, 53, 145, 183; post–Peace Corps career, 182
Belisle, Nga, 53
Berry, Patricia "Trish," 166
Bharati, Agehananda, 67
"Big Bust," 105
Bihawana Secondary School, 193
Biles, Chris, 178, 179
Black Panther Party, 106, 175
Blatchford, Joseph, 127
Bloom, Barry, 141
Bomani, Mark, 136, 147, 199
Bomani, Paul, 97
Bordas, William, 95
Boston Globe, 38
Boston University, 117
Botswana, 5
Bowels, Chester, 10
Boy Scouts, 53
Brain, Jim, 14
Bralic, Marlys, 69t, 163t
Brandeis University, 193
Briggs, Mary, 32; early departure, 163t; in T-2, 69t, 144
British Overseas Survey, 23, 24
Brooklyn Law School, 106
Brose, George, 55, 140
Brown, Earl, 39, 40, 145; post–Peace Corps career, 177; in T-6, 52
Brown, Edward, 60
Brown, Ethel, 69t
Brown, James, 114
Brown, Mary Ann, 52, 145, 177
Brown, Sam, 38, 119–20
Bryceson, Derek, 65, 197
Bunting, Ikaweba, 97
Burgess, Yvette, 55
Burns, John Howard, 111, 136–37
Burns, W. John, 135
Burton, Eleanor Q., 170
Burton, Richard, 14
Burundi, 94, 147
Bush, George, 38
Butts, R. Freeman, 87

Cabral, Amilcar, 108
Cambridge Overseas "O-Level," 90
Camelot, 14

Cameron, Lucille, 54
Cameroon, 34, 89
Canby, William C., Jr., 135
Cardoza High School, 176–77
Cardoza Project in Urban Teaching, 176–77
Carlucci, Frank C., III, 98, 99
Carnegie Corporation, 168
"Cars Out of Place" (White), 148
Carter, Chester, 34
Carter, George, 34
Carter, James "Jimmy" Earl, 37, 98, 183; meeting with Julius Nyerere, 117–18
Carter, Rosalynn, *118*
Carter-Mondale campaign, 183
Cathedral Church, 52
CBS, 42
Center for Assessment and Retraining (CREST), 202
Center for Assessment and Training (CAST), 202
Center for Black Education (CBE), 58–59
Central Intelligence Agency (CIA), 13, 58, 61, 63, 97, 108–9, 182; anti-CIA sentiment in Tanzania, 109–12
Chalmers, Donna (née Abner), 146–48, 190
Chama cha Mapinduzi (CCM), National Executive Committee, 95
Charters, Dean Alexander N., 87–88
Cheche, 108
Chenene Mountains, 24–25
Chicaya, Mary, 51
Children's Homes (Regulation) Act, No. 4 of 1968, 132
Chilonwa Middle School, 89, 93
China, People's Republic of: Beijing, 101, 103; cultural delegation to Tanganyika, 100–101; diplomatic relationship with Tanzania, 97–107; Tanzania's recognition of, 99–100
Chinese Economic and Commercial Mission, 103
Chou Enlai, 101, 103
Chow, Joseph Lawrence, 192
Christianson, Neil, 79–81, 83
City College of New York, 62, 106
Civil Rights Act of 1964, 35
Civil Rights Movement, 13, 35–37, 42, 168, 173
Cleaver, Emmanuel, 107
Clemson University, 182

Clinton, Bill, 37
Cobb, Calvin Coolidge, 105–6
Cobb, Charles, 58, 60
Coffin, Bill, 13
Coleman, Don, 60–61
College for Black Education, 56
College of Agriculture, 21
Colmen, Joseph G., 30–32, 168
Columbia, 129, 195
Columbia University, Teachers College, 86–87, 90
Comitas, Lambros, 75
Commonwealth Assistance, 18
Commonwealth Conference, 109
Community Action Project, 39
Community Analysis and Strategy Tool (CAST), 160
Community Development Program, 151
Congo-Brazzaville, 61
Congo Crisis, 5, 101–2
Congress of Racial Equality (CORE), 106; Suffolk County, 106
Conner, Theophilus Eugene "Bull," 173
Connerly, Ed, 172
Cooper, Malcolm, 95
CORE Securities, 95
Cornell University, 62
Country Management Plan, 158–59
COVID-19, 161
Cox, Courtland, 58, 60
Crawford, James "Jim," 175
Crosby, Bill, 79, 80–81, 83
Crossroads Africa, 34
Croy, Gail: early departure, 163t, 164; in T-2, 69t
Crozier, David, 129
Cuba, 13
Cultural Frontiers of the Peace Corps (Textor and Comitas), 75
Cummins, George, 107, 140, 164, 172, 175; agricultural instruction, 92; in the Army, 173–74; reentry issues, 173–74
Curtis, Erin, 200

Daily News, 125; "Peace Corps to Work Here," 123–24; "People's Forum," 125–26
Dangote, Aliko, 26
Dangote Cement, 26
Dangote Industries Tanzania Limited, 26

Danieli, Dora, 120
Dar es Salaam Anglican Church, 14
Dave Brubeck Trio, 14
Davis, Becky (née Henderson), 163t, 164; in T-2, 69t
Dead Poets Society, 153
Dean, Jimmy, 50
de Goes, Stephanie Joseph, 203–4
Del Mar, David Peterson, 48
Democratic Convention of 1968, 171
Democratic Republic of the Congo, 98, 103,
Dennett, Charlotte Woodall, 135
Dent, Albert, 34
Department of Communications, Power and Works, 17; minister for, 18
Department of Defense, 111
DeSimone, Annie, 145
DeSimone, Peter Salvatore, 21, 32, 145, 163t
Diamond Talkies, 82
Dillard College, 34
Dodoma Secondary School, 93
Douglas, William, 60–61
Dower, Aileen Cochrane, 90
Dower, Hal, 90
Duggan, William R., 73
Dukakis-Benson campaign, 183
Dulake, Robin, 138
Dulles Airport, 135
Duryea, Etta, 54
Dygert, Ruth, 69t

East African Airways, 22
East African Common Services Organization, 91
East African Safari, 29
East African Teachers' Council, 112
Eaton, Patricia, 41
Ecuador, 195
Edgington, George, 95
Education for Self-Reliance, 59, 89, 97, 103, 112–15
Egypt, 48; Cairo, 104–5
Electrical and Mechanical Division, 17
Eliufoo, Solomon N., 113
El Paso Times, 42
English, Joseph, 168, 171
Ephraim, Neema, *188,* 189
Essaye, Anthony F., 135–36

Eswatini (Swaziland), 5
Ethiopia, 5, 34, 42–43
Every Hill a Burial Place (Reid), 137, 192
Executive Order No. 10924, 1
Extradition Act of 1965, 106

Fallen Peace Corps Volunteer Memorial Project, 198–99
Fanti, 48
Federal City College, 58
Fellows, Lawrence, 97
Fels, Charles, 175–76
Ferris, Bob, 81–83
Few Minor Adjustments, A, 202
Ford, Gerald, 117
Foreign Assistance Act of 1961, 112
Foreign Trade Zones, 182
Forman, James, 57, 58
Fourways Grocery Store, 82
Frame, George, 83
Freeman, Bobby, 43
FRELIMO, 66
Friedland, William H., 65, 75–77
Friends of Tanzania (FOT)/Marafiki wa Tanzania, 51, 184–90, 203; General Fund, 185, 187t; Giving Back program, 184–85; Grant Activity, 185t–187t; member-designated fund, 187t; Member Sponsored Funds, 186t; Memorandum of Understanding, 189; newsletter, 184; Projects Committee, 184; scholarships for high school students, Geita, 189; stolen funds, 185
Fuller, Freddy, 13
Fulton, Ruth, 69t
Fumbuka, George Lulenga, 95

Gabiou, Jeff, 83
Gadsden, Marie, 37, 183
Gaither Vocal Band, 54
Galanos Agricultural Secondary School, 92
Galvin, Denis, 150–51
Gambia, 38
Garrett, James P., 58–60, 105
Gaymon (Peace Corps African regional director), 120
Gbenye, Christophe, 101
Gearan, Mark, 161
Gelman, David, 168

General Survey Mission to Tanganyika, 15, 16
Geological Survey of Tanzania (GST), 26; Dodoma headquarters, 51
Ghana, 22, 34, 48, 58, 109, 195–96; anti–Peace Corps sentiments in, 5, 43, 52, 104; independence, 48
Gibbons, Mary, 69t
Goa, 53, 145
Goan Club, 145
Goldmark, Peter C., Jr., 63
Goldwasser, Mike, 89
Goldwater, Barry, 5
Google Maps, 83
Gordon, Robert, 98–99
Government House, 111
Government Notice 478 of 1962, 132
Government of Tanzania (GOT) Ilboru Primary School, 187, 189–90
Great North Road, 151
Griffiths, Gil, 181
Guevara, Ernesto "Che," 102–3
Guinea, 5, 61; Conakry, 5, 94
Gullattee, Alyce, 60–61

Haaren High School, 106
Hagler, Roger, 152
Hanna, William, 53
Hardy, Willie, 39–40
Harkness, John, 129
Harllee-Quattlebaum Company, 182
Harnett, Bertram, 106
Harris, Louis, 35–36
Harris poll, 35–36
Hartery, Fran, 69t
Harvard Tanganyika Project (HTP), 63
Harvard University, 63
Hassan, Samia Suluhu, 189
Hector, Henry, 163t
Hedges, Lee: giraffe incident, 153–54; survey campsite, *152*; in T-1, 150–54
Heidelberg Cement Africa, 26
Hellawell, E. Robert, 30, 69, 100
Helms, Loretta Ann, 45
Helms, Richard, 110
Henderson, D. A., 137
Henry (field aide), 26
Herald Tribune, 42
Hert, Ronald "Ron" Sterling, 104, 107, 117

224 INDEX

High Court of Tanzania, 189
Hill, Sylvia, 60
Hirji, Karim, 108
historically Black colleges and universities (HBCUs), 35, 37
Hobbs, James, 60
Hogan, Pat, 32; early departure, 163t; in T-2, 69t
Hohlstein, Annie, 69t
Holstein, Annie (Patricia), 32, 163t
Hombolo region, 24
Houlihan, Thomas "Tom," 89, 93
House Foreign Affairs Committee, 199
House of Representatives, 54
Howard University, 61
Humphrey, Hubert, 5
Hunter College, 177
Hurley, Bonnie Jo Dopp, 178–79

Ibadakuli Upper Primary School, 90
"import-substitution," 20
India, 17
Institute of Public Administration, 112
International Agencies, 2
International Bank for Reconstruction and Development, 12
International Cooperation Administration (ICA), 10–11
International Development Association (IDA), 15–17
Iowa State University, 92
Issa, Rabia, 141, 200

Jackson, Samuel L., 35–36
Jefferson, Thomas, 47
Jetha, Amirali A., 132
Jitegemee Women in Njombe, 185
Johnson, Anita, 189–89
Johnson, George, 12, 14, 21
Johnson, Jack, 54
Johnson, Lyndon B., 34, 43, 74, 107, 117, 137, 173
Jordan, Everett, 136–37
Josephson, William, 135
Julian, Tereza, 145
Julian, William "Will," 23, 24, 145; in T-1, 53–54
Jumbe, Aboud (vice president), 120

Kabila, Laurent, 103
Kagera Sugar Mills Company, 19
Kaitani, 26

Kambona, Oscar, 98
Kapya, David J. M., 93–94
Kasambala, Jeremiah, 147
Kasindi, Mary Jo, 66
Katua, Herbert, 99
Katus, Thomas "Tom" M., 13–14, 42–43, 190; post–Peace Corps career, 181, 183; reentry issues, 173, 181; in T-1, 20–21, 28–29, 32–33, 53, 100, 144–45, 181
Kawawa, Rashidi M., 96, 101, 103
Kennedy, John F., 10, 13, 35, 57, 110, 112, 196; assassination, 146, 172, 179; creation of the Peace Corps, 1–4, 6; meeting with Julius Nyerere, 11, 73; meeting with Peace Corps volunteers, 13
Kennedy, Padric, 181
Kennedy, Robert, 96
Kenya, 5, 17, 19, 45, 48, 192; Loitokitok, 53; TEA assignments in, 87t
Kenyan Peace Corps, 136
Kenya Rally Drivers Club, 29
Kifungilo Upper Primary School, 49–50; accommodations for teachers, 50–51
Kigahe, Gerald, 21
Kilimanjaro International Airport, 151, 152, 153
Kilombero Sugar Company (KSC), 19, 20
King, Anne, 145
King, Art, 145
King, Barrington, 99
King, John, 32, 163t
King, Martin Luther, Jr., 13, 35, 170; assassination, 96, 179
King, Martin Luther, Sr., 35
King, Martin Luther, III, 35
Kinsey, Peverley "Peppy" Dennett, 130, 134–37, 192, 199; autopsy, 136
Kinsey, William, Sr., 136
Kinsey, William "Bill," 130, 134–35, 137, 142, 192, 199
Koster, Francis "Fran," 166
Kurasini school, 63

Laibu, Issa, 27
Lake Manyara Hotel, 19
Lake Tanganyika, 103
Lake Victoria, 22, 76
Lameck, Lucy, 99
Lauderbaugh, Rita, 69t
Lazar, Katrina, 131–34

INDEX 225

Lazar, Sally, 130–34; adoption of Katrina, 130–34, 163t; reason for joining Peace Corps, 131; in T-2, 69t, 131–34; termination of service, 130, 133, 163t
LeBouisse, Henry R., 10–11
Lee, Spike, 35
Lehman, Gregory T., 192
Lehman, Robert "Robbie" Spencer, 192
Leonhart, William, 99
Liberia, 5
Liberty Cinema, 82
Liebenow, Gus, 67
Life magazine, 167; "Peace Corps' Re-Entry Crisis" (Stolley), 167–68
Life Magazine International, 28, 53
Lihosit, Lawrence, 127
Lin, Harry, 100
Lincoln, Abraham, 47
Lincoln University, 43
Linsmayer, Claire, 69t
Liu Shao-chi, 101
Long-Range Economic and Engineering Plan for Eastern Region's Feeder Road System, 21
Lorna Dadi Foundation, 186
Los Angeles Times, 38
Louisiana State University (LSU), 112
Lounsberry, Bill, 23–25
Lucas, Stephen, 111
Lum, Francis, 43–44
Lumumba, Patricia, 41, 112
Lutengano Middle School, 189
Lutengano Scholarship Fund, 187–89
Lutengano Secondary School, 188–89
Lutheran Church, 190
Lyman, Barb, 69t
Lynch, Wesley, 49

Maasai, 12, 137, 138
Maasai Steppe, 137
Madallali (principal secretary of agriculture), 120
Madhvani Group of Companies, 19
Madison, James, 47
Makerere University, 86
Makonde, 150
Makongoro Secondary School, 186
Malangali Secondary School, 137
Malawi, 5
Mann, Roger, 117

Manpower Development team, 121, 123
Mao Zedong, 99
Martin, Dawn L., 192
*M*A*S*H*, 144
Mason, Patsy, 69t
Masonic Lodge, 106
Maswanya, Said, 65
Mathis, Johnny, 82
Matway, Phaibo, 132
Mawalla, Shose, 146
Mawalla, Vicki, 146
Mays, Benjamin, 34
Mbeya region, 24
Mbuga Primary School, 186
McAteer, William, 32–33
McGovern-Shriver presidential campaign, 183
McHugh, Charles, 135, 136
McNamara, Robert, 5, 107
McNown, Stephen "Steve," 164–65, 175
McPhee, John "Jack," 21, 135, 174; as a Peace Corps volunteer in Tanganyika, 21–22
Medical Missionaries of Mary Sisters, 132
Meisler, Stanley, 113
Metili, Julu, 190
Mgulani Hostel and Conference Center, 90
Mgulani Salvation Army Camp, 69
Microfinance Bank, 189
Mihaly, Eugene, 130, 139–41
Mikumi National Park, 28–29; track, 29
Milhous, Robert "Bob," 21, 22
Ministry of Education, 84, 90–92
Ministry of Finance, 121
Ministry of Justice, 147
Mis-Education of the Negro, The (Woodson), 46
Mkapa, Benjamin, 94
Mohamed, Bibi Titi, 99
Mondlane, Eduardo, 66–67
Moore, Harold, 57
Moravian Church, 188
Morehouse College, 34–35, 59
Morgan State College, 175
Morogoro College of Agriculture, 112
Morogoro European Club, 144–45
Morogoro Girls Upper Primary School, 53
Morrisey, Jim, 165
Morrow, Susan (née Parkins), 138
Moshi Government Hospital, 69t
Moshi Technical School, 89
Mount Kilimanjaro, 12, 70, 151

Mount Meru, 151
Mount View High School, 193
Mowlem Construction Company, 20
Moyers, William D., 13–14, 34, 39
Mozambique, 60, 117, 150; geological survey of, 24; liberation movement, 66
Mpwapwa Secondary School, 89
Mtanda, Ali Tawakali, 94
Mtawali, 69
Muhimbili Hospital, 71, 74, 75, 131, 133, 144, 164
Mullins, Joseph, 168
Mumford, Georgia, 69t
mumiani, 148–50
Museveni, Yoweri, 108
Mwakangale, John B., 96
Mwakikagile, Godfrey, 105
Mwalongo, C., 112–13
Mwanga, Abel, 123–24
Mwangi, Kamau, 66
Mwanza Club, 145–46
Mwanza Hospital, 71
Mzumbe University, 112

Nabudere, Dan, 108
Nairobi, 45
Nakati, Dennis, 93
Namibia, 118
Nangwanda Girls Secondary School, 186
National Aeronautics and Space Administration (NASA), 193
National Association for the Advancement of Colored People (NAACP), 34, 106
Nationalist, 98
Naval Academy, 137
Naval Ordnance Test Station (NOTS), 183
NBC, 42
Ndanda Secondary School, 192
Ndau, Alfred, 27
Ndukeki (Mr.), 121
Nehru, Jawaharlal, 2
New Africa Hotel, 144
New China News Agency, 100
Newsome Communications Center, 107
New Yok Post, 168
New York Times, 11, 38–39, 42, 90, 103, 113; "Once-Ambitious Plan Is Victim of Harsh Political Climate," 97
Ngalabutu, Frank, 51
Ngorongoro Crater, 19

Niger, 34, 39
Nigeria, 34, 48, 104; Enugu, 57
Nipsey Russell Show, 114
Nixon, Richard, 117
Nkrumah, Francis Kwame, 2, 5, 43, 109, 196
Normandy Dam, 118
Noyes, Eliot, 138
Ntiro, Sam, 67
Nyakato Boys Secondary School, 89–90
Nyakirangani, Jackson, 121–23
Nye, Joseph, 78
Nyegina Upper Primary School, 177
Nyerere, Julius, 10, 14, 79, 103–4, 108–9, 146–47; criticism of the Peace Corps, 97, 111–14; plot to overthrow, 98–99; request for Peace Corps volunteers, 6, 22, 59, 61, 96–97, 118–20, 126, 194–96; visit to Beijing, 101–2; visit to Washington, DC, 10, *11*, 73, 117, *118*

Obama, Barack, 107
Oceanside High School, 193
Office of Health Services, 156
Office of Strategic Services, 13
O'Hara, Jim, 21, 145
Ohara, Maria, 145
Ohio State University, 27
Omu-Mura, B., 125–26
O'Neal, Felix "Pete," Jr., 106, 107
Operation Crossroads Africa (OCA), 56, 63; construction projects, 56; measles campaign, 57; medical program, 56–57; in Tanzania, 56–57
Organization of African Unity (OAU), 73, 106; Conference, 48, 104; AGH/Res. 15(1), 105
Our Lady of Premontre High, 137
Outward-Bound Mountain School, 53
Overseas Survey, 23
Overstreet, Lee, 69t, 144

Pac, John B., 98
Page, Thomas S., 135
Pan African Center for Science and Technology (PACST): proposal for, 60, 62–63; purpose of, 62–63
Pan-African Congress: International Secretariat office, 60; Movement, 60; Scientific and Technical Committee, 60–62; Sixth, 60–61, 63

"Pan African Imperative for Increased
  Emphasis on Science and Technology,
  The" (Parker), 61–63
Pan-African Skills Project (PASP), 56, 58, 105
Pan-African Youth Movement, 95
Paraguay, 195
Parker, Neville, 60–63
Parker, Norm (Leon), 174
Parson, Jeremiah "Jerry," 173, 181; in T-1, 20,
  28–29, 32–33, 43, 53, 144–45; treatment in
  El Paso, 29, 41–42; treatment in
  Tanganyika, 29
Payne, C. Lucas, 34, 37
Payton, Carolyn R., 37–38, 119, 127
Peace Corps, 122; advanced training program
  (ATP), 37; African Regional Office, 135;
  anecdotes from volunteers, 143–54;
  Career Information Service (CIS),
  168–69; Career Planning Board, 168; as a
  counter to communism, 1, 3, 12, 73, 103;
  criticism of, 5–6, 38, 40, 97, 103–4, 108–10,
  112–15, 124–26; defense counsel, 199–200;
  "experience," 92, 170, 203; founding, 1–5,
  195; image building, 5; leaflets distributed
  about, 111; mandate, 93–95; Manual,
  155–56, 164; media coverage of, 123–27;
  Medical Division, 129; 1964 annual report,
  138; objective of/goals, 2, 4, 6, 30–33, 54,
  74–77, 127–28, 203–4; Office of the
  Inspector General (OIG), 141–42; project
  criteria and general thrust of program
  after 1979, 127–28; Public Health Service,
  135; and the race factor in Africa, 45–56;
  and the race factor in the United States,
  39–45; racial equality objectives, 34–63;
  reasons against volunteering for, 35–36,
  39–40; recruitment brochures, 36;
  recruitment of African Americans and
  other minorities, 34–63, 97; recruitment
  questionnaires, 35; return of the program
  to Tanzania, 116–28; safety protocols,
  198–99; Second Annual Report, 3–4;
  smallpox eradication program, 137–38;
  socializing with nationals, 145–48; in
  Tanzania, termination of program, 2,
  96–115; thirtieth anniversary conference,
  184; training, 34–63, 120, 121, 123, 127; turf
  fight over control of, 13
Peace Corps Act, 1, 14, 42, 155, 198

Peace Corps Reauthorization Act, 201
Peace Corps Volunteers, 39
Peace Corps volunteers (PCVs): African
  American, 37, 40–41, 48–50, 97, 171,
  174–75; age of, 130; alternatives of, 56–63;
  death in service, 4, 129, 130, 134–42,
  191–93; difficulties in service, 4; drug use,
  130, 157; friendship between, 53–54,
  171–72; interracial relationships, 41,
  53–55, 174; marriage, 32, 52–53, 55, 76–77,
  143–45, 161–63, 165, 172; mishaps in
  Tanzania, 129–42; post-service career
  paths, 171–83; pregnancy, 165; reason for
  starting, 1; reentry experiences, 171–83;
  reentry issues, 167–83; requests for, 2–3,
  10, 11; return of the program to Tanzania,
  116–28; senior volunteers, 160–61; T-1 and
  T-2 reunion, 77; termination of program
  in Tanzania, 2, 96–115; teachers,
  1964-1969, 84–95, 103; trainees, gender,
  41, 201–2; trainees, race, 37, 40–41, 43,
  49–53, 202; training, 4, 12, 40–41, 43,
  49–53, 120–21, 123, 127, 202–3
Peace Corps volunteers, goals of, 4–5; meet
  people's humanitarian needs, 37, 125–28;
  meet people's needs for trained
  manpower, 30–31, 125–28; promote a
  better understanding of the American
  people, 30–31, 53; promote a better
  understanding of other people, 30–31, 54;
  transfer of skills, 93, 127–28
Peace Corps volunteers, teachers, 87–92,
  112–15, 196; growth of education, 85t;
  Peace Corps mandate and, 93–95;
  secondary school enrollment, 86t;
  Standard IV, 84; Standard V, 84; Standard
  VI, 84; Standard VII, 93, 113; Standard
  VIII, 84, 93, 113; training, 85–87, 113
Peace Corps volunteers, termination of
  service, reasons for: administration separation, 156, 165–66; adoptions, 131–34,
  163t; compassionate reasons, 4; cost of,
  161; deaths, 4, 134–42; early termination,
  155–66; early termination management
  exercises, 159; early termination rates,
  157–58; interrupted service, 156–57;
  marriage, 143–45, 161–63, 165; medical
  separation, 4, 156–57, 164–65; policy
  violations, 157; questionnaire, 161;

228 INDEX

Peace Corps volunteers (*cont.*)
  resignation, 156; from Tanzania, 162–66; travel allowances for, 157
Peace Corps Volunteers in Service to America, 38
Peterson, John M., 130, 141–42, 200
Phelps Stokes Fund, 38, 183
Philippines, 55, 175, 177
Pillsbury, Richard, 193
Pillsbury, Rosemary (née Constable), 193
Pillsbury, Wyatt, 193
Platt, Elizabeth, 53
Plummer, Brenda Gayle, 58
Polcyn, Charles, 55
Poole, Robert, 136
Presley, Elvis, 82
Princess Margaret Hospital, 69t, 70–71, 74–76, 131, 144, 146, 164
Proctor, Samuel D., 34
Proctor, Susan (née Tonskemper), 66, 145–46; infant delivery, 71–72; on marriage, 162, 164; reentry issues, 172–73, 177–78; in T-2, 69t, 70–71, 73, 75–77, 172–73; on the Vietnam War, 73–74, 172–73
Project Review and Implementation Strategy Tool (PRIST), 160
Public Works Division/Department (PWD), 17–18, 78, 83; communal labor, 78; construction of dams and roads, 79; education of staff, 17; expatriates in, 17, 18, 28; in Musoma, 79; Provincial, 150, 166; roadworks consultants, 18; training program for Tanzanians, 18, 83
Puerto Rico, 12–13

Quattlebaum, Alex, Jr., 182
Quattlebaum, Alex, III, 182
Quattlebaum, Scott, 182
Quattlebaum Development Company (QDC), 182
Quimby, Thomas H. E., 136
Quink, Ann, 32, 145–46; in T-2, 69t

Rabideau, Susan Hoffma, 89
racism: antimiscegenation laws, 54–55; in El Paso, 29, 41–42; history of Africa and, 46–47; psychological rupture with Africa, 46; school policies, 46–47; stigmatism of African Americans, 46–47, 171–74

Radio Corporation of American, Astro-Electronics Division, 21
Radley, Lawrence, 129
Ratigan, Barbara, 181
Ratigan, John: at Nyakato Boys Secondary School, 89–90; on returning from service, 170–71, 181
Raymaker, Catherine, 139
Raymaker, Chris, 138, 140
Raymaker, Leonard, 139
Raymaker, Mark, 138; disappearance, 130, 137–41; fake death certificate for, *140*
Raymaker, Mike, 138–39
Read, Jean, 69t
Reagan, Ronald, 183
Reid, Peter, 137, 192; in T-2, 69t
returned Peace Corps volunteers (RPCVs), 184
Rhodesia, 60, 103, 117–18
Ries, Eric, 27, 81, 83; in T-5, 27–28
Roads and Aerodromes, 17
Robbins, Eleanora "Nora" Iberall, 26, 51; field crew, 27
Robinson, Fletcher, 60–62, 138
Robinson, James, 34
Robinson, James Herman, 56
Roddenberry, Seaborn Anderson, 54–55
Rodney, Walter, 108
Rose Garden, 13
Ros-Lehtinen, Ileana, 199
Rowe, Bill, 151
Ruaha National Park, 193
Ruark, Robert, 56
Rufiji Basin Development Authority, 118
Ruppe, Loret Miller, 158, 201
Russell, Richard, 83
Russom, Bev, 69t
Rwanda, 5
Rweyemamu, Anthony, 67
Rwezaura, Balthazar A., 132

Sack, Paul, 134, 136, 141, 174
Saidi, *26*
Saint Clement Secondary School, 192
Salvation Army, 90
Samwel, *26*
San Diego Union, 5–6
Santa Monica City College, 130
Sanya Chini plains, 151–53; survey campsite, *152*

Sarakikya, Mirisho S., 148
"Say It Loud—I'm Black and Proud" (Brown), 114
Scancem of Norway, 26
Schaeffer, David, 193
Scheelhaas, Lyle, 119
Schoonover, Brenda (née Brown), 55, 174; post–Peace Corps career, 176–77
Schoonover, Richard "Dick," 55, 174
Schreiber, Gene, 14, 144
Scott, Benjamin F., 59
Scrivener, Richard, 164
Second Baptist Church of Rockville Center, 106
Segal, Aaron, 19
Segall, Burt, 32, 144
Selassie, Haile, 147
Seme, Reuben, 53, 94, 113
Serengeti region, 24
Services Group, Free Zone division, 182
Shalala, Donna, 37
Shariff, Othman, 99
Shiers, Ruther Elizabeth, 72
Shinyanga Secondary School, 95
Shivji, Issa, 108
Shriver, Robert Sargent, 109; as director of Peace Corps, 2, 5–6, 10, 13–14, 30, 37, 42, 54, 87, 110, 136–37, 165; press release of June 1, 1961, 34–35; task force, 34
Sierra Leone, 5, 128
Sievert, Diane, 69t
Simiyu River, 22
Simon (field assistant), 27
Singer, Gayle "Gay," 166
Siriani, Carole, 32, 69t, 145
Smallpox Eradication Program, 137
Smith, Ed, 48, 52
Snyder, Jo, 69t
Sokoine University of Agriculture, 21, 112
Somalia, 61
Songer, Katie, 179–80; reentry issues, 179–81
soul music, 114
South Africa, 60, 103; nurses from, 76; white regime in, 117
South Dakota School of Mines and Technology, Rotary Club, 190
Southern Highlands Participatory Organization (SHIPO), 186
Spain, James W., 119–20, 124–25
Special to CNN, 200

Stafford, Mary, 69t, 163t
St. Agnes Hospital, 130
Star, 6
Star Journal, 5
Stevenson, Adlai, 14
Stewart, Rodgers, 181
St. Joseph Cathedral Convent, 131–32
St. Joseph's Hospital, 130
St. Lawrence, Lee, 10
St. Norbert College, 137
St. Olaf College, 192
Stolley, Richard B., 167–68, 182
Stossel, Scott, 10, 109–10
Student Nonviolent Coordinating Committee (SNCC), 56, 58
St. Vincent's College of Nursing, 130
Sun, 31
sundowners, 147
Sutherland, Bill, 105
Swai, Nsilo, 146
Syracuse University, 27, 65–68, 72, 87, 89, 107, 113, 178; Maxwell School, 137; Research Committee on East African Studies, 67; School of Nursing, 67–68; University College, Adult Education Division, 87

Tabora Boys Secondary School, 53, 93–95, 113
Tabora Club, 53
Taiwan, 100
Tamura, Allen, 43–44; campsite at Dulu, *24*; survey crew, 25, *26*, 149–50; in T-1, 23–25, 31, 45, 100, 149–50
Tanga Government Hospital, 69t, 72
Tanganyika. *See* Tanzania
Tanganyika African National Union (TANU), 60, 99, 101; Youth League, 108
Tanganyika Five (T-5) PCVs, 26–28, 51, 78–83, 107, 172; civil engineers, 26, 78–83; cultural sensitivity, lack of, 77; culverts, *81;* drifts, *80;* geologists, 26; in Musoma, 79–83; nurses, 77; questions on impact of, 82–83; secondary teachers, 90; surveyors, 26, 79; 2011 reunion, 166; water development, 27, 28; Water Development and Irrigation Division and, 79–80
Tanganyika Geological Survey, 23, 45
Tanganyika News Review, 78
Tanganyika One (T-1) PCVs, 10–33, 53, 76, 116, 181, 190, 194, 196, 203; attitude of British

Tanganyika One (*cont.*)
toward, 30–31; boycott, 41–42; civil engineers, 14–15, 78; concrete survey markers, 152; dating and relationships, 32, 144, 203; geologists, 14, 23–28, 148–50; graduation ceremonies, 42; meeting with President Kennedy, 13–14; morale, 31–32; objectives of, 18, 30–31; pioneer status of, 31; predeparture training, 12–13, 45, 65; qualifications, 15; questionnaire for, 30–31; rural marketing feeder road survey, 20–21; surveyors, 14, 15–22, 150–54; suspected of being *mumiani* (vampires), 148–50; Swahili language training, 14; training director, 13; training in El Paso, Texas, 12, 29, 41–44; training in Puerto Rico, 12–13; wooden survey markers, 151–52

Tanganyika Planting Company (TPC), 19

Tanganyika Seven (T-7) PCVs, 53, 181

Tanganyika Six (T-6) PCVs, 49–50, 52–53, 89, 164–65, 175; residences, 50–51

Tanganyika Standard, 32–33; Malcom X interview in, 48–49, 105; "Tom na Jerry: The Safari Wonders," 28

Tanganyika Three (T-3) PCVs, 189; agricultural secondary schools, 92; American Studies and World Affairs, 88, 89–92; Area Studies, 88; Cambridge Overseas "O-Level" examinations, 90; Health and Medical Training, 88; housing, 91; Peace Corps Orientation, 88, 90; Philosophy, Strategy, Tactics and Menace of Communism, 88; Physical Education and Recreation, 88; primary school teachers, 90; school supplies, 90; secondary school teachers, 89; Swahili Language Training, 88, 90–91; teachers, 84–95; Technical Studies, 88; trainee evaluations, 90; training at Syracuse, 87–88; transportation, 91; upper primary school teachers, 89

Tanganyika Two (T-2) PCVs, 116, 196–97; American Studies and World Affairs, 66–67, 74; Area Studies, 66–67, 72, 74; British nurses and, 74, 197; challenges faced by, 69–74; dating and relationships, 32, 144, 203; director of area studies for, 75; early departure rates, 162–66; housing, 75; initial hospital assignments, 69t; longevity verses attrition, 76–77, 165; male attention and nurses, 73; Medical Studies and Personal Hygiene, 66; morale, 76, 77; Nursing Procedures and Techniques, 66–68; nurses, 32, 64–77, 131–34, 190, 203; Peace Corps mandate and, 74–77; Peace Corps Orientation, 66, 68; Physical Conditioning and Recreation, 66; relationships with Tanzanian staff nurses, 75–76; Swahili language training, 66, 69; tour of duty, 73; training at Syracuse University, 65–68, 72, 75

Tanzania, 2, 5, 38, 48; agribusiness, 19, 20; agricultural development needs, 118; American embassy in Dar es Salaam, 2, 97–98, 119–20; anti-CIA sentiment in, 109–12; army mutiny, 73, 101; Arusha, 14, 19, 21, 108, 150–51, 153; Arusha-Chini, 19; Bagamoyo, 144; Bukoba, 15, 91, 122; cement factories, 25–26; Central Province, 21; Chalinze, 21; China relations, 97–107; closure of the Peace Corps program, 2, 89, 103, 108; colonial government, 20; credit and financial aid requests, 15–18; Crisis of 1969, 2; Dar es Salaam, 14, 21, 22, 25–27, 55, 58–59, 61, 63, 69–70, 73–74, 90, 91–92, 95, 100–103, 105–6, 112, 123, 125, 131–36, 142, 144, 146–47, 164, 194, 197, 204; Dodoma, 15, 21, 23, 26–28, 51–52, 81, 145, 165, 176, 193; Eastern Province, 20; Eastern Trunk Road, 21; fisheries, 127–28; growth of education, 85t; economic development, 14; economic survey of, 11–12; education, 84–95; farm-to-market feeder road projects, 14, 20; Five-Year Development Plan, 18, 195; Geita, 22, 189; geological survey and maps of, 23–28; high bridges, 20; "high priority" status, 11–12; Ifakara-Mahenge road, 20, 28; Ikizu-Ikoma road, 79; independence, 2, 14–15, 17, 19–20, 51, 64–65, 70, 73–74, 77, 84, 89, 99, 112, 149, 150, 194, 196; infrastructure, 14–16; interconnected highway system, 17; Iringa, 112; Kigoma, 103, 122; Kilombero, 20; Kiomboi, 132; Kitete, 19; Korogwe, 164; Lyamungu, 176; Makiungu, 132; Maswa, 135–36; Mbeya, 113, 192; Mbozi, 186; Mbulu District, 19; medical

staff shortage, 64–65, 70; Mikumi, 20; Mikumi-Kilombero road, 20; Morogoro, 15, 20–22, 59, 92; Moshi, 70, 74, 140, 153, 197; motor vehicles in, 16; Msasani, 61; Mtwara, 15, 21, 25–26; Musoma, 52, 79–83, 145, 186; Mwanza, 22, 76, 80, 81–82, 122, 135–36, 197; Mwanza-Musoma Road, 22; Nachingwea, 73; Newala, 186; 1964 mutiny, 147–48; Njombe, 15; Northern Province, 19; Nyegina, 52, 145; OCA in, 56–57; Pangani, 144, 149; Parliament, 95–96; Peace Corps Volunteer mishaps in, 129–42; request for Peace Corps volunteers, 10–11; relations between Peace Corps and, 77; return of the Peace Corps program to, 116–28, 197; "roads-to-markets" program, 10, 16–20, 30, 196; Saadani, 24; secondary school enrollment, 86t; Segera, 21; Shinyanga, 90, 122; Singida, 132; socialism, 93, 102, 114, 124, 126; Southern Province, 21; sugar production in, 19–20; Tabora, 73, 148, 166, 197; Tanga, 25, 70, 74, 100, 144, 164, 197; Tanga-Moshi trunk road, 21; Tengeru, 12, 14, 21; termination of Peace Corps program in, 96–115, 197; Three-Year Development Plan, 11, 84, 88, 195; union with Zanzibar, 2, 89; US relations, 96, 97–107, 117–23; "villagization" program, 18–19; West Lake Province, 91
Tanzania Bar Association, 136
Tanzanian Criminal Investigation Division, 136
Tanzania People's Defense Force, 148
Tanzania Portland Cement Company (TPCC), 25, 26
Tanzania Ten (T-10) PCVs, 137, 140
Tanzania Twelve (T-12) PCVs, 90
tanzanite, 25
Teachers for East Africa (TEA), 76, 85–87, 113, 163t; British teachers in, 85, 112; primary school teachers, 112; in Tanganyika, 86–87, 94; training, 87; US teachers, 112
Teacher's Training Colleges, 196
Technical College, 21
"Technology of Liberation" (Scott), 59–60
Tennessee Valley Authority (TVA), 118
Texas Western College, 12, 21, 41
Textor, Robert B., 75
Thailand, 38

Thomas, Roosevelt, 37
Thomas, Sanna Poorman, 164–65
Tibandebage, Andrew, 98
Times-Union, 6
Togo, 128
Torrey, Barbara, 189
Toure, Sekou, 5
Toynbee, Arnold, 5
Trescott, Jacqueline, 118–19
Tshombe, Moise, 101, 103
Tusker beer, 79
Twiga Cement Factory, 25–26

Uganda, 5, 122; Kampala, 86; TEA assignments in, 87t
Ugly American, The (Burdick and Lederer), 5, 12–13, 67
Ulimwengu, Jenerali, 95
United Kingdom, 15, 67, 109; nurses, 74, 76
United Nations, 2, 14, 17; Educational, Scientific and Cultural Organization (UNESCO), 182; General Assembly, 117; High Commission for Refugees (UNHCR), 94; Trusteeship Council, 10, 194
United States, Tanzania embassy in, 99
United States Army Nurses Corp, 130
United States Agency for International Development (USAID), 18, 112, 120, 128, 182–83; financial assistance from, 18
United States Constitution, 54–55, 119
United States Department of Justice, 142
United States Department of State, 58, 98, 104, 110–11, 135
United States General Accounting Office (GAO), 122–23
United States Geological Survey (USGS), 27
United States Information Agency, 55
United States Public Diplomacy and Public Affairs, 55
University College, Dar es Salaam (UCD), 111–12; Department of Sociology, 111
University of California, 183
University of California, Berkeley, 43
University of California Los Angeles, 130
University of Cambridge, 94
University of Chicago, 59
University of Dar es Salaam, 60, 62, 93–95, 108, 189; Department of Civil Engineering, 62; Muhimbili Medical School, 94

University of Georgia, 119
University of Ghana, 104
University of Ibadan, 104
University of Miami, 37
University of Michigan, 1, 193
University of Texas at El Paso, 41
University of Wisconsin, Milwaukee, 181
University Students African Revolutionary Front (USARF), 108
U Nu, 2
Usambara Mountain, 50; geological survey of, 24
USA Today, 141, 200

Van Loenen, Richard, 23, 24
Vasquez, Gaddi H., 37–38
Vaughn, Jack, 127, 135
Veech, Alex, 53, 145
Veech, Linda, 53
Veterans Hospital in Lost Angeles, 130
Vietnam War, 73–74, 93, 96–97, 107–9, 171–73, 176, 197; Gulf of Tonkin, 107
Voluntary Service Overseas (VSO) volunteers, 138
Volunteer Training Specialists Inc. (VTSI), 181

Wagogo tribe, 31, 51–52
Waldinger, Natalie, 193
Walker (Mr.), 120
Warner, Candy, 51, 185
Washington Post, 38, 42, 96, 118, 119
Water, Sanitation, and Hygiene (WASH), 186
Water Development and Irrigation Division (WD&ID), 27, 81; Engineering Geologists, 28; surveys, 80; T-5 in, 79–80; volunteers in, 79–80
Watson, Willie Mae, 49
Wazo Hill, 25
Welsing, Francis, 60
White, John, 165
White, Luise, 148
Wiggins, Anne (née Thompson), 138

Wiggins, Warren W., 135
William (field aide), *26*
Williams, Franklin H., 2, 10, 34, 42, 183; as ambassador to Ghana, 43; as Peace Corps director, 42–43
Williams, Robin, 153
Wilmore, Jacques, 121, 123
Winkelman, Joe, 93
Winkelman, Lowel, 53
Wisconsin Law School, 137
WOL, 39
Wolfensberger, Donald, 138
Woodson, Carter Godwin, 46
Wooford, Harris L., 2
Word, Carol, 38; culture shock, 50; in T-6, 49–50
World, 6
World Bank, 15, 18, 22, 182
World Health Assembly (WHA), 137
World Health Organization (WHO), 131, 137–38
World War I, 194
World War II, 13, 17, 28, 44, 106, 194
Wright, M. Peter, 23–24

X, Malcolm, 40, 106, 179; on Peace Corps volunteers, 48–49, 58, 104; visit to African continent, 48–49, 58, 104–5

Yale University, 13
Yamat, Loy, 189–90
Yates, Dwight, 53, 93
YMCA, 174
York, Allan, 95
Young, Arthur, 20, 32, 144
Young, Estelle, 106
Youssoufou, Oumarou, 39–40

Zambia, 117
Zanzibar, 2, 89, 98, 120; revolution, 101; TEA assignments in, 87t; union with Tanganyika, 2
Zimmerman, Jonathan, 40–41, 55